ANGELS AND DEVILS

"And another angel came, and stood before the altar, having a golden censer; and there was given to him much incense, that he should offer of the prayers of all saints upon the golden altar, which is before the throne of God. And the smoke of the incense of the prayers of the saints ascended up before God from the hand of the angel."
—The Apocalypse 8:3-4

The Blessed Virgin Mary crushes the head of the serpent, Satan, through the power of her Immaculate Conception.

ANGELS AND DEVILS

By

Joan Carroll Cruz

"For he hath given his angels charge over thee; to keep thee in all thy ways."
—Psalm 90:11

TAN BOOKS AND PUBLISHERS, INC.
Rockford, Illinois 61105

OTHER BOOKS BY THE AUTHOR

Mysteries, Marvels, Miracles
Miraculous Images of Our Lord
Miraculous Images of Our Lady
Secular Saints
The Incorruptibles
Prayers and Heavenly Promises
Eucharistic Miracles
Relics
Desires of Thy Heart

Nihil Obstat: Rev. Terry T. Tekippe
Censor Librorum

Imprimatur: ✠ Most Rev. Francis B. Schulte
Archbishop of New Orleans
October 28, 1998

Library of Congress Catalog Card No.: 98-61407

ISBN 0-89555-638-3

Printed and bound in the United States of America.

TAN BOOKS AND PUBLISHERS, INC.
P.O. Box 424
Rockford, Illinois 61105
1999

"And there was a great battle in heaven, Michael and his angels fought with the dragon, and the dragon fought and his angels . . . And that great dragon was cast out, that old serpent, who is called the devil and Satan . . ."

—*The Apocalypse* 12:7-9

Our Lady is pictured crushing the head of the serpent, Satan, on the front of the Miraculous Medal. The design for the Miraculous Medal was given to St. Catherine Labouré by the Blessed Virgin Mary in 1830. Although this famous medal was originally titled the "Medal of the Immaculate Conception," the numerous miracles associated with it led to the popular title of the "Miraculous Medal." The prayer which Our Lady wanted included on the Medal (shown here in French) indicates her victory over the devil from the first moment of her Conception:

"O Mary, conceived without sin,
pray for us who have recourse to thee."

CONTENTS

—Part I—
ANGELS

—Part II—
DEVILS

AUTHOR'S NOTE

In this work I have endeavored to give information regarding the most frequently asked questions about angels and devils, and perhaps at the same time to give unbelievers a little something to think about regarding the existence of angelic helpers and devilish tormentors. To prove the various points, I have relied on the very best of references: Holy Scripture and Sacred Tradition, the teachings of the Church, the writings of Popes and Doctors of the Church, the opinions and visions of saints as well as the writings of esteemed theologians.

Why another book about angels? The subject is so vast and interesting, it seems unlikely that it can be adequately explored in any one volume. Each writer attempts to present a different perspective of the subject. Perhaps we each hope to present various facets that might not have been explored enough by others. Whatever the case, I have attempted, as have many others, to explore the subject in a trustworthy, instructive, interesting and helpful manner.

While it is a worthwhile occupation to read and learn about our angelic companions who are with us now and will remain with us in Heaven, it was not my intention to dwell in a lengthy fashion on the devil. Concerning this, C. S. Lewis, author of *The Screwtape Letters*, wrote: "There are two equal and opposite errors into which our race can fall about the devils. One is to disbelieve in their existence. The other is to believe, and to feel an excessive and unhealthy interest in them." In trying to avoid an "unhealthy interest" in the devils, I have nevertheless felt it necessary to discuss their origins, what they are like, what they can do, and to warn about some of the wiles they use to entrap unsuspecting souls in our day. This knowledge is necessary, since we must know something of this mortal enemy before we can present a defense.

It is my prayer that the reader will find some merit in this work and that all will successfully combat against the devil and grow ever closer to their own angel guardians.

Joan Carroll Cruz

ANGELS AND DEVILS

"For our wrestling is not against flesh and blood; but against principalities and powers, against the rulers of the world of this darkness, against the spirits of wickedness in the high places." —Ephesians 6:12

— Part One —

ANGELS

"The existence of the spiritual, non-corporeal beings that Sacred Scripture usually calls 'angels' is a truth of faith. The witness of Scripture is as clear as the unanimity of tradition."

—*Catechism of the Catholic Church,* No. 328

ANGELS

1. What Are Angels?

St. Augustine (354-430) instructs us that the word "angel" is the name of their office, not of their nature. Their nature is known as "spirit." The word "angel," as translated from the Greek, means "one going," "one sent" or "messenger." St. Augustine adds that "the spirits called angels were never, in any sense, at any time, partakers of darkness, but from the moment of their creation, they were made beings of light. They were not merely created in order to exist and to live, but they were also illumined, so that they might live in wisdom and happiness."[1]

According to **St. Bernard** (1090-1153) in his *De Consideratione*, angels are

> mighty, glorious, blessed, distinct personalities, of graduated rank, occupying the order given them from the beginning, perfect of their kind . . . endowed with immortality, passionless . . . being of pure mind, benignant affections, religious and devout; of unblemished morality; inseparably one in heart and mind, blessed with unbroken peace, God's edifice dedicated to the divine praises and service. All this we ascertain by reading, and hold by faith.[2]

According to Fr. Pascal P. Parente, "Even though not yet an article of faith, it is Catholic doctrine that the Angels are pure spirits, incorporeal substances, free and independent from any material body . . ."[3]

As to their "form," we accept the descriptions of Scripture and Tradition and the revelations of the Saints which reveal that when they appear on earth, angels have a form similar to that of men, but of an ethereal, spiritual nature. At least that is how they appear in various apparitions in both the Old and New Testaments and in the apparitions of saints.

St. John Damascene (c. 675-c. 749), a Doctor of the Church, writes: "An angel is an intellectual substance, endowed with liberty, perpetually active, without a body, serving God, having the form and the limits of whose substance only its Creator knows."[4]

We believe that each angel is a distinct being, an individual, having distinct features (as we will learn from the revelations of the Saints), who has his own place in a hierarchy and who has an intellect far superior to human intellect. This is manifest in their many apparitions. Agreeing is **St. Thomas Aquinas**, who maintains that the Angels differ from each other specifically.

2. How Do We Know that Angels Exist?

The answer can be briefly summarized in this manner: we know that angels exist from the teaching of the Church, which is based both on Sacred Scripture—the Old and the New Testaments—and on Tradition, from the unanimous teachings of the Saints and Doctors of the Church, and from the innumerable well-authenticated accounts of apparitions.

That the Angels were created was defined by the Fourth Lateran Council (1215). The decree "*Firmiter*" against the Albigensian heresy declared both the fact that they were created and that men were created after them. Given free will and a high intelligence at their creation, they are often called the "sons of God."

In the Bible, angels are represented as a large gathering of spiritual beings intermediate between God and men. Angels are the servants and messengers of God, doing all as God pleases, serving the accomplishment of the divine plan. As **St. Paul** cites in his letter to the Hebrews: "Are they not all ministering spirits, sent to minister for them, who shall receive the inheritance of salvation?" (*Heb.* 1:14).

In addition, there are angels who minister not only to man, but principally to God Himself. In the book of *Daniel*, the Prophet tells of a vision of angels: ". . . thousands of thousands ministered to him, and ten thousand times a hundred thousand stood before him." (*Dan.* 7:10). Our Lord Himself reveals the following: "See that you despise not one of these little ones: for I say to you, that their angels in heaven always see the face of my Father who is in heaven." (*Matt.* 18:10).

The first great wealth of information regarding angels is given us in both the Old and New Testaments, as well as through the teachings of Holy Mother Church. Tradition has handed down from the earliest days important truths regarding them, while numerous Doctors of the Church have enlightened us on this doctrine. But probably the greatest wealth of information has been given us by the saints who have been privileged to view them and sometimes to communicate with them in wonderful visions that have been recorded for our edification.

Before we consider these wonderful visions we will first consider the testimony about the Angels as given in the Old Testament.

3. Angels in the Old Testament

Of the forty-six books of the Old Testament, angels are mentioned in thirty-one. In these books we learn about the activities of the Angels as they are directed by God. They adore, rebuke, reprove, comfort, instruct, chastise, prophesy, destroy, protect, assist, guard, interpret, advise, announce births, locate the lost and deliver messages of God; they also intercede and pray for us, they afflict, punish and even kill.

We are reminded of the following well-known activities of angels:

When **Adam and Eve** were cast out of the Garden of Eden for their sin, God "placed before the paradise of pleasure cherubims, and a flaming sword, turning every way, to keep the way of the tree of life." (*Gen.* 3:24).

Three angels visited **Abraham**, and when he saw them, "he ran to meet them from the door of his tent, and adored down to the ground." After eating the meal that was prepared for them, they prophesied that Abraham's wife Sara, even though well advanced in years, would nevertheless bear a son. (*Gen.* 18:2-14). The prophecy was fulfilled when Sara gave birth to a son whom Abraham named Isaac.

We learn later that Sara had a servant girl who ran away from her stern mistress, but "the angel of the Lord having found her, by a fountain of water in the wilderness . . . said to her: Return to thy mistress, and humble thyself under her hand." (*Gen.* 16:7-9).

Yet another intervention of an angel took place when Abraham was about to slay his son for a holocaust, as instructed by God. While the knife was poised to strike, ". . . an angel of the Lord from heaven called to him, saying: Abraham, Abraham . . . Lay not thy hand upon the boy, neither do thou anything to him . . ." (*Gen.* 22:11-12).

After Abraham, we learn that **Lot** and his wife, while entertaining two angels in their home, were warned by them about the destruction of Sodom:

> And when it was morning, the angels pressed him, saying: Arise, take thy wife, and the two daughters which thou hast: lest thou also perish in the wickedness of the city . . . And they brought him forth and set him without the city: and there they spoke to him, saying: Save thy life: look not back, neither stay thou in all the country about: but save thyself in the mountain, lest thou be also consumed . . . And his wife looking behind her, was turned into a statue of salt. (*Gen.* 19:15-17, 26).

When **Moses** was learning from God the laws that would be observed by the people, God assured him, "Behold I will send my angel, who shall go before thee, and keep thee in thy journey, and bring thee into the place that I have prepared . . . If thou wilt hear his voice, and do all that I speak, I will be an enemy to thy enemies and will afflict them that afflict thee. And my angel shall go before thee . . ." (*Ex.* 23:20, 22-23).

When **Josue** was in a field of the city of Jericho, he lifted up his eyes and saw a man holding a drawn sword. After the man answered that he was not an enemy but "prince of the host of the Lord," Josue recognized him as an angel and "fell on his face to the ground." The angel then said, "Loose thy shoes from off thy feet: for the place whereon thou standest is holy. And Josue did as was commanded him." (*Jos.* 5:13-16). The Lord then announced that Josue could lay claim to the city of Jericho. (*Jos.* 6:2).

We read in *4 Kings* (*2 Kings*) that **Ezechias** prayed for God's help against his enemy, the Assyrians: "And it came to pass that night, that an angel of the Lord came, and slew in the camp of the Assyrians a hundred and eighty-five thousand." (*4 Kgs.* 19:35).

The prophet **Elias** went one day's journey into the desert and slept under a juniper tree. He was later awakened by an angel, who said to him, "Arise and eat." Elias looked, "and behold there was at his head a hearth cake, and a vessel of water: and he ate and drank, and he fell asleep again."

For a second time the angel touched him and said, "Arise, eat: for thou hast yet a great way to go." And Elias arose, ate and drank, "and walked in the strength of that food forty days and forty nights, unto the mount of God, Horeb." (*3 Kgs.* [*1 Kgs.*] 19:4-8).

When Nabuchodonosor had **Sidrach**, **Misach** and **Abdenago** cast into the burning furnace for not adoring a golden statue, they walked unharmed among the flames; the angel of the Lord "drove the flame of the fire out of the furnace, and made the midst of the furnace like the blowing of a wind bringing dew, and the fire touched them not at all, nor troubled them, nor did them any harm." The three young men sang the praises of God and prayed, "O ye angels of the Lord, bless the Lord: praise and exalt him above all forever." (*Dan.* 3:49-50, 58).

In the book of *Zacharias* we are told about a vision in which the prophet saw four chariots driven by angels. The horses, "grisled and strong," were black, white and red. An angel, who was his companion during the vision, informed **Zacharias** that they were the four winds of the heaven, "which go forth to stand before the Lord of all the earth." (*Zach.* 6:1-5).

The *Catechism of the Catholic Church* teaches that angels "closed the earthly paradise; protected Lot; saved Hagar and her child; stayed Abraham's hand; communicated the law by their ministry; led the People of God; announced births and callings; and assisted the prophets, just to cite a few examples. Finally, the Angel Gabriel announced the birth of the Precursor and that of Jesus himself."[5]

4. Angels in the New Testament

In the entire New Testament, including the four Gospels, the Epistles and *The Apocalypse*, the words "angel" or "angels" are mentioned more than 158 times.

From the Incarnation to the Ascension, we know that **Our Lord** was surrounded by the adoration and the service of angels. "Thinkest thou that I cannot ask my Father, and He will give me presently more than twelve legions of angels?" (*Matt.* 26:53). Before His birth they advised Joseph to accept Mary as his wife; they warned him to take Mary and the Child to Egypt and announced when it was safe to return. At Our Lord's birth they announced the good news to the shepherds; they served Him in the desert and in the Garden of Olives; they were present at His Resurrection. "For an angel of the Lord descended from heaven, and coming, rolled back the stone, and sat upon it." (*Matt.* 28:2).

Angels will also be indispensable at the Lord's Second Coming because Jesus tells us: "For the Son of man shall come in the glory of his Father with his angels, and then will he render to every man according to his works." (*Matt.* 16:27). "The harvest is the end of the world. And the reapers are the angels." (*Matt.* 13:39). "So shall it be at the end of the world. The angels shall go out, and shall separate the wicked from among the just." (*Matt.* 13:49).

Angels continued to perform their services for the benefit of the Church and the Apostles, as noted in the *Acts of the Apostles*.

An angel awakened **Philip** and instructed him: "Arise, go toward the south, to the way that goeth down from Jerusalem into Gaza." Philip went immediately and met the eunuch of Ethiopia, who was reading the prophet Isaias. After explaining the book to him, Philip baptized the eunuch, and the eunuch "went on his way rejoicing." (*Acts* 8:26-39).

We learn of an angel's visitation in the fifth chapter of the *Acts of the Apostles*, when **the Apostles** were cast into the common prison by the high priest. But that very night an angel opened the doors of the prison and, leading them out, said: "Go, and standing speak in the temple to the people all the words of this life." (*Acts* 5:20). The next morning, when the high priest and the council had gathered, they gave orders for the Apostles to be brought to them for questioning. But when the ministers came to the prison, they found the cell empty. They reported: "The prison indeed we found shut with all diligence, and the keepers standing before the doors; but opening it, we found no man within." (*Acts* 5:23). The Apostles were later found in the temple preaching.

The devout **Cornelius**, a centurion and a Gentile, was visited by an angel who instructed him to send his servants to invite St. Peter to his home. When Peter arrived, Cornelius told him, "Four days ago unto this hour, I was praying in my house, at the ninth hour, and behold a man stood before me in white apparel and said, 'Cornelius, thy prayer is heard, and thy alms are had in remembrance in the sight of God.' " (*Acts* 10:30). Peter preached to him and those in the house and baptized them—the first Gentiles to be admitted into the Church.

Next we find **St. Peter** again in prison, this time at the hands of King Herod. Perhaps the King had heard of his miraculous escape from prison when the high priest had him apprehended. This time the King took extra precautions that the Apostle would not escape and "delivered him to four files of soldiers to be kept." (*Acts* 12:4). But one night while Peter slept between two soldiers, bound with two chains and with jailers before the door, an angel appeared in a great light. While the soldiers were in a mysterious slumber, the chains miraculously fell from the Apostle. Peter was told to dress, to put on his sandals and to follow the angelic apparition. "And passing through the first and the second ward, they came to the iron gate that leadeth to the city, which of itself opened to them. And going out, they passed on through one street: and immediately the angel departed from him." (*Acts* 12:10).

The **Apostle Paul** also had an experience when he was aboard a ship, which was "being mightily tossed with the tempest." (*Acts* 27:18). After many days, St. Paul spoke to the passengers and crew: "Now I exhort you to be of good cheer. For there shall be no loss of any man's life among you, but only of the ship. For an angel of God, whose I am, and whom I serve, stood by me this night saying: 'Fear not, Paul, thou must be brought before Caesar; and behold God hath given thee all of them that sail with thee.'" (*Acts* 27:22-24). After some days of difficulty the ship was run aground, and the stern "was broken with the violence of the sea." (*Acts* 27:41). Just as the angel had predicted, all the "two hundred threescore and sixteen souls" were saved and only the ship was lost. (*Acts* 27:37-44).

Angels are repeatedly mentioned in *The Apocalypse* written by **St. John** while at Patmos. In the Saint's vision of things yet to come, we find the Angels adoring and ministering before the throne: "And I beheld, and I heard the voice of many angels round about the throne . . ." (*Apoc.* 5:11). "And all the angels stood round about the throne, and the ancients, and the four living creatures; and they fell down before the throne upon their faces, and adored God." (*Apoc.* 7:11).

In the events yet to come we also find angels dispensing God's justice: "And I saw another angel ascending from the rising of the sun having the sign of the living God; and he cried with a loud voice to the four angels, to whom it was given to hurt the earth." (*Apoc.* 7:2). "And the four angels were loosed, who were prepared for an hour, and a day, and a month, and a year: for to kill the third part of men." (*Apoc.* 9:15). "And I saw another sign in heaven, great and wonderful: seven angels having the seven last plagues. For in them is filled up the wrath of God." (*Apoc.* 15:1). "And I heard a great voice out of the temple, saying to the seven angels: Go, and pour out the seven vials of the wrath of God upon the earth." (*Apoc.* 16:1).

We learn too that angels are assigned to guard various places, especially in the New Jerusalem: "And it had a wall great and high, having twelve gates, and in the gates twelve angels . . ." (*Apoc.* 21:12).

And finally, in the book of *The Apocalypse*, angels are mentioned in 13 of the 22 Chapters.

5. What the Church Teaches about Angels

The Church continues to benefit from angelic services, since angels are recognized in her prayers and rubrics. In the funeral liturgy we pray, "May the Angels lead you into Paradise." The words of Gabriel are given in the *Hail Mary*, and the announcement is repeated in the *Angelus*, which the Church recites at 6 a.m., noon and 6 p.m.

The Angels are appealed to for prayer at the beginning of Holy Mass in the words: "And I ask Blessed Mary, ever Virgin, all the Angels and Saints, and you, my brothers and sisters, to pray for me to the Lord our God." *The Confiteor* in the Traditional Roman Rite of the Mass invokes "Holy Michael the

Archangel." The Preface of Holy Mass also appeals to "all the choirs of Angels in Heaven" to join with us in praising God. And after the Consecration, we pray: "Almighty God, we pray that Your angel may take this sacrifice to Your altar in Heaven . . ."

The Church has traditionally designated September 29 as the Feast of (the Dedication of the church of) St. Michael the Archangel. This feast has now been expanded to include St. Gabriel and St. Raphael also. In the traditional Roman calendar, May 8 commemorated "The Apparition of St. Michael the Archangel" at Monte Gargano in Apulia, Italy, in 492. The guardian angels are remembered on October 2. Besides these remembrances, there are also other prayers in which the Church mentions angels. In addition, there are novenas, chaplets, litanies, beloved hymns and prayers of the Saints.

In an address given by Pope John Paul II on July 9, 1986, the Holy Father stated regarding angels: "All of the Church's tradition is unanimous in affirming that they do exist. One would have to alter Sacred Scripture itself if one wished to eliminate this teaching . . . At certain points in salvation history, angels have had a fundamental role to play in the unfolding of human events."

In the same year, on July 23, the Holy Father further instructed:

> The Angels are purely spiritual beings, created by God and given intelligence and free will. Through an immediate intuition of the truth, their intelligence grasps its object in a way that is much more complete than is possible for man . . . The world of the pure spirits is divided into good angels and bad ones. And this division has happened precisely as a result of their freedom to choose. God was present to their intelligence and free will as the Supreme Good. He also wished to give them, through grace, a share in the mystery of His divinity. The good angels have chosen God. But the others . . . have turned against God and the revelation of His grace. Their decision

was inspired by a false sense of self-sufficiency, and it emerges as hatred and rebellion against God.

It is traditional Catholic teaching (though not a defined dogma) that each individual is given a guardian angel, who will accompany, guard and teach him throughout his life. After death this angel will accompany the soul to its judgment, visit it if it is detained in Purgatory, and accompany it to the glory of Heaven. (See #64-76.)

6. When Were the Angels Created?

St. Jerome, St. John Damascene, the Greek Fathers and many Doctors of the Church hold that the creation of the Angels took place previously to that of the corporeal world. Other theologians and Catholic writers believe that the Angels were created at the same time the world was created, although *before* the creation of man. This latter point was upheld by the Fourth Lateran Council of 1215, which stated: "God, by His almighty power, created together in the beginning of time both creatures, the spiritual and the corporeal, namely the angelic and the earthly, and afterwards the human, as it were an intermediate creature, composed of body and spirit." (D 428).

Despite the opinions of those previously mentioned, the issue is still being debated among theologians and writers of religious material as to exactly when the Angels were created—before the heavens, the stars? But the common opinion of theologians is that the Angels and the material world were created at the same time.

St. Thomas Aquinas (1225-1274) writes on this subject: "God alone, Father, Son and Holy Ghost, is from eternity. Catholic Faith holds this without doubt, and everything to the contrary must be rejected as heretical. For God so produced creatures that He made them from nothing, that is, after there had been nothing."[6] From this we know that there was a time when angels did not exist and that they were created in the beginning of time and before man was created. Exactly when they were created, whether before the earth and the skies, is known to God alone.

7. Before the Angelic Battle in Heaven, Were All the Angels Admitted to the Full Vision of God?

It is the belief of many theologians and Doctors of the Church that the Angels were all created in the state of grace in *a* heaven, but one separated from the Heaven of the Holy Trinity. The Angels had to give proof of their fidelity to God before being admitted to His presence. It was at this time that the bad angels rebelled. Had they seen the majesty and magnificence of God—the full impact of the Beatific Vision—they would never have entertained thoughts of being equal to or superior to God, nor would they have dared to be rebellious.

After the fall of the angels—who then became devils—the good, faithful angels were admitted to the Heaven of the Holy Trinity, where they were permitted to gaze on the unveiled beauty of God. All of the above, as mentioned, is the belief of many theologians, and was also that of **St. Thomas Aquinas**, a Doctor of the Church. The Saint writes that the faithful angels, since their entrance into the Heaven of the Trinity, could not and cannot now sin or rebel because they now see God "in His essence," which he also calls "the union of beatitude."[7]

8. Has the Number of Angels Increased Since Their Creation?

It is the universal Catholic belief that after the battle in which the defeated angels were transformed into devils, the number of angels has remained the same. Their number was complete from that time to this.

9. How Many Angels Are There?

Some learned men have maintained that they surpass in number all the stars of Heaven, all the birds of the air, all the drops of water, all the blades of grass . . . that is, their number seems to us to be infinite and is known to God alone. **St. Gregory of Nyssa** (c. 330-c. 395) declares that there are millions of them. The **Prophet Daniel** apparently seems overwhelmed and at a loss to describe the number of angels in a vision he was granted, but nevertheless wrote that before the throne of God, "thousands of thousands ministered to him, and ten thousand times a hundred thousand stood before him." (*Dan.* 7:10).

St. Luke writes that, after the birth of the Saviour was announced to the shepherds, "Suddenly there was with the angel a multitude of the heavenly army praising God . . ." (*Luke* 2:13). In his letter to the *Hebrews*, **St. Paul** speaks of many thousands of angels. (*Heb.* 12:22). **St. Thomas Aquinas** (1225-1274) cites the opinion of Pseudo Dionysius that the number of angels surpasses the feeble and limited range of our material numbers.

Bl. Angela of Foligno (c. 1248-1309), a great mystic of the Church, once wrote of a vision:

> I experienced a clear perception of how Christ comes in the Sacrament of the Altar, that never before or after has it been so clearly demonstrated to me. It was shown to me how Christ comes accompanied by a mighty throng, or host . . . I was told that this host was the thrones [one of the nine choirs of angels], but I did not understand what this word meant. This host formed an array so imposing, a militia of such great number, that if I did not know that God does all things according to measure, I would believe that the number of this host was without measure, indeed countless . . . they could not be measured either by its length or its breadth. It was ineffable.[8]

Fr. Pascal P. Parente, in his book *The Angels* (formerly titled *Beyond Space*), reports that the number of the angelic spirits "must exceed beyond all comparison the number of human souls created from the beginning of the world until now and those to be created from now to the end of the world."[9]

In describing his vision, **St. John**, in *The Apocalypse*, wrote: "And I beheld, and I heard the voice of many angels round about the throne, and the living creatures, and the ancients; and the number of them was thousands of thousands." (*Apoc.* 5:11).

Once more in *The Apocalypse* we read that the Apostle saw a man clothed "with a garment sprinkled with blood; and his name is called THE WORD OF GOD. And the armies that are in heaven followed him on white horses, clothed in fine linen, white and clean." (*Apoc.* 19:13-14).

St. Paul, in his letter to the *Hebrews*, wrote: "But you are come to Mount Sion, and to the city of the living God, the heavenly Jerusalem, and to the company of many thousands of angels." (*Heb.* 12:22). **St. Denis** (d. c. 250) maintains that God alone knows their number. With this we may confidently agree.

10. After Death Will Men Be Equal to the Angels in Heaven?

The Psalmist wrote: "What is man that thou art mindful of him? or the son of man that thou visitest him? Thou has made him a little *less* than the angels." (Emphasis added.) (*Ps.* 8:5-6). We were made a little less than the Angels, but if and when we reach Heaven, apparently our status will be elevated. **St. Luke** quotes the words of Jesus: "Neither can they die any more: for they are equal to the Angels, and are the children of God, being the children of the resurrection." (*Luke* 20:36). **St. Thomas Aquinas** writes: "By the gift of grace men can merit glory in such a degree as to be equal to the Angels, in each of the angelic grades; and this implies that men are taken up into the orders of the Angels."[10]

This does not mean that we will become angels. Men, after the purification in Purgatory, if that was necessary, become saints, not angels. By this quotation St. Thomas means that, according to the degree of holiness reached on earth, we will be equal to those angels in the higher, or the middle or lower choirs of angels. This would explain the vision of **St. Frances of Rome** (1384-1440) in which she saw her dead son, Evangelista, who was accompanied by an angel who was to be St. Frances' constant, visible companion. Evangelista is reported to have said, "There are nine choirs of angels in Heaven, and the higher orders of angelic spirits instruct in the divine mysteries the less exalted intelligences. If you wish to know my place amongst them, my Mother, learn that God, of His great goodness, has appointed it in the second choir of angels, and the first hierarchy of archangels. This my companion is higher than I am in rank, as he is more bright and fair in aspect."[11]

11. Are There Male and Female Angels?

Since angels are pure spirits, they are neither male nor female—although they have qualities that we associate with masculinity, or femininity, as when St. Frances of Rome tells that her angel had "beautiful golden hair which fell in soft curls over the shoulders." When angels are sent by God to earth to perform a particular function, they assume an appearance which in most cases is identified as male. This is well demonstrated in the prophet **Daniel's** description of the Angel Gabriel: "And it came to pass when I, Daniel, saw the vision, and sought the meaning, that behold there stood before me, as it were, the appearance of a man." (*Dan.* 8:15).

When **Tobias** was searching for someone to accompany him on a journey, he, "going forth, found a beautiful young man, standing girded, and as it were, ready to walk." (*Tob.* 5:5). The young man was, of course, the Archangel Raphael. And as to the women who visited Our Lord's tomb on Easter Sunday, upon "entering into the sepulchre, they saw a young man sitting on the right side, clothed with a white robe: and they were astonished." (*Mark* 16:5). And so it goes with many of the angelic visitations recorded in Scripture.

Again, in the lives of the Saints, angels are almost always identified as male. The children of Fatima described the Angel of Peace as "he": "Kneeling on the ground, he bowed down until his forehead touched the ground . . . "

However, it has been the consistent teaching of the Church that angels are neither male nor female because of their nature as pure spirits. This is upheld in the gospel of **St. Mark**: "For when they shall rise again from the dead, they shall neither marry, nor be married, but are as the angels in heaven." (*Mark* 12:25). This Scripture reading indicates that angels were not created for procreation and therefore do not need to be assigned a particular gender.

Angels are perhaps identified as male because of their extraordinary majesty and their projection of power and great strength.

12. What is the Reaction of Some Who Have Seen Angels?

When angels appear on earth to accomplish a particular assignment, they assume a bodily form and earthly garments as an accommodation to the visionary. Their heavenly splendor is then muted or hidden altogether while performing their earthly assignments given by God, until their project is accomplished. It is then that their appearance gives some hint of their heavenly citizenship, which is sometimes met with fear.

Such is the case when **Tobias and his family** learned that the young man who had accompanied the younger Tobias on his journey was an angel. After Raphael introduced himself, he must have then appeared resplendent because, when they heard who he was, "they were troubled, and being seized with fear, they fell upon the ground on their face." The Angel was then "taken from their sight and they could see him no more. Then they, laying prostrate for three hours upon their face, blessed God: and rising up, they told all his wonderful works." (*Tob.* 12:16, 21-22).

The prophet **Daniel** experienced an apparition of the Archangel Gabriel, and "when he was come, I fell on my face trembling . . . And when he spoke to me, I fell flat on the ground." (*Dan.* 8:17-18). And again, Daniel writes: "And I heard the voice of his words: and when I heard, I lay in a consternation upon my face, and my face was close to the ground." (*Dan.* 10:9). Daniel concludes: ". . . he that looked like a man touched me and strengthened me." (*Dan.* 10:18).

In the New Testament we learn that the angel who announced to the **shepherds** the birth of Jesus stood by them, ". . . and the brightness of God shone round about them [the shepherds]; and they feared with a great fear. And the angel said to them: 'Fear not; for behold, I bring you good tidings of great joy, that shall be to all the people . . .'" (*Luke* 2:9-10). Then on Easter morning, "an angel of the Lord descended from heaven, and coming, rolled back the stone, and sat upon it. And his countenance was as lightning, and his raiment as snow. And for fear of him, the guards were struck with terror, and became as dead men." (*Matt.* 28:2-4). Mary Magdalen "and the other Mary," after arriving at the sepulchre, upon being told by the angel to go quickly and "tell ye his disciples that he is risen: . . . went out quickly from the sepulchre with fear and great joy." (*Matt.* 28:7-8).

In the *Acts of the Apostles*, we learn that **Cornelius**, a centurion, "a religious man, and fearing God with all his house," was visited by an angel during the ninth hour of the day, and Cornelius "was seized with fear." (*Acts* 10:1-4).

But later apparitions of angels, as described in the lives of the Saints, are rarely met with fear, but are accepted with joyful appreciation and admiration, as we will later learn.

13. Angels as Children

In all the cases mentioned from the Old and New Testaments, angels appeared as adults, but we learn to our edification that they sometimes appeared to the Saints as children.

In the depths of a pine forest near Lake Lucerne in Switzerland, **St. Meinrad** (797-861) built a small hermitage where he could devote himself entirely to his Creator. Eventually, his remote dwelling was discovered by a monk from Reichenau. After speaking with the monk about religious matters, the Saint invited him to return for a similar conversation. Sometime later the monk approached the hermitage at night and saw a brilliant light filtering through. Looking in, he saw the Saint reciting the night office, while a young child, surrounded by brilliant rays, supported the book and recited the alternate verses. The monk did not enter, but returned to his monastery and made known to his fellow monks that Meinrad's retreat had been visited by an angel.[12]

An angel who appeared as a small child also visited **St. Catherine Labouré** (1806-1876). The Saint was still a postulant in the Order of the Sisters of Charity when she went to bed the night of July 18, 1830, the eve of the feast of St. Vincent de Paul, the founder of her order. After only two hours of sleep, she was awakened by the small voice of a child: "Come to the chapel, the Blessed Virgin awaits you." She was unafraid, but concerned that she would be discovered. The child replied to her thoughts, "Do not be uneasy. It is half past eleven; everyone is asleep. Come, I am waiting for you." After dressing hurriedly, she followed the child down the hall where, to her surprise, the lights were burning brightly. In fact, all along her journey to the chapel, the lights were lit. On arriving at the chapel, the heavy door opened easily at the mere touch of the child's hand. Again Catherine was surprised to see the lights in the chapel and the candles burning brightly, as though for a midnight Mass.

After waiting for a few minutes, the child's voice changed to a deep, reverential tone when he announced, "Here is the Blessed Virgin." There was a rustling of fabric and then the appearance of Our Lady, who walked to the director's chair and sat down. Realizing that the apparition resembled a picture of St. Anne that hung over the sacristy door, Catherine's eyes moved from the painting back to the Lady, until the child reassured her once again in a man's deep, but trembling voice, "This is the Blessed Virgin." This vision, which lasted over two hours, was the first of a number of visions that would result in the introduction to the world of the Miraculous Medal. After the vision, the child, whom Catherine recognized as her guardian angel, accompanied her back to the dormitory. When they arrived at the side of Catherine's bed, the child faded from sight, just as Our Lady had done.[13]

A vision of an angelic child is given in the biography of **St. Anthony Mary Claret** (1807-1870), a mystic, visionary, founder of two religious orders and later archbishop of Santiago, Cuba. One stormy day, when the holy priest was on his way to give a mission, he approached a stream that he had to cross; but due to the storm, the stream had developed into a turbulent river. Refusing to cancel the mission, the Saint nevertheless decided to wade across and was in the act of removing his shoes when an unknown, modest and courteous boy appeared. With a smile and soft words, the child told the priest, "Don't take off your shoes, for I will take you across the river." The priest almost laughingly told the child that it was impossible for a child of his small size to do such a thing and recommended that he return home because of the rain. But the child insisted that he could bring the priest to the other side without him becoming wet.

And so it happened that the child took the missionary on his shoulders, quickly waded the turbulent stream and transported Fr. Claret to the opposite bank, much to the astonishment of the holy priest. As a little token of appreciation, Fr. Claret opened his breviary to give the child a holy card, but found that the angelic child had disappeared.[14]

One year after the death of her young son, Evangelista, **St. Frances of Rome** (1384-1440) was praying in her oratory when a mysterious light shone in the room, and "its radiance seemed to pervade not only her outward senses, but the inmost depths of her being, and to awaken in her soul a strange sensation of joy." Suddenly standing before her was Evangelista, full of joy and peace, as was his companion, who stood by his side. The companion was introduced to her as an angel sent by God who would remain with her in visible form for many years. After her son vanished, the angel followed her wherever she went, the whole time surrounded with a dazzling radiance. Upon the advice of her spiritual director, Don Antonio, the Saint described the angel in this way: "His stature is that of a child of about nine years old; his aspect full of sweetness and majesty; his eyes generally turned towards Heaven: words cannot describe the divine purity of that gaze."[15] (See #16.)

We learn that **Bl. Padre Pio** (1887-1968) as a youngster frequently saw his guardian angel, who appeared as a child. In his later writings, Padre Pio often spoke of his angel as "the companion of my infancy." Padre Agostino, Padre Pio's spiritual director, notes that "his camaraderie with his guardian angel is without doubt." Eavesdropping during an ecstasy of Padre Pio in 1911, Padre Agostino wrote down what Padre Pio said to his angel, including the words, "Well done, little child." During another ecstasy the same year, Padre Pio was heard to exclaim when answering a knock at his door, "Ah, it is you, my Little Angel? It is you, Little Boy." Another time, when asking a question of his angel, he addressed him, "Now then, Little Man . . ."[16]

14. Angels as Adolescents and Adults

When the father of **Tobias** thought he would die, he instructed Tobias to journey to Medes to obtain money that had been loaned to Gabelus who lived in that city. Telling his son to find a traveling companion, Tobias went out and "found a beautiful young man, standing girded, and as it were ready to walk." (*Tob.*

5:5). Not knowing he was an angel, Tobias asked if the young man would accompany him, since he said he knew the way. After the successful completion of the journey, the young man identified himself, "I am the angel Raphael, one of the seven who stand before the Lord." (*Tob.* 12:15).

In the Old and New Testaments angels always appear to be handsome young men, and that is how they most often appear to the Saints. It was in this form that they appeared to **St. Dominic** (1170-1221). The convent in the city of Faenza, Italy preserves ancient memoirs regarding the angels' appearance to the Saint. Albert, the Bishop of Faenza, on learning that St. Dominic would be journeying through the city, insisted that the Saint lodge in the episcopal palace. According to his custom, the Saint continued his regular practices and rose every night at the hour of Matins and proceeded to the nearest church to assist at the Divine Office. The attendants of the Bishop watched secretly to see how it was that the Saint was able to leave the palace without arousing the servants.

What they witnessed left them astonished, since they saw two beautiful youths with lighted torches standing by the door of the Saint's chamber, waiting for him to leave. They then led the way for him, every door opening for them as they went along. In this way they conducted him safely to the church of St. Andrew and, after Matins, returned in the same fashion. The servants informed the Bishop, who himself witnessed the angelic companions of the Saint. The Bishop soon bought the land between the episcopal palace and the church of St. Andrew and named the area "The Angels' Field" in memory of what they had witnessed.[17]

Another event in the life of **St. Dominic** regarding the appearance of an angel took place in Rome when he visited the sisters of his order. Although it was very late when he finished his visit with them, he decided to go to Santa Sabina, a church which has been in the custody of the Dominican Order from that time to the present day. His companions were afraid they would be harmed at such a late hour, but the Saint insisted that the good Lord would send an angel to guard them. And so He did, since a young man "of great beauty presented himself, having a staff in his hand, as if ready for a journey." When they reached the door of the church, they found it locked, but the young man leaned against the door, which immediately opened. He entered first, then the brethren, and then the Saint. The young man then went out and the door closed. When the Saint's companion, Brother Tancred, inquired about the identity of the mysterious young man, the Saint replied, "My son, it was an angel of God, whom He sent to guard us."[18]

The companions of the Saint had reason to worry about his safety. As was his custom, the Saint was one night praying by a low pillar located at the bottom of the nave near the door in the church of Santa Sabina. That night a round black stone was hurled at him by an invisible hand from the upper part of the roof. It grazed his head, tore his hood and buried itself in the ground beside him. This pillar, with the stone atop it, is still found in the same location in the church of Santa Sabina.[19]

St. Lydwine of Schiedam (1380-1433) had a close relationship with the Angels and frequently saw them under the form of adolescents, marked on the forehead with a bright cross. This sign of our redemption distinguished the Angels from the demons, who often impersonate angelic spirits but who are unable to wear this blessed symbol. Although the Angels were always visible to her, they disappeared when the Saint had visitors and returned only when the visitors were gone.

One day the widow, Catherine Simon, who nursed the Saint and knew about the visible presence of the Angels, told the Saint of her desire to see an angel, as Lydwine saw them. Being grateful for the loving care given her by the widow, Lydwine told her to kneel down, saying, "Here is the angel whom you desire to know." The Saint's biographer, H. K. Huysmans, tells us that "an angel then appeared in the room under the form of an adolescent whose dress was woven of threads of white fire." The woman was unable to utter a single word to express her happiness. Then St. Lydwine asked the angel, "My brother, will you authorize my sister to contemplate the splendor of your eyes, if only for a moment?" When the angel looked at the woman, she was so taken out of herself that for some time she continued to groan and weep for love without being able to sleep or eat. Lydwine sometimes told her friends, "I know no affliction, no discomfort that a single look from my angel does not dissipate; his look acts on grief like a ray of sun on the dew of the morning, dissipating it altogether."[20]

St. Martin de Porres (1579-1639) was a Dominican lay brother who labored in Peru. His biographer, J. C. Kearns, O.P., records that the Blessed Mother often sent to him angels who were in the form of comely youths with lighted candles to accompany him from the dormitory to the choir. This remarkable privilege was witnessed by many of Martin's fellow religious.[21] The priests and brothers of the community once saw St. Martin in the company of two angels who were assisting the Saint one night when, according to custom, the Little Office of the Blessed Virgin was being recited in the dormitory before Matins. "At another time the Saint was seen walking in the cloister of the convent in the visible company of four angels, who looked like handsome young men who carried lighted torches in their hands."[22] The Saint was much devoted to his guardian angel, to whom he often turned in prayerful petition and for supernatural assistance.

The father of **Anna Maria Redi** tells how one day, after the maid had locked the child in her room while she went to Mass, Anna Maria knelt in prayer and saw at her side two singularly beautiful young men. She was about to speak to them when one of them said to her, "Anna Maria, always be cheerful and happy, for Jesus is to be your Spouse." They then disappeared, leaving the child's heart flooded with sweetness. Anna Maria later entered the Discalced Carmelite Monastery at Florence and is now known as **St. Theresa Margaret of the Sacred Heart of Jesus** (1747-1770).[23]

When **St. Anthony Mary Claret** (1807-1870) was traveling from Vich to Orista with a servant named Ramon Prat, the snow was falling heavily and hiding every trace of a road. When the Saint realized that Ramon was far from his home in Vich, he insisted that the servant return. Ramon, however, refused to return home, citing that the priest was still far from his destination and would surely lose his way without a guide. Suddenly, a distinguished young man appeared. He announced that he was going to Orista and would see the priest safely to the city. Ramon agreed to return to Vich, but on examining the path over which the youth was supposed to have traveled, he noticed that there were no footprints in the snow. Amazed by this, Ramon watched the two travelers as they went along, and no doubt reported the unusual incident. As for the Saint, when the city of Orista was reached and the priest had no further need of a guide, the young man promptly vanished. His traveling companion was undoubtedly an angel sent to see the Saint safely to his destination.[24]

Ven. Mary of Agreda (1602-1665) in *The Mystical City of God,* the "autobiography" of the Blessed Mother that is said to have been dictated to her by Mary herself, writes that, to assist the Blessed Virgin, "nine hundred angels were chosen from the nine choirs, those who had distinguished themselves by their esteem, love and reverence for the most holy Mary. They were made visible to the Blessed Virgin under the form of young men in their early years, but of the most exquisite beauty and courteousness."[25]

Closer to our own time, when the three **Fatima children** were one day enjoying a game, a strong wind began to shake the trees. Since the day had been unusually calm, the children looked about and saw a figure coming toward them above the olive trees. Lucia writes in her *Memoirs,* "As the figure drew nearer, we were able to distinguish its features. It was a young man about fourteen or fifteen years old, whiter than snow, transparent as crystal when the sun shines through it, and of great beauty

. . . On reaching us, he said: 'Do not be afraid! I am the angel of Peace. Pray with me.' After kneeling and touching his face to the ground, he repeated three times the words: 'My God, I believe, I adore, I hope and I love Thee! I ask pardon of Thee for those who do not believe, do not adore, do not hope and do not love Thee.'" Lucia adds, "His words engraved themselves so deeply on our minds that we could never forget them."[26]

Some months later, as Lucia writes: "Suddenly, we saw beside us the same figure, or rather angel, as it seemed to me." The angel this time identified himself as "the angel guardian, the Angel of Portugal," and recommended that they "bear with submission the suffering which the Lord will send you." Still another time the angel appeared to them in a great light, carrying a chalice and a Host, which he suspended in the air before he knelt beside the children. After reciting the prayer that begins: "Most Holy Trinity, Father, Son and Holy Spirit, I offer Thee the most precious Body, Blood, Soul and Divinity of Jesus Christ," he offered Lucia the Host and shared the Blood of Jesus between Jacinta and Francisco. Since Lucia does not give us a different description of the angel in the second and third apparitions, he apparently appeared in the same fashion as in the first apparition, "a young man about fourteen or fifteen years old," and seems to have been the same angel in all three occurrences.[27]

15. Angels in Unusual Aspects

"And hospitality do not forget; for by this some, being not aware of it, have entertained angels." (Heb. 13:2).

Sometimes angels have resembled ordinary people, as beggars, the poor, as shepherds, but as soon as they disappeared, their angelic nature was realized and the recipients of such favors were filled with a joy not easily described. Such was the case of the angelic visit to **St. Zita** (1218-1278), the patroness of domestic workers.

St. Zita never wore shoes and only the poorest of clothing. So it was that, on one cold Christmas Eve, she insisted on going to church in spite of the wishes of the family for whom she worked. Unable to dissuade her, the master threw his costly fur coat over her, cautioning her not to lose it. At the entrance of San Frediano Church, she saw a shabbily dressed old man suffering from the cold. Without hesitation she threw her master's fur coat over the poor man, making him promise to return it to her after the service. When the service was over, the poor man and the coat were nowhere to be found.

The Saint returned home to the unhappy disposition of her master. A few hours later, when the family sat down to the Christmas dinner, a stranger appeared at the door, carrying the missing fur coat on his arm. With a gracious deportment and with a heavenly smile he thanked Zita for the use of the coat and then disappeared. All who had seen him were filled with celestial joy. Butler tells us that from that day on the people of Lucca called the entrance door "The Angel Door" in honor of the event.[28]

The biography of **St. Felix of Valois** (1126-1212), co-founder of the Trinitarian Order, reveals that he was a hermit when St. John of Matha visited him in the forest to propose founding an order for the redemption of captives. The story is told that St. Felix was traveling one wintry day in the company of his uncle, Thibaud of Blois, searching for the indigent, when they met a man half-naked and shivering from the cold. It was the uncle who addressed the beggar first: "What do you want me to give you?" To this the man mentioned the mantle. He also admired the uncle's ring, which was given to him, and the knightly insignia he wore, which also was given to him. The beggar, it was revealed, was an angel who had no need of what was surrendered to him, but was sent only to test the charity of the travelers.[29]

Another beggar, in the same century, approached Brother John of Calabria and Brother Albert of Rome when **St. Dominic** (1170-1221) sent them into the city to beg alms for the abbey. They had been unsuccessful all day, but when they were returning home, an elderly woman gave them a loaf of bread. They were soon met by a beggar who implored them for help. Realizing that the one loaf would be insufficient for the whole abbey, they decided to give it to the beggar with their blessing. On their return to the abbey, they related to the Saint what had taken place, who immediately recognized the significance of what had occurred. "It was an angel of the Lord. The Lord will know how to provide for His own. Let us go and pray."

In spite of having nothing with which to feed his followers, the Saint nevertheless ordered the brethren to assemble for dinner. While St. Dominic sat with them at table and prayed, suddenly "two beautiful young men" appeared in the refectory, carrying loaves in two white cloths which hung from their shoulders. They began to distribute the bread, starting at the lower rows and placing a loaf in front of each one. When they reached St. Dominic, they also placed a loaf in front of him. They then bowed their heads and disappeared, "without anyone knowing, even to this day, whence they came or whither they went."[30] On this occasion, wine was also miraculously provided. Both the wine and the bread, which were of "excellent quality," provided meals for three days.

A record of those who witnessed this miracle was carefully recorded. Not only was some of the bread kept as relics, but in commemoration of this event, it became the custom in houses of the Order to serve the lowest tables first, moving upward to the place of the prior. This custom was afterwards made a law of the Order, being introduced into the constitutions.[31] Moreover, this same miracle is said to have been repeated twice at Rome and twice at Bologna. In recounting this miracle to Pope Gregory IX, one of the members of the Order reported that on one occasion a handful of dried figs had also been given to each of them. And he added that "never had he eaten better figs."[32] St. Dominic was known to have warned his brethren that they were "never to distrust the Divine goodness, even in time of greatest want."

16. Descriptions of Angels

Perhaps the best description of an angel given in the Old Testament is that of the prophet Daniel, who was ending a fast when he had the vision which he describes. The prophet explains: "I was by the great river which is the Tigris. And I lifted up my eyes, and I saw: and behold a man clothed in linen and his loins were girded with the finest gold: And his body was like the chrysolite, and his face as the appearance of lightning, and his eyes as a burning lamp: and his arms, and all downward even to the feet, like in appearance to glittering brass: and the voice of his word like the voice of a multitude." (*Dan.* 10:4-6).

With the exception of *The Apocalypse,* where some details are given, no really detailed descriptions of angels are given in the New Testament. We know, however, as recounted earlier, that at the Resurrection "there was a great earthquake. For an angel of the Lord descended from heaven, and coming, rolled back the stone, and sat upon it. And his countenance was as lightning, and his raiment as snow." (*Matt.* 28:3). The appearance of the angel must have been magnificent, since ". . . for fear of him the guards were struck with terror, and became as dead men." (*Matt.* 28:4).

Although the New Testament does not give detailed descriptions of the Angels, we do have many details given by the Saints.

In *The Mystical City of God,* **Ven. Mary of Agreda** (1602-1665) gives this description of the Archangel Gabriel at the time of the Incarnation:

> The appearance of the great prince and legate was that of a most handsome youth of rarest beauty; his face emitted resplendent rays of light, his bearing was grave and majestic, his advance measured, his motions composed, his words weighty and powerful, his whole presence displayed a pleasing, kindly gravity and more of godlike qualities than all the other angels until then seen in visible form by the heavenly Mistress. He wore a diadem of exquisite splendor and his vestments glowed in various colors full of refulgent beauty. Encased on his breast, he bore a most beautiful Cross, disclosing the mystery of the Incarnation, which He had come to announce.[33]

Another time, in writing about the angels who were given to the Blessed Mother to guard and assist her, Ven. Mary of Agreda writes that "Twelve of the angels appeared in the same corporeal shape as those which I have first mentioned [young men in their early years], except that they bore palms and crowns reserved for the devout servants of the Mistress."[34]

When **St. Frances of Rome** (1384-1440) experienced a vision of her deceased son, Evangelista, as described earlier, he was accompanied by an angel. The Saint described the heavenly being as a child of about nine years old, "his aspect full of sweetness and majesty; his eyes generally turned toward Heaven: words cannot describe the divine purity of that gaze." Evangelista introduced the archangel as being a gift from God. He was to be St. Frances' spiritual guide, her defender and helper in every difficulty and would remain as her companion for many years. Following the apparition, when she left the oratory, "The angel followed her and, enveloped in a halo of light, remained always visible to her, though imperceptible to others. The radiance that surrounded him was so dazzling, that she could seldom look upon him with a fixed gaze. At night, and in the most profound darkness, she could always write and read by the light of that supernatural brightness." When in prayer or in conference with her director, or while struggling with the devil, she was enabled to see his form with perfect distinctness. The Saint adds these descriptions of the angel:

"His brow is always serene; his glances kindle in the soul the flame of ardent devotion . . . He wears a long shining robe, and over it a tunic, either as white as the lilies of the field, or of the color of a red rose, or of the hue of the sky when it is most deeply blue. When he walks by my side, his feet are never soiled by the mud of the streets or the dust of the road."

The angel helped St. Frances of Rome in many other ways as well. When she committed a fault, he seemed to disappear, and he reappeared only when the Saint expressed sorrow for what she had done. He looked kindly upon her when she was disturbed and guided her when she was tempted to perform penances that were beyond her strength. The Saint tells us that when he spoke, she saw his lips move; and a voice of indescribable sweetness, but which seemed to come from a distance, reached her ears. The light of the angel also gave her a marvelous insight into the thoughts of others, so that their sins and errors, or their evil inclinations, were supernaturally revealed to her. Because of this gift, she was enabled to help many return to the reception of the Sacraments.[35]

The most astounding feature of the angel was his beautiful golden hair, which fell in soft curls over his shoulders and had a glow all its own. According to the sources of Frances Parkinson Keyes, "When demons came to attack the Saint, the angel tossed back his curls and the sparkling rays that escaped from these put to flight those creatures of darkness, who could not endure the light."

Another passage of the same author reveals that:

> A great part of the beauty and power of the celestial protector lay in his hair, which as to color resembled molten gold; it fell in ringlets long enough to cover his neck and wave over his shoulders. If demons molested the Saint, he sometimes lowered his gaze so that it would rest on her and calm her; and sometimes to conjure the plots of their hatred against their innocent victim, he shook his flaming locks, an action which sufficed to put the monsters from hell to flight.[36]

The angel remained with her for twenty-four years, until she founded a religious order. It was then that he was replaced with one of taller stature. "In appearance, there was little difference between them; the newcomer also wore a dalmatic, but of more precious tissue than that worn by the previous protector. The light which surrounded him was even more dazzling, and his power was so great that he did not need to shake his locks in order that they might emit sparks and thus put demons to flight—his very glance was sufficient to do this!"[37]

An interesting aspect of angels is given by **Père Lamy** (1855-1931), who was on familiar terms with many angels. He tells us that "they have a great light and sometimes none at all. In their great light, even when I was almost blind, I used to see the holy chapel and the trees and the leaves, and the other side of the trees. The eye no longer is obverse or reverse. Often I call upon them when I am too tired, so as to be able to go out and do such or such a thing. They send me their light and I am comforted whilst there is need."[38]

Père Lamy continues by telling us that "The Angels, like the Saints, have no body like the real bodies of the Blessed Virgin and Our Lord. They have bodies that are not of our sphere. Each angel has his own face. The figures in which the Angels show themselves to our eyes often have black hair, and their hair is well cut. I have never seen curly hair among the Angels. My guardian angel has a fairly round head, a very beautiful face, black and wavy hair . . ."[39]

St. Teresa of Avila (1515-1582) gives us a description of an angel in her *Autobiography*:

> I saw an angel close by me, on my left side, in bodily form. He was not large, but small of stature, and most beautiful—his face burning, as if he were one of the highest angels, who seem to be all of fire: they must be those whom we call cherubim. Their names they never tell me; but I see very well that there is in Heaven so great a difference between one angel and another, and between these and the others, that I cannot explain it.[40]

We learn that **St. Cecilia** (d. second or third century) had vowed her virginity to God before her marriage. Afterward, in the bridal chamber, she told her husband of the vow and persuaded him to respect it, telling him that if he were baptized, he would be able to see the angel that protected her virtue. In order to be baptized, Valerian, her husband, sought out Pope Urban, who then resided in the catacombs to escape the persecutions that constantly harassed the Church at that time. (This pope was later martyred for the Faith.)

After his Baptism, Valerian found Cecilia prostrate in prayer with the angel of God beside her. The angel is described in this way: "His face was resplendent as lightning, his wings brilliant with the most gorgeous colors. The blessed spirit held in his hand two crowns interwoven with roses and lilies, one of which he placed upon the head of Cecilia and the other upon that of Valerian, whilst with the musical accents of Heaven [he said], 'Merit to preserve these crowns, by the purity of your hearts and the sanctity of your bodies. I bring them fresh from the garden of Heaven. These flowers will never fade, nor lose their celestial fragrance; but no one can see them who has not endeared himself to Heaven, as you have done by virginal purity.' "[41] Cecilia, Valerian and his brother, Tiburtius, who was also converted by Cecilia, later died as martyrs for the Faith.

Sr. Lucia of Fatima (b. 1911), when describing the first vision of the angel, writes in her *Memoirs*: "Then we saw coming toward us, above the olive trees, the figure I have already spoken about. Jacinta and Francisco had never seen it before, nor had I ever mentioned it to them. As it drew closer, we were able to distinguish its features. It was a young man, about fourteen or fifteen years old, whiter than snow, transparent as crystal when the sun shines through it, and of great beauty." The angel identified himself as the angel of Peace and asked the children to pray with him.[42]

And finally, **St. Bridget of Sweden** (1303-1373) tells us, "If we saw an angel clearly, we should die of pleasure."[43]

17. Angels' Wings

Some have expressed the opinion that winged angels are the invention of artists who intend to distinguish the heavenly figures from other figures in their works of art. However, wings were not their invention, but that of God, who often wills that angels appear to men as winged beings. The first mention of angelic wings is given in the book of *Exodus*, when God gave **Moses** the instructions for the making of the Ark of the Covenant. After describing the length and design, God told the people to make "two cherubims of beaten gold, on the two sides of the oracle. Let one cherub be on the one side, and the other on the other. Let them cover both sides of the propitiatory, spreading their wings, and covering the oracle, and let them look one towards the other." (*Ex.* 25:18-20).

When **Solomon** began building of the temple in Jerusalem, angels were also included. "And he made in the oracle two cherubims of olive tree, of ten cubits in height. One wing of the cherub was five cubits, and the other wing of the cherub was five cubits: that is, in all ten cubits, from the extremity of one wing to the extremity of the other wing." (*3 Kgs.* 6:23-24).

"The second cherub also was ten cubits: and the measure, and the work was the same in both the cherubims." (*3 Kgs.* [*1 Kgs.*] 6:25). That is to say, one cherub was ten cubits high, and in like manner the other cherub. "And he set the cherubims in the midst of the inner temple: and the cherubims stretched forth their wings and the wing of one touched one wall, and the wing of the other cherub touched the other wall: and the other wings in the midst of the temple touched one another. And he overlaid the cherubims with gold." (*3 Kgs.* [*1 Kgs.*] 6:27-28).

The earliest known artistic depictions of winged angels in post-Biblical times are found in a fourth century bas-relief at Carthage and a fourth century representation in ivory of St. Michael that can be viewed in the British Museum.

Closer to our own day, we learn of the remarkable vision of angels with Our Lady at the apparition in **Knock, Ireland**. On the rainy night of August 21, 1879, the Blessed Virgin appeared with St. Joseph and St. John the Evangelist, along with an altar, on which stood a Crucifix and a lamb. The Blessed Mother remained in an attitude of prayer, while St. John moved his lips and raised his hand as if preaching, although not a sound was heard. For two hours the vision remained by the gable of the parish church, surrounded by a brilliant light. Fifteen inhabitants of the village gave sworn testimony as to what they saw, including Patrick Hill, who gave the most detailed deposition.

Patrick examined the figures "for the space of one hour and a half or longer." He looked carefully into the eyes of the Blessed Mother. He reported, "I saw her eyes: the balls, the pupils, and the iris of each." The crown she wore had "a golden brightness . . . inclined to a more mellow yellow than the striking whiteness of the robes she wore . . . the upper parts of the crown appeared to be a series of sparkles, or glittering crosses." He saw that the figures were raised two feet from the ground. He examined the feet of both St. Joseph and the Blessed Virgin and noted that St. John "wore no sandals." He explained in detail the attitude and position of each figure and mentioned that St. John was dressed like a bishop, preaching and holding a book. "I came so near that I looked into the book; I saw the lines and the letters." His examination of every aspect of the vision was detailed and exact.

He describes other aspects which the others either did not see or failed to mention in their depositions. Patrick saw angels. He testified: "On the altar stood a lamb, the size of a lamb eight weeks old . . . behind the lamb a large Cross was placed erect or perpendicular on the altar; around the lamb I saw angels hovering during the whole time, for the space of one hour and a half or longer; I saw their wings fluttering, but I did not perceive their faces, which were not turned to me."[44]

Patrick Hill's deposition, as well as the other fourteen, was given in October 1879, almost two months after the apparition. The first official Church commission of inquiry in 1879, and also that of 1936, found that "the testimony of the witnesses, taken as a whole, was trustworthy and satisfactory." Since the time of the vision many cures have taken place, and pilgrims from throughout Ireland and the whole world have visited the Shrine. Today, at the gable end of the church, white marble statues stand exactly where the figures were located during the vision, and winged angels are depicted hovering above the altar that supports the crucifix and the lamb.

In addition to Scriptural references and the vision of Knock, winged angels have appeared to numerous saints. The guardian angel of **St. Cecilia** (d. second or third century) was seen standing beside the Saint, "his face resplendent as lightning, his wings brilliant with the most gorgeous colors."[45] **St. Gertrude the Great** (1256-c. 1302) writes in her *Revelations,* "While the Antiphon *Fundamenta templi ejus* was chanted at the Benedictus during the week, angelic spirits appeared around the walls, as if they had been deputed to guard the church and to repel the attacks of all enemies. Their golden wings touched each other and emitted a most exquisite melody . . . each descended in turn from the top to the bottom, to show with what vigilance they guarded their fellow citizens, and preserved them from every evil."[46]

St. Gemma Galgani (1878-1903) saw an angel with wings while she was praying in church one evening. She tells us what she saw in an entry in her diary. Suddenly realizing that it was growing late, "I saw when I rose up that my guardian angel was over my head with outspread wings, and he himself accompanied me home."[47] **Ven. Anne Catherine Emmerich** (1774-1824), while contemplating a vision of Heaven, saw a "luminous winged figure."[48] While not mentioning the wings of his angel, **Padre Pio** (1887-1968) writes that after being beaten violently by a demon, "I turned to my angel and . . . at length he appeared and flew all around me, and with his angelic voice, sang hymns to the Divine Majesty."[49]

18. Angels with Four Wings

In addition to angels who have two wings, there are apparently others with *four* wings. The prophet **Ezechiel** tells of a vision in which he saw God surrounded by the glories of Heaven. There were four living creatures, that is, four angels who had "the likeness of a man in them." (*Ezech.* 1:5). He describes the angels as having four wings each: "and every one [had] four wings." (*Ezech.* 1:6).

Ezechiel then writes: "And their faces, and their wings were stretched upward: two wings of every one were joined, and two covered their bodies." (*Ezech.* 1:11). Ezechiel gives many other mysterious details about these living creatures. He then adds: "And I heard the noise of their wings, like the noise of many waters, as it were the voice of the most high God. When they walked, it was like the voice of a multitude, like the noise of an army, and when they stood, their wings were let down." (*Ezech.* 1:24).

Ven. Anne Catherine Emmerich (1774-1824), the recipient of many extraordinary visions, reports that when men make progress in the spiritual life, they receive guardian angels of a higher order. She then adds that there are *four-winged* angels, and she names them as "the Elohim [one of the three common names used in the Hebrew Old Testament for God], who distribute God's graces." According to Ven. Anne Catherine, angels belonging to this group are known as "Raphiel, Etophiel, Salathiel, and Emmanuel,"[50] whom she describes as four great, luminous angels whose wings move constantly around them. "They are the administrators and distributors of God's superabundant graces, which they receive from the three archangels and scatter throughout the Church, to the four points of the compass . . ."[51]

19. Angels with Six Wings

We have noted that there are angels with one pair of wings, other angels with two pairs of wings, and now we shall see that there are angels with *three* pairs of wings.

We read in *Isaias*: "In the year that king Ozias died, I saw the Lord sitting upon a throne high and elevated: and his train filled the temple. Upon it stood the seraphims: the one had six wings, and the other had six wings: with two they covered his face, with two they covered his feet, and with two they flew." (*Is.* 6:1-2).

In centuries-old glass, a window in the great Chartres Cathedral depicts seraphim and cherubim each with six wings of red and blue. Also depicted in this window are other choirs of angels: Dominations, Powers and Principalities. This window is located on the south transcept near a window depicting Saint Apollinaris of Ravenna. In addition to these descriptions we have those of the Saints and Blesseds of God.

St. John the Evangelist writes in *The Apocalypse* that he saw four living creatures, "and each of them had six wings . . . And they rested not day and night, saying: 'Holy, holy, holy, Lord God Almighty, who was, and who is, and who is to come.'" (*Apoc.* 4:8).

We will recall that the most unusual vision of a being with wings was that witnessed by **St. Francis of Assisi** (1181-1226). Whether it was Our Lord Himself or an angel representing Our Lord is really unclear. The Saint's companion and biographer, Thomas of Celano, writes:

> Two years before Francis gave his soul back to Heaven, while he was living in the hermitage called Alverna, after the place on which it stood, he saw in the vision of God a man standing above him, like a seraph with six wings, his hands extended and his feet joined together and fixed to a cross. Two of the wings were extended above his head, two were extended as if for flight, and two were wrapped around the whole body. When the blessed servant of the Most High saw these things, he was filled with the greatest wonder . . . he was filled with happiness and he rejoiced very greatly because of the kind and gracious look with which he saw himself regarded by the seraph, whose beauty was beyond estimation."[52]

This parallels the vision of Isaias which was recounted above, in which he, too, saw angels with six wings.

Another view about angels and wings is given by **Père Lamy** (1855-1931), the holy mystic who was favored with countless visions, especially of angels. He relates that he never saw an angel with wings.

20. Angels and the Holy Eucharist

It is the opinion of St. Gregory, St. Augustine and St. John Chrysostom that Heaven opens at the time of Holy Mass and that multitudes of angels descend to assist and adore during the celebration of the Holy Eucharist. **St. John Chrysostom** speaks of angels crowding around, bowing profoundly, "worshiping Him who lies on the altar." Since God in the person of Jesus is then present on the altar, He is adored by the Angels as He is revered by them in Heaven. Angels who cluster in the sanctuary and around the altar during Holy Mass were sometimes seen by privileged saints, such as **St. Bridget** (1303-1373), who wrote in her *Revelations*: "One day, when I was assisting at the Holy Sacrifice, I saw an immense number of holy angels descend and gather around the altar, contemplating the priest. They sang heavenly canticles that ravished my heart; Heaven itself seemed to be contemplating the great Sacrifice. And yet, we poor, blind and miserable creatures assist at the Mass with so little love, relish and respect!"

Angels in visible form often appeared when **Bl. Henry Suso** (1295-1366), the holy Dominican, was offering the Holy Sacrifice. As the angels gathered around the altar, it was noticed that those who came near to him gazed at the Host in raptures of love.

One can only imagine the symphonies of praise and love these blessed spirits sing in adoration of what is often called "the Bread of Angels." The activity of the ministering spirits at Holy Mass involves a special assignment. **Fr. Alessio Parente**, who was an assistant to Padre Pio (1887-1968), tells that he was one morning distributing Holy Communion when he finished before another priest, who was also distributing the Holy Eucharist.

After returning to the altar, Fr. Alessio had just completed the purification of the ciborium when he saw, ". . . on my right side, a Host, in mid-air, heading for the ciborium, and It dropped in. Automatically, my head jerked towards the right, but there was no one there. The other priest was still at the altar rail. I was a little shocked, to say the least, and when my brother friar returned from the altar rails, I took the Host and put It into his ciborium."

Later, he told **Bl. Padre Pio** of his experience, to which Padre Pio replied: "Be more careful and don't rush when you distribute Holy Communion. Thank your guardian angel, who did not let Jesus fall on the floor." This brought to Fr. Alessio's mind another incident, when a brother friar had said to Padre Pio, "Father, our eyes are not so good that we can see any small particles of the Sacred Species which fall down while we distribute Holy Communion." To this Padre Pio replied, "What do you think the angels do around the altar?" Fr. Alessio then understood that the angels are ever ready to safeguard the smallest particle from falling on the floor and return it safely to the ciborium.[53] But it is not only during Holy Mass that angels are present. Because of the presence of Jesus in the Tabernacle, angels are always adoring at the altar, just as they adore Jesus in Heaven.

21. Angels with the Lamb of God and the Blessed Mother

Since our **Blessed Mother** is surrounded by angels in Heaven, it would seem proper that they accompany her during her earthly visitations, most of the time remaining invisible, but at least on one occasion appearing active in adoring the Lamb of God. Such was the case when the Blessed Virgin appeared at Knock, Ireland, as mentioned earlier.

Seen at the south gable wall of the church, the Blessed Virgin was clothed in white garments and was wearing a large brilliant crown. Her hands were raised as if in prayer, and her eyes were turned heavenward. **St. Joseph** stood at her right and **St. John the Evangelist** on her left. Next to St. John was an altar, on which stood a Cross and a lamb. Not a word was spoken by the vision, and even though rain was falling heavily, the ground around the apparition remained dry. The figures were life-size, three dimensional and moved slightly. One could almost walk between the figures, but could not touch them since they would then recede.

In his deposition, Patrick Hill gave a thorough description of everything and declared, "On the altar stood a lamb, the size of a lamb eight weeks old—the face of the lamb was fronting the west, and looking in the direction of the Blessed Virgin and St. Joseph; behind the lamb a large cross was placed erect or perpendicular on the altar; around the lamb I saw angels hovering during the whole time, for the space of one hour and a half or longer; I saw their wings fluttering, but I did not perceive their faces, which were not turned to me."[54]

Perhaps the Angels are not always seen hovering around the altars in our churches, but we know that myriads of heavenly hosts adore the Holy Eucharist at every Holy Mass and at each exposition of the Blessed Sacrament and that they are ever ready to assist the Blessed Mother of God.

22. Angels and the Blessed Mother

The guardian angel assigned to the Blessed Virgin at her birth must have been one of the highest order, but we can safely assume that multitudes of angels also protected her from her birth, she being destined to have a unique and exalted position both in Heaven and on earth.

Ven. Mary of Agreda (1602-1665) reveals in the book, *The Mystical City of God*, that a large number of angels were assigned to Mary. She writes: "The nine hundred Angels, which were chosen from the nine choirs, one hundred from each, were selected from the number of those who had distinguished themselves by their esteem, love and reverence for the most holy Mary. They were made visible to the Blessed Virgin under the form of young men in their early years, but of the most exquisite beauty and courteousness."[55]

We know that the Archangel Gabriel received Our Lady's consent to be the Mother of God; angels counseled St. Joseph on at least three occasions when it concerned the Blessed Mother; angels attended when she gave birth to the Saviour; and we can be assured that they assisted her during her lifetime and that they were present at her death and Assumption into Heaven. Since an angel consoled Our Lord in the Garden of Olives, can we not assume that angels also consoled the Blessed Mother during her many sorrows? And since angels are always present around our dear Mother in Heaven, surely they are present during her visitations on earth.

One such visit involved **St. Teresa of Avila** (1515-1582), who tells of an extraordinary vision she received during the first year in which she served as the prioress of the convent of the Incarnation. Indicating that the Blessed Mother was the real prioress, the Saint had placed a picture of her in the prioress' stall in the choir. The Saint writes that

> at the beginning of the *Salve*, I saw the Mother of God descend with a multitude of angels to the stall of the prioress, where the image of Our Lady is, and sit there herself. I think I did not see the image then, but only Our Lady. She seemed to be like that picture of her which the Countess gave me, but I had no time to ascertain this because I fell at once into a trance. Multitudes of angels seemed to me to be above the canopies of the stalls and on the desks in front of them; but I saw no bodily forms, for the vision was intellectual. She remained there during the *Salve* and said to me: "Thou hast done well to place me here; I will be present when the sisters sing the praises of my Son and will offer them to Him." After this I remained in that prayer which I still practice and which is that of keeping my soul in the company of the most Holy Trinity.[56]

In other sections of this book we learn that angels were often heard serenading the Blessed Mother when her miraculous images were discovered. They were heard in some of her shrines, and especially during the apparition of Our Lady of Guadalupe. The angels who appeared during the apparition of St. Joseph, St. John and the Blessed Mother at Knock, Ireland, were silent, but, as recounted earlier, there was an apparition of a little angel, who appeared about the age of four or five years, who spoke several times to **St. Catherine Labouré** (1806-1876).

The little angel came one night to the bedside of the Saint and awakened her by repeating her name. Then he said, "Come to the chapel. The Blessed Virgin awaits you." After dressing hurriedly and following the little angel to the chapel, the Saint stood waiting. After a few moments, there was a sound like the rustle of a silk dress. The angel then bowed, and curiously, his voice, which only moments before was sweet and like that of a child, suddenly became deep, mature and reverent as he announced, "Here is the Blessed Virgin."

After Our Lady told the Saint that she would be charged with a special mission, and after confiding other matters concerning the community and the world, the vision departed. The little angel then escorted the Saint back to her bed and disappeared. When the clock struck two, the Saint realized that the apparition had lasted over two hours.

This vision of 1830 resulted in the manufacture of medals that would be the instruments of so many graces that the medal became known as the "Miraculous Medal."[57]

23. Angels and the Priesthood

St. John Chrysostom (347-407), a Doctor of the Church, writes in his *Treatise on the Priesthood* in what high regard he holds the vocation of the holy priesthood. Therein he writes: "For the priestly office is indeed discharged on earth, but it ranks amongst heavenly ordinances, and very naturally so: for neither man, nor angel, nor archangel, nor any other created power, but the Paraclete Himself, instituted this vocation and persuaded men while still in the flesh to represent the ministry of angels. Wherefore the consecrated priest ought to be as pure as if he were standing in the heavens themselves in the midst of those powers."

This saint also speaks of angels crowding around the priest, bowing profoundly and "worshiping Him who lies on the altar."

St. Francis de Sales (1567-1622), a Doctor of the Church, gives us another example of the high regard which Heaven reserves for the priesthood. He once saw a young seminarian being accompanied by his guardian angel. After the young man's ordination, the Saint saw the angel walking *behind* the priest, in respect and reverence for his priestly dignity.

St. Thomas Aquinas (1225-1274) writes: "It is reasonable to suppose that different angels are appointed to the guardianship of different men . . . A guardian is assigned to a man for two reasons: first, inasmuch as a man is an individual, and thus to one man one guardian is due; and sometimes several are appointed to guard one." He continues: "Although men are equal in nature, still inequality exists among them, according as Divine Providence orders some to the greater, and others to the lesser things, according to the book of *Ecclesiasticus*, 'Some of them hath he blessed, and exalted: and some of them hath he sanctified, and set near himself: and some of them hath he cursed and brought low . . .' Thus it is a greater office to guard one man than another."[58] This is why many theologians believe that a young man, upon his ordination, is given an angel of a higher order in addition to the original guardian angel.

24. No Two Angels Alike

The saintly **Father Paul of Moll** (1824-1896), a Flemish Benedictine who is known as the "Wonder-worker of the Nineteenth Century," once said that "There are no two angels alike in Heaven. How great then must be the power of God to have been able to create in a single instant these innumerable legions of heavenly spirits!"[59] **St. Teresa of Avila** (1515-1582) had frequent visions of angels and reports in her *Autobiography* that angels "do not tell me their names, but I am well aware that there is a great difference between certain angels and others, and between these and others still, of a kind that I could not possibly explain."[60] **Père Lamy** (1855-1931), a French mystic and visionary priest, tells that the Blessed Virgin was given thousands and thousands of angels . . . and she knows them all by name. Concerning these thousands of angels, the holy cleric adds, "Each angel has his own particular cast of countenance and all are so beautiful!"[61] He again insists: "Each angel has his own face."[62]

25. Do Angels Know the Future?

St. Thomas Aquinas (1225-1274) tells us in his *Summa Theologica* that future events are known to God alone and that "the intellect of an angel, and every created intellect, fall far short of God's eternity; hence the future as it is in itself cannot be known by any created intellect."[63] However, this saint speaks of knowing the future "by the cause." For instance, if a person jumps into a pool of water, the short term "future" is that he will get wet. If we mail a letter, the "future" is that it will be delivered. The Saint continues: "Men cannot know future things, except in their causes, or by God's revelation. The angels know the future in the same way, but much more acutely." Thus, something that we do will have a result in the future, which is unknown to us, but which is known to the Angels. Future events not related to a cause are unknown to the Angels, *unless they are revealed to them by God*. The Saint adds, however, that "events which proceed from their causes in the minority of cases are quite unknown, such as casual and chance events."[64]

St. Augustine (354-430), in his *City of God*, explains the Angels' knowledge of "the historical future" in a different way: "Their knowledge even of the world of time and change is greater than the demons' because, in the Word of God, through whom the world was made, they contemplate the ultimate reasons why, in the cosmic order, some things can be used while others are refused, and nothing is confused." The Saint writes that angels are never mistaken: "They foresee, in the living laws of God's eternal and unchangeable Wisdom, the historical future and know, by a participation in the Divine Spirit, that most infallible of all causes, God's will. The special privilege of such knowledge God has rightly reserved to the holy Angels. Thus, they are not only eternal but also blessed. And the good which gives them blessedness is God Himself, who created them, for their perfect and unfailing bliss is to share in the Vision of God."[65]

26. Do Angels Know Our Secret Thoughts?

Scripture relates: "The heart is perverse above all things, and unsearchable, who can know it? I am the Lord who search the heart, and prove the reins: who give to every one according to his way." (*Jer.* 17:9-10). After quoting this passage, **St. Thomas Aquinas** states emphatically, "Therefore angels do not know the secrets of hearts."

The Saint continues that even though the Angels do not know the secrets of hearts, they can deduce them to a certain extent in two ways. One way is that "thought is sometimes discovered not merely by outward act, but also by change of countenance." The second way, and in this the Saint quotes from **St. Augustine**, is that angels can "sometimes with the greatest faculty learn man's dispositions, not only when expressed by speech, but even when conceived in thought, when the soul expresses them by certain signs in the body." St. Augustine then adds, "It cannot be asserted how this is done." St. Thomas Aquinas writes further, "But it does not follow that, if the angel knows what is passing through man's sensitive appetite or imagination, he knows what is in the thought or will."[66] St. Thomas then repeats that "God alone can know the thoughts of hearts and affections of wills."

27. Do Angels Have Names?

As just mentioned by **Père Lamy** (1855-1931), the Blessed Virgin was given thousands of angels for attendants, "and she knows them all by name." We know for certain the names of the three archangels which are given in Scripture. We know that the **Archangel Raphael** introduced himself to Tobias: "For I am the angel Raphael, one of the seven, who stand before the Lord." (*Tob.* 12:15). We know the name of **St. Gabriel** since he introduced himself to Zachary: "I am Gabriel, who stand before God; and am sent to speak to thee, and to bring thee these good tidings." (*Luke* 1:19). The **Archangel Michael** did not introduce himself as the others did, but his name was known to Daniel the prophet, who wrote: "Michael, one of the chief princes, came to help me, and I remained there by the king of the Persians." (*Dan.* 10:13).

Since the Archangel Raphael told Tobias that he was one of the seven who stand before the throne of God, many have wondered about the names of the other four archangels. The following have been suggested: Uriel, Sariel, Raguel and Jeremial. It must be noted, however, that the last four names appear in the apocryphal book of *Enoch* and the fourth book of *Esdras* (*4 Esd.* 4:1), which the Church does not recognize as being canonical. The names of angels not found in the canonical books of the Bible were rejected under Pope Zachary in 745 and were again rejected in a synod held at Aix-la-Chapelle in 789.

Do all the other angels have names? Probably so. We read in the *Psalms* that the Lord "telleth the number of the stars: and calleth them all by their names." (*Ps.* 146 [147]:4). If the stars have names, then surely the Angels do. If, as it is claimed, the Blessed Virgin knows the names of those angels given to her, would this indicate that all the angels have names? Spiritual writers have often suggested that we give a name of our choosing to our guardian angel, not that it would replace the name given him by God, which it would not, but that we might have in this way a closer relationship with our guardian angel.

28. Do Angels Speak with One Another?

We know that when angels are assigned the task of delivering a heavenly message to man, they often speak with words, such as in the message of St. Gabriel to the Blessed Mother, the message of St. John the Baptist's conception to Zachary, and the counsels of St. Raphael to Tobias. We are told that **St. Frances of Rome** (1384-1440), who was given the constant vision of her angel, heard his messages in an audible form: "When he spoke, she used to see his lips move; and a voice of indescribable sweetness, but which seemed to come from a distance, reached her ears."[67]

Tradition constantly reports that angels sing the praises of God. But do they speak among themselves in Heaven? Commonly called "the language of angels," their communications with one another do not require words of the mouth, according to **St. John Damascene** and **Dionysius**, but rather what are called "illuminations." **St. Gregory the Great** speaks of this as "interior speech."

According to **St. Thomas Aquinas**, angels "talk" to each other by a mere act of the will, opening their minds and revealing whatever ideas or thoughts they wish to share. The Saint also describes this as "the interior word." The Saint further writes, "External speech, made by the voice, is a necessity for us, on account of the obstacle of the body. Hence, it does not befit an angel; but only interior speech belongs to him, and this includes not only the interior speech by mental concept, but also its being ordered to another's knowledge by the will."[68]

St. John Damascene writes that "Angels need neither tongue nor ears, but without the help of any spoken word, they exchange with each other their thoughts and their counsels."[69] **Dionysius** writes that angels are "enlightened" in the divine mysteries by God Himself.

As **Fr. Pascal Parente** writes: "Symbols and words are very often inadequate in expressing the full thought, or they are ambiguous or not well understood by the hearer. To be able to open one's mind and reveal the whole thought, as it is there, without the channel of symbolism, sound and words, is a higher and better form of expression. Such is the wordless exchange of ideas, the language of the angels."[70] (See #74.)

29. Angelic Activities

Announcing good news seems to have been the happy assignment given to the Archangel Gabriel. We learn of the conception of **St. John the Baptist** when his father, **Zachary**, was visited in the Temple by the archangel, who was "standing on the right side of the altar of incense. And Zachary seeing him, was troubled, and fear fell upon him. But the angel said to him: Fear not, Zachary, for thy prayer is heard; and thy wife Elizabeth shall bear thee a son, and thou shalt call his name John." The angel then identified himself: "I am Gabriel, who stand before God; and am sent to speak to thee, and to bring thee these good tidings." (*Luke* 1:11-13, 19).

When **St. Elizabeth** was in her sixth month, the Archangel Gabriel was sent once again with good news. The gospel of St. Luke mentions the visit of the archangel to the Blessed Virgin, who was told of the birth of the Saviour. We learn next that an angel visited **St. Joseph**, who was instructed to take the expectant Mary as his wife. Some have speculated that this unidentified angel was again the Archangel Gabriel. The angel appeared to Joseph again when he was instructed to retreat with Mary and the Child to Egypt, and again after the death of Herod when Joseph was instructed to return to Israel. All the messages of the angel were given while St. Joseph was asleep, and all were immediately acted upon.

We must not forget the angel who appeared to the shepherds and announced the birth of Jesus: "And behold an angel of the Lord stood by them, and the brightness of God shone round about them; and they feared with a great fear." (*Luke* 2:9). Other activities of angels in Scripture were the appearance of a comforting spirit who attended Jesus in the Garden of Olives and that of the angel who appeared at the tomb after the Resurrection. An activity of a different nature is recorded in the New Testament when we learn of the miraculous cures that took place in Jerusalem at the pool called Probatica (or Bethsaida) that had five porches: "In these lay a great multitude of sick, of blind, of lame, of withered; waiting for the moving of the water. And an angel of the Lord descended at certain times into the pond; and the water was moved. And he that went down first into the pond after the motion of the water, was made whole, of whatsoever infirmity he lay under." (*John* 5:2-4).

Of the many activities of angels, one is to guide a soul to perform a service for the spiritual benefit of another. Such was the case reported in the *Acts of the Apostles* in which the deacon **Philip** heard the voice of an angel, who instructed him saying: "Arise, go towards the south, to the way that goeth down from Jerusalem into Gaza." Rising immediately Philip went as he was told and met a man of Ethiopia, a eunuch, who was reading the book of *Isaias*. Philip was asked by the eunuch to explain the prophecy to him, which he did. The result was the baptism of the Ethiopian and the prompt disappearance of the deacon, since "the Spirit of the Lord took away Philip; and the eunuch saw him no more. And he went on his way rejoicing." (*Acts* 8:26-40).

One of the most dramatic events in the *Acts* involves the imprisonment of **St. Peter**, which was mentioned earlier. After his arrest, he was delivered to "four files of soldiers to be kept." He was definitely well guarded, having been bound with two chains and made to sleep between two soldiers. To further insure he would be well guarded, "keepers" were placed before the door. During the night, however, an "angel of the Lord stood by him: and a light shined in the room: and he striking Peter on the side, raised him up saying: Arise quickly. And the chains fell off from his hands." The angel told St. Peter:

> Gird thyself, and put on thy sandals. And he did so. And the angel said to him: Cast thy garment about thee, and follow me. And going out, he followed him, and he knew not that it was true which was done by the angel: but thought he saw a vision. And passing through the first and the second ward, they came to the iron gate that leadeth to the city, which of itself opened to them. And going out, they passed on through one street: and immediately the angel departed from him. (*Acts* 12:4-10).

Not only in the Old and New Testaments do we hear of the activities of angels, but also in the lives of the Saints, wherein they perform all manner of services. Due to dire necessity, **St. Isidore the Farmer** (1070-1130) was placed by his parents in the employ of John de Vergas while Isidore was still a boy. For the rest of his life, he worked for the same wealthy landholder, plowing the fields with extreme care. Before reporting to the fields each day, however, Isidore attended Holy Mass and often lingered later than he should have. Eventually, reports reached John de Vergas that Isidore was often not only late for work, but was often absent from the fields during working hours.

Since Isidore was a hardworking and trusted employee, John de Vergas decided to test the truth of the accusations. Hiding himself one morning, John de Vergas discovered that while Isidore was in fact late for work because of his lingering in church, his plowing was nevertheless accomplished by unseen hands that guided snow-white oxen across the fields. Many witnesses agreed with the landowner that angels performed Isidore's chores while the Saint was rapt in prayer. In fact, more work was accomplished than if Isidore had done the work himself. Thereafter, Isidore was revered by all and was placed in responsible positions of trust.[71]

The small angel who was the visible companion of **St. Frances of Rome** (1384-1440) for twenty-four years left her with a heavenly smile and was replaced by another, "more refulgent still." This took place after the Saint founded a religious community, to which she retreated after the death of her husband. When this angel appeared, he held "three golden boughs, such as grow at the top of palm trees and from which hang the fruit; from these he continually drew golden threads, which he wound about his neck or made into balls, to provide for a mysterious tissue that would be used later on."[72] By day and by night it seemed to be the special assignment of this angel continually to weave this mysterious fabric, the threads of which seemed to grow out of the mystical palm that he carried.

The meaning of the symbols was given to the Saint during a vision of St. Benedict, who revealed that "the gold was the type of the love and charity which was to govern her dealings with her daughters, while the palm implied the triumph she was to obtain over human weakness and human respect. The unceasing labors of the angel were to mark the unwearied efforts she was to use for the right ordering and spiritual welfare of the community entrusted to her care." Some years later, while on her deathbed, St. Frances saw the bright angel hurrying as he worked on the mysterious fabric, and then she saw him finish the work as he adjusted the last threads. "The halo of light which surrounded him grew brighter and brighter, and Frances' dying form reflected that splendor."[73]

Another being from Heaven with a similar occupation was the guardian angel of Anna Maria Rose Gallo, later to be known as **St. Mary Frances of the Five Wounds** (d. 1791). Devout as a child, with a special interest in the Holy Eucharist, the Saint frequently saw a beautiful boy whom she believed to be her guardian angel. It is affirmed by her mother and her director that frequently a most beautiful boy would appear to her and relate to her heavenly things, instructing and counseling her. According to the Saint, the angel would appear at her side when she was laboring at the loom for her father's business. Frequently, while she was contemplating the mysteries of Heaven, the angel would continue her work so that the exacting father would be pleased with the amount of work expected of Frances. Declining a noble marriage, she joined the Third Order of St.

Peter of Alcantara and remained at home continuing her work at the loom, this time spinning golden thread with the help of her guardian angel.[74]

St. Paul of the Cross (1694-1775), the founder of the Passionist Order, experienced on two occasions the power of the holy Angels. One wintry day, the Saint was returning on foot to the house of his order on Mount Argentaro when he grew very weak and experienced convulsions and trembling. Falling to the ground, he prayed with confidence, "Lord, I would not wish to die in this place without the assistance of my religious." In an instant he felt himself lifted from the ground and saw at his side two angels of surpassing beauty. Then, carried by the heavenly creatures, he immediately found himself within the enclosure.

Another time he was traveling with Fr. John Baptist when both began to suffer from the severity of the cold. Walking with their feet bare against the icy roads, their feet became so stricken as to be unable to proceed. With great confidence, the Saint called upon the holy Angels and was immediately transported to the end of his journey. His companion, however, was not transported. But after he asked the holy Angels to assist his traveling companion, Fr. John Baptist was presently beside him.[75]

Angels are also known to bring comfort to God's distressed children, as one did to **St. Joseph of Cupertino** (1603-1663). This Saint for two years had suffered a great dryness of spirit and a sadness of heart until the good Lord rewarded His servant, who had remained faithful to Him during the trial. The Saint's biographer writes: "One day, when feeling far removed from all help and lying on his bed, he cried out amid many sobs and tears: 'My Lord, why hast Thou forsaken me?' " It was then that a stranger in religious garb, whom the Saint immediately recognized as his guardian angel, stood before him and gave him a new habit. No sooner had the Saint put on this habit than all sadness left him and his former joyousness of heart returned.[76]

Bl. Sebastian of Apparicio (1502-1600) was married twice, but after the death of his second wife, even though he was then seventy years old, he gave all he had to the Poor Clares and entered the monastery of the Friars Minor of the Observance in Mexico. Later transferring to the monastery at Pueblo, he spent the last twenty-six years of his life there in the humble role of a begging brother. It was said that angels were seen to accompany the holy monk on his long journeys and to guide him when he did not know the way. This holy brother died at the age of ninety-eight.[77]

St. Stephen of Rieti (d. c. 560) was the abbot of a monastery near Rieti in Italy and was admired for his holiness and great patience. St. Gregory the Great (540-604), in writing of this saint, tells us that eyewitnesses testified they saw angels standing beside the Saint while he was on his deathbed. It was piously believed that the angels afterward carried his soul to Paradise. It is also reported that those who witnessed this apparition were so awe-stricken that they could not remain beside the dead body.[78]

Two angels also wonderfully assisted **St. Thomas Aquinas** (1225-1274) after he joined the Dominican Order at the age of nineteen. It seemed that his mother and brothers had wanted him to join the Benedictine Order and plotted to have him imprisoned in the castle of San Giovanni in order to persuade him to change his mind. His brothers devised a scheme to introduce into his room a woman of evil character, which they did. On seeing the woman, the Saint immediately seized a burning brand from the hearth and chased her from the room, then falling on his knees, he implored God for the grace of perpetual chastity. As Butler relates, "He immediately fell into a deep sleep, during which he was visited by two angels, who girded him around the waist with a cord so tight that it awoke him." It is reported that the Saint never alluded to this event until he was on his deathbed, when he described the vision to his confessor, Fr. Reginald. The Saint confided that thenceforth he was never tried by temptations of the flesh.[79]

Bl. Benvenutus of Recanati (d. 1289) was a lay brother in the Franciscan Conventuals Order. Remarkable for his piety and humility, he always and gladly assumed the lowliest offices. Often during Holy Mass, and especially after having received Holy Communion, he would fall into an ecstasy so that he seemed to be totally insensible. One day he remained for a long time in one of these communions with Our Lord, so that afterward he realized it was long past the time when he should have been preparing the brethren's meal. Rushing to the kitchen, he was greeted by an angel who had been engaged in doing his work. Afterward, the diners agreed that they had never been served a better meal.[80]

An angel as a letter carrier? Such was really the case noted and tested in the life of **St. Gemma Galgani** (1878-1903). Favored with extraordinary graces and with heavenly revelations, this saint was also favored at times with the visible presence of her angel. While living under the charity of the Giannini family, Gemma disliked asking them for stamps with which to send letters to her confessor and advisor, Fr Germano. One day she asked the priest's angel to take the letter she had written to him. This letter and all the letters that followed were safely delivered by the angel without one being lost. And in fact, Fr. Germano called them angelic letters because they reached him by angelic means. At first, however, he was very skeptical of this means of conveyance.

To test that the letters were really delivered by spiritual beings, Fr. Germano had Gemma give a letter addressed to him to her Aunt Cecilia, who locked it in a place unknown to Gemma. Nonetheless, this letter was miraculously delivered to him. Once again, on June 11, 1901, Gemma gave a letter for him to her aunt, who in turn gave it to Don Lorenzo Agrimonti (a priest who was living with the Giannini family). He, in turn, locked it in a chest of drawers in his own room and put the key in his pocket. The next day the Saint sensed that the angel had passed with her letter in his hands. Aunt Cecilia and Don Agrimonti went at once to look for it and found the letter missing. Once again there was the same result when two other hidden letters were found missing. Fr. Germano then wrote, "Both letters were brought to me by the guardian angel." It is known that countless other letters were also delivered by angelic assistance.[81]

In addition to the actions mentioned above, angelic activities also include adoring and worshipping God; such a case was witnessed by **Sr. Mary Martha Chambon** (d. 1907), who is awaiting beatification. One day during a vision of Our Lord, He called her attention to a group of angelic spirits pressing around the altar during Holy Mass. He revealed: "They are contemplating the beauty, the sanctity of God! They admire, they adore . . ."[82]

Bl. Padre Pio (1887-1968) gives us a great deal of information about the activities of angels. To our minds, tears are important in relieving grief and are present when remembering heartfelt situations. When tears dry they are forgotten, but they are apparently remembered by the Angels and are of some worth in the next life, as revealed by Padre Pio. To someone who had been crying a great deal, this holy priest said, "Your tears were collected by the Angels and were placed in a golden chalice, and you will find them when you present yourself before God."[83]

Père Lamy (1855-1931) was on such familiar terms with many angels that he could depend on them to help him in various situations. He himself tells that "I have been upheld by the holy Angels many a time when I have been exhausted with weariness, and have been brought from one place to another without knowing anything about it. I used to say, 'My God, how tired I am.' I was in my parish, far away, often at night, and I found myself carried to the Place St. Lucian all at once. How it happened I don't know." His experiences can be described as one of the helpful activities of the heavenly spirits.[84]

Here, the triumphant warrior St. Michael the Archangel is shown crushing Satan's head and pushing him into the fires of Hell. Note the chains in St. Michael's left hand, which he uses to bind Satan and render him powerless.

Art Resource: New York

Angels kneel humbly, rapt in adoration of the divine mysteries, their haloes proclaiming the unending angelic hymn of praise: *Adoramus Te, glorificamus Te*—"We adore Thee, we glorify Thee." *(Detail from a Gozzoli masterpiece).*

Above: Adam and Eve are expelled from Eden. An angel guards the door, bearing a flaming sword.
Below: An angel stops Abraham, who, in obedience to God, is about to sacrifice his son Isaac.

Above: Lot's wife disobeys the angels' command not to look back on perishing Sodom.
Below: As Jacob sleeps, he sees angels ascending and descending a ladder to Heaven.

Above: An angel passes by an Israelite family's house at the first Passover, sparing the firstborn son.
Below: The Hebrews carry the Ark of the Covenant, which God commanded be decorated with winged cherubim.

Above: The Archangel Raphael instructs Tobias on how to catch a deadly fish.
Below: An angel went down into the fiery furnace, rendering the flames harmless to the three holy youths.

An angel in human form wrestled with Jacob all night; this strange wrestling match showed Jacob that, with divine assistance, he could overcome any human obstacle. The angel said to Jacob, "For if thou hast been strong against God, how much more shalt thou prevail against men?" (*Gen*. 32:28).

Habacuc was cooking pottage when an angel grabbed him by the hair of his head and transported him—and his pottage—to the hungry Daniel, who was waiting for release from the lion's den. (*Dan.* 13).

"Hail, full of grace!" The Archangel Gabriel points to Heaven, indicating that it is the Holy Spirit who will overshadow the Blessed Virgin and cause her to conceive. Other angels protect Our Lady and hold a canopy that both veils the sacred event and frames Mary's unsurpassed beauty.

“And there were in that same country shepherds . . . keeping the night watches over their flock. And behold an angel of the Lord stood by them, and the brightness of God shone round about them; and they feared with a great fear. And the angel said to them: Fear not; for behold, I bring you good tidings of great joy . . .” (*Luke* 2:8-10).

A “multitude of the heavenly army” appeared at the birth of the Saviour, crying out, “Glory to God in the highest; and on earth peace to men of good will.” (*Luke* 2:14).

An angel appeared in a dream to warn St. Joseph to flee Herod's slaughter of the Holy Innocents. Above, St. Joseph guards the sleeping Madonna and Child and keeps his staff in his hand, ready for flight. The angel beckons St. Joseph and points to a vision of the Holy Family on the road to Egypt.

As Our Lord endured His Agony in the Garden of Gethsemane—while His beloved disciples slept—"there appeared to him an angel from heaven, strengthening him. And being in agony, he prayed the longer." (*Luke* 22:43).

Our Lady of Sorrows is surrounded by sorrowful angels carrying the instruments of the Passion.

"And entering into the sepulchre, they saw a young man sitting on the right side, clothed with a white robe; and they were astonished. Who saith to them: Be not affrighted; you seek Jesus of Nazareth, who was crucified: he is risen, he is not here, behold the place where they laid him." (*Mark* 16:5-6).

30. Angels Going Up and Down

In the Old Testament, when **Jacob** "was come to a certain place," he decided to rest; taking some stones and putting them under his head, he fell asleep. "And he saw in his sleep a ladder standing upon the earth, and the top thereof touching heaven: the angels also of God ascending and descending by it." (*Gen.* 28:12). The Lord God at the top of the ladder then announced to Jacob that the land would be given to him and all his descendants.

Not only Jacob, but some of the Saints have also had a similar vision, including the following. While he was visiting Osimo with a priest companion, the attention of **St. Joseph of Cupertino** (1603-1663) was directed in the distance to the cupola of the Holy House of Loreto. On seeing it, the Saint suddenly exclaimed, "Do you not see the angels who ascend and descend from Heaven to yonder sanctuary?"[85]

The same vision was accorded to **St. Rita of Cascia** (1381-1457) as she was praying one day before a crucifix. There appeared to her a ladder, with God at the top, inviting her to ascend. There were also angels ascending and descending. A voice then spoke to her: "Rita, if you wish to unite yourself to God in Heaven, you must climb this ladder." After the vision, St. Rita contemplated its meaning and understood that she should build at once a spiritual ladder, on whose steps, made of virtues, she would ascend to the joys of eternity.[86]

When **St. Angela Merici** (1474-1540) was thirty-two years old and a laywoman, she experienced a vision in which she saw a staircase reaching to the heavens and a number of young women and angels ascending and descending. One of the young ladies approached her and delivered this message: "Know, Angela, that our Divine Lord has sent you this vision to teach you that before you die, you are to found in Brescia a company of young virgins like these. This is His will for you." The ladies who joined her in catechetical work remained in their homes, took no vows and only gathered for prayer and teaching. After the Saint's death, **St. Charles Borromeo**, Bishop of Milan, reorganized the secular group into a religious organization that eventually developed into the Ursuline Order, the first teaching order in the Church.[87]

A heavenly ladder is also mentioned in the life of **St. Dominic** (1170-1221). It happened one day that Fr. Guallo Romanoni, prior of the monastery of Friars Preachers in Brescia, fell asleep leaning against the bell tower of his church. In his dream he saw two ladders let down from an opening in the sky above him. At the top of one stood Our Lord, and at the top of the other was His Blessed Mother. Angels were going up and down on them, and at their foot was seated one in the habit of the Order, but his face was covered with his hood, after the fashion in which the friars are accustomed to cover the face of the dead when they are carried out for burial. The ladders were drawn up into Heaven, and Fr. Romanoni saw the unknown friar received into the company of the Angels, surrounded by a dazzling glory, and borne to the very feet of Jesus. When the prior awakened, he was puzzled about the meaning of the vision, but he soon learned that at the same time he had experienced the dream, St. Dominic had died in Bologna.[88]

31. The Speed of Angels

The prophet **Isaias** speaks of angels as being swift (*Is.* 18:2), while Ezechiel speaks of them as traveling as "flashes of lightning." (*Ezech.* 1:14). Rev. Pascal P. Parente, in his book, *The Angels* (formerly *Beyond Space*), writes that the heavenly creatures "pass from one place to another with the rapidity of thought . . . an instantaneous change of place." An angel can move from one distant place to another "with the speed of lightning, or the speed of thought."[89] Fr. Paul O'Sullivan, in his book *All About the Angels,* notes that light travels at the speed of 186,000 miles a second. "Light comes from the sun to our earth at the same rate and takes 8 minutes and 15 seconds to arrive, but the movement of the Angels is unspeakably more rapid—

they come in one instant."[90] Their speed exceeds that of the heavens and of the winds, says **Tertullian** (b. c. 160). And he adds, "In an instant they pass from one end of the world to another." **St. Thomas Aquinas** (1225-1274) writes in his *Summa Theologica*, "An angel can be in one place in one instant and in another place in the next instant, without any time intervening."[91]

32. Special Assignments

The Bible sanctions the idea of certain angels being in charge of special districts, as recorded in the book of *Daniel,* where we read: "The prince of the kingdom of the Persians resisted me one and twenty days . . ." (*Dan.* 10:13). The prince in this passage is regarded as the Angel Guardian of Persia.

It is piously believed by the Church and many saints that our churches and our altars are guarded by angels. Especially do they guard and revere our dear Saviour, who reposes in our Tabernacles. It is also our belief that angels guard our homes, our towns, our countries. This seems to be confirmed by **Père Lamy** (1855-1931), visionary and mystic, who states that there are angels who guard every home, every town, every province, every state.[92] **St. Augustine** (354-430) believed that angels preside over every visible thing, whether animate or inanimate. He believed further that the heavens and the stars have their directing angels. In *The Apocalypse* we learn that there are angels who guard the winds: "After these things, I saw four angels standing on the four corners of the earth, holding the four winds of the earth, that they should not blow upon the earth, nor upon the sea, nor on any tree." (*Apoc.* 7:1).

There are angels who guard the waters: "And I heard the angel of the waters saying: Thou art just, O Lord . . ." (*Apoc.* 16:5). And one of the angels even has power over fire: "And another angel came out from the altar, who had power over fire . . ." (*Apoc.* 14:18).

St. Clement agrees that every country, town and village has an angel to guard it.

This seems to be confirmed by **St. Vincent Ferrer** (1350-1419), who was one day approaching the city of Barcelona when he had a vision of an angel. Later, in the pulpit, he related his experience. He said that he had just met a most beautiful angel who introduced himself as the special guardian of the city. The announcement was met with great excitement. An artist was quickly commissioned to portray the angel, and as soon as his work was completed, the statue was erected in a public square. It is now known as the beautiful Plaza of the Angel.

In the second chapter of *The Apocalypse*, **St. John** mentions the angels who guard the churches of Ephesus, Smyrna, Pergamus and Thyatira. In the third chapter, the angels guarding the churches of Sardis, Philadelphia and Laodicea are mentioned. In the 21st chapter of *The Apocalypse*, we also find angels guarding the gates of the New Jerusalem: "And it had a wall great and high, having twelve gates, and in the gates twelve angels." (*Apoc.* 21:12). Angels, it seems, even guard rivers: "And I heard a voice . . . saying to the sixth angel, who had the trumpet: Loose the four angels, who are bound in the great river Euphrates." (*Apoc.* 9:13-14).

That angels are appointed to guard countries we have for proof the vision of the **children of Fatima**, who in the second vision of the angel in 1916 were told by the apparition that sacrifices of reparation and supplication for the conversion of sinners "would draw down peace upon your country." The vision identified himself: "I am its angel guardian, the Angel of Portugal."[93]

This was the same angel who appeared to the children once before and whom Lucia described as being "a young man, about fourteen or fifteen years old, whiter than snow, transparent as crystal when the sun shines through it, and of great beauty."[94]

Ven. Anne Catherine Emmerich (1774-1824) was also of the opinion that angels are also given special assignments on earth.

She revealed: "I have seen the angels that protect the fruits of the earth, spreading something over the trees and plants and over cities and countries. I have seen angels hovering over them, guarding and defending them, and sometimes abandoning them."[95]

It has also been written that communities and confraternities have their angels who watch over their members. A pious story is told by the confessor of a certain young man who lay dangerously ill. Two angels, all resplendent with majesty and beauty, appeared to him and consoled him until the moment of his death. One angel revealed that he was the young man's guardian angel; the other told him he was the tutelary angel of the Confraternity of the Blessed Virgin, to which the young man belonged. This latter angel said that he had been sent by the Mother of God to assist him because he had faithfully observed the rules of the Confraternity.

St. John of Avila (1499-1569) confirmed the truth of the following incident. The Rev. Centenares, in 1585, was a member of the St. John community when he was awakened one stormy night with a request to take Holy Communion to a man who was dying. Even though he was not certain of the way and the storm complicated his difficulty, the priest nevertheless set out, taking with him two consecrated Hosts. Immediately after he left the church, two beautiful youths with a heavenly appearance and bearing arranged themselves on either side of the priest as guards of honor. The priest was amazed that the candles they held were not extinguished, in spite of the heavy rainfall. The two led the way to the house of the dying man and then led the priest back to the church. After he placed the remaining Host in the Tabernacle, the two youths disappeared. St. John later assured the priest that the two youths were angels sent by God to reward his zeal.

33. The Power of the Angels

The Psalmist writes, "Bless the Lord, all ye his angels: you that are mighty in strength, and execute his word, hearkening to the voice of his orders." (*Ps.* 102:20). Since the Angels of God are pure and perfect in all respects, it would follow that they are also strong enough to enforce the mighty will of God, as the Psalmist reports. The power of a single angel was demonstrated when **Ezechias** was threatened by the Assyrian army and he prayed to God for help. "And it came to pass that night, that an angel of the Lord came, and slew in the camp of the Assyrians a hundred and eighty-five thousand." And when the King of the Assyrians arose the next morning, "he saw all the bodies of the dead." (*4 Kgs.* 19:35).

When **Daniel** was in the den of lions for six days without food, an angel of the Lord visited the prophet Habacuc, who had boiled pottage and had broken bread in a bowl. "And the angel of the Lord said to Habacuc: Carry the dinner which thou hast into Babylon to Daniel who is in the lions' den . . . And the angel of the Lord took him by the top of his head and carried him by the hair of his head, and set him in Babylon over the den in the force of his spirit." After Daniel ate, "The angel of the Lord presently set Habacuc again in his own place." (*Dan.* 14:33, 38).

In the time of **David**, "The Lord sent a pestilence upon Israel, from the morning unto the time appointed, and there died of the people from Dan to Bersabee seventy thousand men." But then the Lord "had pity on the affliction, and said to the angel that slew the people: It is enough: now hold thy hand. And the angel of the Lord was by the thrashing floor of Areuna the Jebusite." (*2 Kgs.* 24:15-16).

In the book of *The Apocalypse* we learn that God gave the command to the Sixth Angel to "Loose the four angels, who are bound in the great river Euphrates." And God gave these four angels the power "to kill the third part of men." (*Apoc.* 9:14-15). That is, God gave these angels power to kill, in a short space of time, millions of people. Although the angels mentioned here were given extraordinary strength, less "energy" was needed by the angel who freed **St. Peter** from chains and led him out of prison while passing between Roman guards who were, no doubt, in a mysterious sleep.

This also brings to mind the little angel who awakened **St. Catherine Labouré** (1806-1876). As the angel led the Saint through passages on the way to the chapel to meet the Blessed Mother, doors opened at a mere thought from the angel. We also recall the angels who did the plowing and various chores for **St. Isidore the Farmer** (1070-1130).[96] Scripture and the lives of the Saints give countless examples of angels who used unusual strength, as well as of those who apparently used only a thought-command to perform services for God and man.

34. Angels and Fire

It seems strange that fire, which can be so destructive on earth and so painful in Hell and in Purgatory, should be mentioned many times in Scripture and in the lives of the Saints as having properties that are unusual, or even very pleasant. We learn of **Moses** and the burning bush that was not consumed (*Ex.* 3:2) and of the pillar of fire that went before the Israelites during their journey from Egypt. (*Ex.* 13:21-22). Fire appeared over the Ark of the Covenant (*Num.* 9:16), and we read of the fiery chariot and the fiery horses that took **Elias** up "by a whirlwind into heaven." (*4 Kgs.* 2:11). And there was the fiery furnace that did not harm **Sidrach**, **Misach** and **Abdenago**. In fact, the atmosphere in the furnace was "like the blowing of a wind bringing dew, and the fire touched them not at all, nor troubled them, nor did them any harm." (*Dan.* 3:50). These conditions existed through the intervention of an angel. (*Dan.* 3:49-50).

In the third chapter of *Genesis* we read of the expulsion of **Adam** and **Eve** from Paradise. The Lord God "placed before the paradise of pleasure cherubims, and a flaming sword, turning every way, to keep the way of the tree of life." (*Gen.* 3:24). During the time that the children of Israel were oppressed by the Madianites, **Gedeon** heard the word of God and was visited by an angel, who instructed him concerning the sacrifice he should prepare. When the lamb and the loaves were ready and were placed upon a rock as instructed by the angel, "The angel of the Lord put forth the tip of the rod, which he held in his hand, and touched the flesh and the unleavened loaves: and there arose a fire from the rock, and consumed the flesh and the unleavened loaves: and the angel of the Lord vanished out of his sight." (*Jgs.* 6:21).

Isaias had a vision of the Lord sitting upon a throne, "high and elevated and his train filled the temple." The prophet saw seraphim each with six wings who sang, "Holy, holy, holy, the Lord God of hosts, all the earth is full of his glory." (*Is.* 6:1-3). When Isaias beheld the splendor of the Lord, he bemoaned his unworthiness and his unclean lips. It was then that one of seraphim "flew to me and in his hand was a live coal, which he had taken with the tongs off the altar. And he touched my mouth, and said: Behold this hath touched thy lips, and thy iniquities shall be taken away, and thy sin shall be cleansed." (*Is.* 6:5-7).

St. John the Evangelist in *The Apocalypse* frequently mentions heavenly fire. About angelic fire, he wrote: "And I saw another mighty angel come down from heaven, clothed with a cloud, and a rainbow was on his head, and his face was as the sun, and his feet as pillars of fire." (*Apoc.* 10:1). Again the Evangelist writes: "And thus I saw the horses in the vision: and they that sat on them, had breastplates of fire and of hyacinth and of brimstone." (*Apoc.* 10:17). In this vision even the horses produced fire: "And the horses were as the heads of lions: and from their mouths proceeded fire, and smoke, and brimstone." (*Apoc.* 9:17). In addition to the riders wearing breastplates of fire in the preceding quotation, we learn that fire is also used to clothe various angels.

St. Lydwine of Schiedam (1380-1433), who frequently beheld her guardian angels, tells that she once saw an angel that appeared in her room "under the form of a young boy whose dress was woven of threads of white fire."[97] Another time, during a vision of Heaven, the Saint saw angels whose clothing "flamed in draperies of fire, bordered by shining orphreys, and flowers of fabulous gems flashed upon the moving fire of their robes."[98] Still another time she saw an angel near her bed who shone resplendently "in his tunic of pale fire."[99] Yet another time, while enraptured by a vision of Heaven and the veneration paid to the maternity of the Blessed Virgin Mary, the Saint saw that "great seraphim flamed, unloosing from harps of fire the gorgeous pearl of sound; others offered vessels of gold full of sweet essence, which are the prayers of the just . . . others standing near the archangel . . . saw to the lighting of the incense and wove with threads of blue smoke the warm linen with which they should envelop the Holy Child . . ."[100]

St. Teresa of Avila (1515-1582) writes in her *Autobiography* of an experience involving fire that caused both pain and sweetness. The Carmelites celebrate the feast of this mystical event, called the Transverberation, on August 27. The Saint writes that she saw an angel

> who was not tall, but short, and very beautiful, his face so aflame that he appeared to be one of the highest types of angel who seem to be all afire . . . In his hands I saw a long golden spear, and at the end of the iron tip, I seemed to see a point of fire. With this he seemed to pierce my heart several times, so that it penetrated to my entrails . . . The pain was so sharp that it made me utter several moans; and so excessive was the sweetness caused me by this intense pain that one can never wish to lose it.[101]

Another time, St. Teresa writes of a vision of Heaven in which she saw "A great multitude of angels, whom I thought of incomparably greater beauty than others I have seen. I wondered if they were seraphim or cherubim, for they were very different in their glory and they seemed to be all on fire."[102]

35. Angelic Music and the Blessed Mother

It is most appropriate that the Mother of God should be serenaded in Heaven by a host of angels with their heavenly songs of her praise. It was these songs of praise that were often heard at the miraculous discoveries of her various portraits.

One of the earliest such incidents relating to a miraculous image of Our Lady took place at Einsiedeln, Switzerland. It was there that the hermit **St. Meinrad** (797-861) established the hermitage and chapel mentioned earlier, in which the Saint was seen reciting the night Office with his guardian angel. (See #13.)

After St. Meinrad's death, the chapel was seldom visited, but in 903 Benno, a canon of Strasburg, made a pilgrimage there and decided to restore it. Later, a community of Benedictine monks erected a handsome church, which was so arranged that the chapel remained as a separate little building within the church. When the structure was completed in 948 and its consecration planned for September 14, a most astounding miracle occurred.

St. Conrad, the Bishop of Constance, who was to perform the consecration, decided to spend part of the night in prayer before the image of the Blessed Virgin. With him were some of the clergy. Shortly after midnight a bright light illuminated the sanctuary, while heavenly voices began to sing. Looking up, the prelate saw two choirs of angels chanting the hymns appointed by the Church for the solemn consecration of a church. He then beheld Our Lord Himself, the Blessed Virgin and several saints. Amazed by what he was witnessing, the bishop was not too awestruck to notice that the angels made a slight alteration in the prayers. Instead of the words: "Blessed is He that cometh in the name of the Lord," the angels substituted: "Blessed be the Son of Mary, who has come down to this place; who reigns world without end." The following day, when the first words of the consecration of the church were about to be uttered, a voice was distinctly heard by all present: "Cease, for the church has been divinely consecrated."

The deposition of St. Conrad regarding the vision, the singing and the consecration, dated 948, is still intact and preserved at the Abbey. Additionally, the miraculous events were confirmed by a bull of **Pope Leo VIII** (963-964).[103]

Another early manifestation involving an image of Our Lady took place at **Montserrat, Spain** while shepherd boys were tending their sheep at the foot of the mountains on a Saturday evening in the year 890. During the night the shepherds were amazed to see lights and to hear singing coming from the mountain. When this was repeated the following night, the shepherds reported the situation to their priest, who soon investigated. When he too heard the singing and saw the mysterious lights, he informed the bishop, who subsequently also witnessed the phenomenon.

Inside a nearby cave they discovered a statue of Our Lady. According to documents later discovered, it was learned that the statue had been hidden there for safekeeping in the year 718 to protect it from invading Saracen infidels. A small church was soon erected for the enshrinement of the statue. This developed into the magnificent sanctuary which houses the statue that is now known as the Miraculous Image of Our Lady of Montserrat.[104]

Another miraculous image was discovered on April 25, 1467, a special feastday in **Genazzano, Italy.** An immense crowd had filled the Piazzo of Santa Maria at 4 o'clock when "suddenly, above the murmur of the crowd, there sounded up in the clear blue sky the strains of exquisite music . . . Soon, above the church spires and lofty turrets, they beheld a beautiful white cloud which darted forth vivid rays of light in every direction amidst the music of Heaven." Gradually the cloud descended and "to their amazement rested upon the furthest portion of the unfinished wall of the chapel of St. Biaggio . . . Gradually it cleared away, and to their astonished eyes a most beautiful object was revealed. It was the image of Our Lady, holding her Divine Son in her arms." This portrait is now known as the Miraculous Image of Our Lady of Good Counsel, not only because of this miraculous presentation, but also because of its composition and unusual preservation.[105]

An image of the Blessed Virgin that was accompanied by angelic singing and sparkling stars is that which is revered in **El Puig, Spain.** When the monastery church was completed on a hillock at El Puig—where the appearance of seven brilliant stars had indicated the place where the holy image of the Blessed Mother was to be enshrined—angelic voices were heard, joining in with the chants of the monks. Especially on Sundays during the recitation of the *Salve Regina (Hail Holy Queen)*, the invisible singers joined their voices to those of the congregation.

Eventually, the sanctuary became known as the "Angels' Room." The stars that had appeared on the hillock once more appeared, but this time over the steeple of the church. In addition to the people of El Puig who saw the stars and heard the angelic voices, the people of Valencia were likewise favored when the image was carried from El Puig to Valencia in the year 1588. During a sixteen-day celebration in honor of the image, angelic voices were heard each day, while the seven stars were visible each night, traveling mysteriously along the route taken by the statue from the "Angels' Room" at El Puig to the cathedral of Valencia, where the image was temporarily enshrined.[106]

From Italy we turn to Mexico to learn of an event that took place there. Because of the many miracles that occurred as a result of prayer before the shrine of Our Lady of the Angels in **Tecaxic, Mexico,** a new sanctuary was built in 1650 to accommodate the crowds of Our Lady's devotees. Miracles continued to be performed by Our Lady in the new church, but the most charming of these involved the mysterious singing and the display of lights that emanated from the shrine.

It is told that Pedro Millan Hidalgo, a highly respected citizen of Almoyola, was accustomed to doing business in Toluca. The road that stretched between the two pueblos passed through Tecaxic. While passing the chapel of Our Lady of the Angels, especially on Wednesdays and Saturdays, he heard music of remarkable beauty. Sometimes he felt compelled to investigate the identity of the singers, but each time he entered the shrine he discovered only silence and solitude. Sometimes when he passed the shrine at night, he saw lights flickering through the windows. Thinking that services were being conducted and that the light was coming from numerous candles, he decided one night to take part in the service, only to find a darkened church when he opened the doors. Another night, thinking that the Indians had extinguished the candles in fear of him, he called out, entered the church and walked around only to find that he alone was there.

Pedro Hidalgo related these incidents to his friends, and because of his unblemished character and the great respect with which he was regarded, they believed all he told them. Some out of curiosity, and others out of devotion, went at night to the shrine. Some heard the singing and saw the lights; others did not.

Of all the numerous miraculous images of Our Lady in Mexico, the most famous is that of **Our Lady of Guadalupe** in Mexico City, a likeness miraculously impressed on a tilma worn by the poor Indian, **Juan Diego**. The history reports that Juan Diego, on the cold morning of December 9, 1531, was walking from his village to attend Holy Mass at the Franciscan Monastery in Tlaltelolco. While walking on Tepeyac hill, he stopped abruptly and listened. According to Francis Johnston in his book *The Wonder of Guadalupe*, "he was startled to hear strains of music in the still morning twilight . . . the music was real, and what was even more astonishing, the strains were beautiful beyond words, like a choir of mellifluous birds, filling the chilly air with ravishing sweetness . . . Juan gazed up in wonderment at the dark outline of Tepeyac Hill from where the blissful harmony flowed down like liquid silver."[107] It was then that he saw the brightness that enveloped the vision of the Mother of God, who requested that a chapel be built at the site.

After another vision, Bishop Zumarraga required a miracle to prove the truthfulness of what Juan Diego claimed. Miraculous roses were collected during still another vision and gathered in the apron-like cloak worn by the visionary. When the bundle of roses fell from the cloak in the presence of the Bishop and others, the miraculous image was revealed. Having obtained the proof that he wanted, the Bishop had a chapel built. It developed through the years into the magnificent Basilica of Our Lady of Guadalupe that is besieged at all times of the year by Mexican devotees and pilgrims from around the world.

Twenty-six years after the first apparition, the archbishop of Mexico canonically established the truth of the visions. Rome added its approval in 1754 when the Sacred Congregation of Rites issued a decree approving an Office and Mass for Our Lady of Guadalupe. Several popes have since expressed in one way or another their admiration of the miraculous image, as did Pope John Paul II, who visited the image in 1979.

Many other images of Our Lady were either serenaded at their discovery, during their transfer to another church or during an apparition. There are really too many to list here. For now let us explore the many incidences in which the Saints were rhapsodized by the voices of angels.

36. Angelic Music and the Saints

Angelic music was often heard at the deathbeds of various saints, but what is perhaps the earliest recorded incident of this kind is that which took place before the death of **St. Chad** (d. 672), a holy Bishop who first served the bishopric of York and then that of Mercia. St. Chad was a friend of **St. Owen**, who lived with several other monks in a house near Lichfield, which the holy Bishop visited when his episcopal duties were satisfied. Seven days before the death of St. Chad, St. Owen heard heavenly music proceeding from the oratory in which the Bishop was meditating. Later in the day, he asked the holy Bishop about the joyful music he had heard coming from the oratory. St. Chad, who was at the time in perfect health, informed him that the music had come from angelic spirits who announced his impending death. St. Chad then became sick with a "languishing fever," from which he died seven days later.[108]

Bl. Lucy of Narni (1476-1544) was also serenaded by angelic voices before her death, and "seraphic music" was heard in the church before the funeral of **St. Louis Bertran** (1526-1581). Two monks traveling from Toulouse were sleeping one night in the ruins of a castle near Pibrac when they were awakened by angelic melodies. The next day they learned of the death of **St. Germaine Cousin** (1579-1601). And so it goes in many biographies of the Saints. The angelic voices confirmed, as it were, the sanctity of the dying and recently dead, and thoroughly enthralled those who were privileged to hear the melodies of Heaven.

Angelic voices not only announced the death of certain saints, but were also heard by many saints who were very much alive. During an ecstasy in which she was admitted to Heaven and saw its beauty and those of the inhabitants, **St. Lydwine of Schiedam** (1380-1433) heard heavenly music and the voices of the Angels. The Saint's biographer describes the music of Heaven in this way: "Great seraphim flamed, unloosing harps of fire, the gorgeous pearl of sound . . . others chanted messianic psalms and sang in alternate choirs transporting hymns. . . . In humble imitation she repeated the language of praise; but how differently from the chords of those harps, the power and subtility of those fragrances, the thundering zeal of those voices."[109]

While **St. Margaret Mary Alacoque** (1647-1690) was busy picking hemp one day with the community, she withdrew into a courtyard near the Blessed Sacrament, where she continued her work on her knees. "I became enraptured," she said, "and I saw the Adorable Heart of my Jesus," which appeared brighter than the sun. Encircled about it were seraphim, "who sang in marvellous harmony: 'Love triumphs, love enjoys, the love of the Sacred Heart rejoices!' " The Saint was invited to join in the chorus, "but I did not dare to do so." The apparition of the Sacred Heart, as well as the accompanying music of the Angels, "lasted from two to three hours, and I have felt the effects thereof throughout my life."[110]

One day **St. Colette** (1381-1447), reformer of the Poor Clares, was speaking with her spiritual director on the manner in which the Canonical Hours should be recited in choir. Immediately, they heard angelic voices chanting the Divine Office in melodious tones, with an inflection at the end of each verse. It was then apparent to the abbess and her Franciscan director that Heaven was indicating the exact mode of chant they were to adopt. This plain chant was ever after observed by the reformed monasteries of the Poor Clares. The Saint's love of chant from her early years and this Heaven-sent suggestion, together with her inspired leadership of the community, led her sisters and novices to share her joy in this manner of chanting God's praises.

During the early expansion of the Dominican Order, there arrived in Bologna in the year 1218 **Bl. Reginald of Orleans**, whose talents included an extraordinary power of government and "a burning and vehement eloquence." Within six months of his arrival, more than a hundred men joined the Order, including distinguished doctors and students of the university. So many joined that a common saying among the people was that "it was scarcely safe to go and hear Master Reginald, if you did not wish to take the friar's habit." The community soon outgrew its small monastery, so that all were moved in 1219, two years before the death of the founder, St. Dominic, to San Nicholas delle Vigne. Before this move, however, the site was indicated as a place of future holiness and pilgrimage when miraculous signs appeared and angelic singing was heard by workers in the nearby vineyards.[111]

When **St. Anthony Mary Claret** (1807-1870) visited Madrid, he made the acquaintance of the pious Viscountess of Jorbalan, who was a member of the religious order known as the Adoratrices. The Viscountess was favored by Heaven in an extraordinary manner, since she revealed to the Saint that she heard angels sing the Trisagion every day at four-thirty in the afternoon, no matter where she would happen to be. The Saint asked the holy religious to implore Our Lord to grant him the favor of also hearing the Angels in their praise of the Holy Trinity.

The Viscountess prayed, and one day, a little before four-thirty, the Saint went into a room next to the one in which the Viscountess was working. Exactly at half past four, they were delighted by the angelic harmonies, which repeated: "Holy, Holy, Holy Lord God of hosts! The heavens and the earth are full of Thy glory! Glory be to the Father, glory be to the Son, glory be to the Holy Ghost!" Thereafter it became the pious custom of the Adoratrices to say the Trisagion every day at half past four in the afternoon, no matter where they happened to be.

In thanksgiving for this rare privilege, St. Anthony Mary Claret recited the prayer every day in honor of the Most Holy Trinity. In addition, he composed a book which contained fervent prayers that became popular as the official text for this holy exercise.[112]

Ven. Anne Catherine Emmerich (1774-1824) once saw in Heaven the seraphim and cherubim, with many other spirits, standing around the throne of God, "hymning incessant praise."[113] It is reported that the holy lay brother, **Bl. Simon Ballachi** (1260-1319), who left a promising career to enter the Dominican Order, was often visited by saints and often heard angelic voices in his little cell.[114] **Père Lamy** (1855-1931), who was blessed with many visions of angels and had a holy familiarity with them, heard three or four angels in the church of La Courneuve. "I heard their voices without seeing them. As you do with people you know, I recognize them by their voices."[115]

We turn now to **Bl. Padre Pio** (1887-1968), to whom angelic harmonies were a familiar, welcomed occurrence. Fr. Alessio Parente, who was for many years the priest's constant companion and helper, tells us that on one occasion in the Friary of Our Lady of Grace, a number of friars heard heavenly voices singing beautiful harmonies, but could not tell from whence they came, since at that hour during the day there would be no singing in the church. When they asked Padre Pio about it, the holy friar replied, "Why are you surprised? They are the voices of the angels who are taking souls from Purgatory into Paradise."[116]

On another occasion, two of Padre Pio's spiritual children were sitting on the beach when they began hearing unexplained voices coming from the direction of the Gargano mountain. It seemed like a heavenly choir singing harmonies they had never heard before. Their souls were lifted, and they experienced unearthly delight before the music began slowly to fade away. The two young men were so overcome by the experience that they visited Padre Pio and asked him about the singing. The Padre replied: "Silly boys, you didn't understand? It was the angels who were praising Our Lady from above the friary. Thank the Lord for the special grace which you received."[117]

37. Musical Instruments and the Angels

We are familiar with pictures of angels playing musical instruments, and we are familiar with *Psalm* 150, which reads: "Praise ye the Lord in his holy places: praise ye him in the firmament of his power. Praise ye him for his mighty acts, praise ye him according to the multitude of his greatness. Praise him with sound of trumpet: praise him with psaltery and harp. Praise him with timbrel and choir: praise him with strings and organs. Praise him on high sounding cymbals: praise him on cymbals of joy: let every spirit praise the Lord. Alleluia." (*Ps.* 150).

Holy Scripture mentions many musical instruments—harps, timbrels, cymbals, organs, strings, lutes, pipes and "divers kinds of musical instruments"—but does not mention the Angels playing any of these instruments.

There is, however, one instrument, undoubtedly the instrument of choice, which Scripture *does* describe angels as playing—the trumpet. We read in the gospel of *St. Matthew:* "And he shall send his angels with a trumpet, and a great voice: and they shall gather together his elect from the four winds, from the farthest parts of the heavens to the utmost bounds of them." (*Matt.* 24:31). **St. Paul** writes in his first letter to the *Corinthians*: "In a moment, in the twinkling of an eye, at the last trumpet: for the trumpet shall sound, and the dead shall rise again incorruptible:

and we shall be changed." (*1 Cor.* 15:52). St. Paul instructs again: "For the Lord himself shall come down from heaven with commandment, and with the voice of an archangel, and with the trumpet of God: and the dead who are in Christ, shall rise first." (*1 Thess.* 4:15).

St. John, in *The Apocalypse,* tells of things to come, and angels play a large part in the drama. In describing his vision the Saint writes:

> And I saw seven angels standing in the presence of God; and there were given to them seven trumpets . . . the seven angels, who had the seven trumpets, prepared themselves to sound the trumpet. (*Apoc.* 8:2, 6). And the first angel sounded the trumpet, and there followed hail and fire. (*Apoc.* 8:7). And the second angel sounded the trumpet: and as it were a great mountain, burning with fire. (*Apoc.* 8:8). And the third angel sounded the trumpet, and a great star fell from heaven. (*Apoc.* 8:10). And the fourth angel sounded the trumpet, and the third part of the sun was smitten. (*Apoc.* 8:12). And the fifth angel sounded the trumpet, and I saw a star fall from heaven upon the earth. (*Apoc.* 9:1). And the sixth angel sounded the trumpet: and I heard a voice. (*Apoc.* 9:13). And the seventh angel sounded the trumpet: and there were great voices in heaven. (*Apoc.* 11:15).

Going back to the book of *Exodus,* we read that while **Moses** was receiving the Ten Commandments an angel was again sounding a trumpet: ". . . all the people saw the voices and the flames, and the sound of the trumpet, and the mount smoking: and being terrified and struck with fear, they stood afar off." (*Ex.* 20:18).

With the exception of **St. Lydwine of Schiedam,** whose biographer mentions "great seraphim flames, unloosing from harps of fire the gorgeous pearl of sound,"[118] this author could only find one other incident in which an angel was heard with a musical instrument.

Thomas of Celano, a companion of **St. Francis of Assisi** (1181-1226), writes that there was a follower of the Saint who had been a lute player in the world. The Saint one day asked him to obtain a lute and to play it for him, but the brother answered, "I am afraid men may suspect that I am being tempted to frivolity." The Saint answered that it would be better to forget about it so that the opinion of others might not be harmed. The next night, while the Saint was at prayer, he heard the sound of a lute "of wonderful harmony and very sweet melody." No one was seen, but the angelic sounds moved back and forth with the movement of the player. The next morning the Saint revealed to the brother what had taken place and added: "I who could not hear the lutes of men have heard a far sweeter lute."[119]

It seems that angels rarely play instruments for men. Perhaps they are saving the exhibition of their talents for the audiences who will hear their exquisite melodies as they perform before the throne of God.

38. Thoughtful Considerations

Both **St. Basil the Great** and **St. John Chrysostom** testify to having seen many hosts of angels in human form when the Blessed Sacrament was exposed. They were clothed with white garments and standing around the altar as soldiers stand before their king. "Their heads were bowed, their faces covered, their hands crossed, and the whole body so profoundly inclined as to express the deepest sense of their own unworthiness to appear before the Divine Majesty."

As Fr. Michael Muller, C.SS.R. writes:

> These angels, those pure spirits, shrink before the infinite holiness of God, and we allow vain, worldly and even sinful thoughts to insinuate themselves into our mind in His presence. The Angels tremble before His greatness, and we fear not to talk and

> laugh in His presence. The Angels, those princes of Heaven, are all humility and modesty, and we, the dust of the earth and miserable sinners, all impertinence and pride! The Angels veil their faces before His splendor, and we do not even so much as cast down our eyes . . . The Angels bow down to the earth, and we will not bend our knee! The Angels, full of awe, fold their hands upon their breasts, and we allow ourselves every freedom of attitude and movement! What humiliating reflections! What an impressive lesson![120]

Pope St. Leo I, a great devotee of the Angels, exhorts us to make friendships with the holy Angels, as did **St. Denis**, a contemporary of the Apostles and a disciple of St. Paul. St. Denis personally assumed the title of Philangelus, that is, "Friend of the Angels." Friendship with the Angels is also encouraged because of the assistance and the loving attentions that they always give us. As **St. Augustine** tells us,

> The Angels go in and out with us, having their eyes always fixed upon us and upon all that we are doing. If we stop anywhere, they stop also; if we go forth to walk, they bear us company; if we journey into another country, they follow us; go where we will, by land or by sea, they are ever with us. While we sleep, they keep watch by us . . . they never tire of being with us all day long and all night long, and during every moment of our life. And if we are so happy as to be saved, after our death, they will visit us in the prison of Purgatory.[121]

How often have we received enlightenment from them regarding both spiritual and temporal matters: sudden impressions which surprise us when we least expect them; moments when our hearts feel urged to offer love to God; reminders about prayers to be said or forgotten duties or kindnesses that were neglected, but which should be performed; a sudden answer seemingly coming from nowhere to a question that perplexes us; a recollection of a friend long forgotten who might be in need of prayer; a pious thought or remembrance while we are in the midst of recreation, amusement or some busy occasion. All of us at one time or another have experienced these moments, but did not realize where they came from. Perhaps while we endeavor to grow closer to our guardian angel, we can be more attentive to these "inspirations" that suddenly come upon us and then realize that it is our "heavenly friend" who is responsible for them.

39. The Nine Choirs of Angels

We obtain our information about certain ranks of the heavenly army from hints given us in Scripture. In the Old Testament books of *Exodus* and *Isaias* we are introduced to the Seraphim and Cherubim. In the New Testament we learn of Angels and Archangels. The remaining choirs are given us by St. Paul, who wrote that all things were created by God in Heaven and on earth, whether visible or invisible, whether "thrones or dominations, or principalities, or powers . . ." (*Col.* 1:16). And again, "Above all principality, and power, and virtue, and dominion, and every name that is named." (*Eph.* 1:21). These, plus other statements in Scripture, firmly established the existence of *nine* choirs of angels as early as the time of **St. Ignatius the Martyr** (d. 107), who mentions the hierarchies and the ranks of angels in his *Epistle to the Trallians*: "I am in chains and able to grasp heavenly things, the ranks of the Angels, the hierarchy of principalities, things visible and invisible."[122]

While St. Ignatius the Martyr knew there were ranks of angels in Heaven, and while others mention fewer choirs, by the time of **St. Ambrose** (340-397), the present number of nine choirs had become established in Christian piety. Agreeing to this is **St. Gregory the Great** (540-604), who wrote, "We know on the authority of Scripture that there are nine orders of angels: These we know to be Angels, Archangels, Principalities, Virtues, Powers, Dominations, Thrones, Cherubim and Seraphim."[123] The matter was confirmed in the thirteenth century by **St. Thomas Aquinas** (1225-1274), who gave the number and names of the various choirs and even gave the biblical references where the names could be found. Moreover, in his *Summa Theologica*, he not only interpreted the names of the choirs, but continued at length in describing the attributes and function of each.

The Church recognizes and mentions some of these angel choirs in the Preface for Sundays recited during the traditional Latin Mass. Part of it reads: "This the Angels and Archangels, the Cherubim and the Seraphim do praise; day by day they cease not to cry out as with one voice, saying: Holy, Holy, Holy . . ." The Preface for weekdays, however, mentions other choirs: ". . . Through Him the Angels praise Your Majesty, the Dominations adore it, the Powers are in awe. The heavens and the heavenly hosts and the blessed Seraphim join together in celebrating their joy . . ."

The choirs of Principalities, Virtues and Thrones were not mentioned in the above prayers, but we know they are included in the heavenly choirs, which are divided into three groups.

The first group includes the Seraphim, Cherubim and Thrones, those closest to the throne of God. The second group embraces the Virtues, Dominations (or Dominions) and Powers. The third group includes the Principalities, Archangels and Angels. According to Pseudo-Dionysius, the Angels "know what they have by way of power and enlightenment, and they know their place in this sacred, transcendent order."[124]

Pope Leo XIII (1878-1903), in his encyclical *Quod Apostolici Muneris*, mentions the distinct nature of the different choirs of angels when he writes: "Just then as the Almighty willed that, in the heavenly kingdom itself, the choirs of angels should be of differing ranks, [and] subordinated the one to the other; again just as in the Church, God has established different grades of orders with diversity of functions, so that all should not be Apostles, all not Doctors, all not Prophets . . . ." Later, **Pope Pius XI** (1922-1939) writes on the same theme in his encyclical *Studio-*

rum Ducem: "Ineffable Creator, Who out of the treasuries of Thy wisdom hast appointed three hierarchies of angels and set them in admirable order high above the heavens . . ."

We are also informed that each rank of angels is directed in sacred matters by its predecessors, and that, in turn, it directs those which come after it. **St. Ignatius Loyola** (1491-1556) notes that "Among the Angels there is likewise this graded subordination of one hierarchy to another, and in the heavenly bodies and all their movements an orderly and close connection and interrelation is kept, all movement coming from one Supreme Mover in perfect order, step by step, to the lowest."

Some of the Saints have also noted the differences in the Angels, including **St. Teresa of Avila** (1515-1582), who had many visions of angels. This saint writes in her *Autobiography* of the variations in these heavenly beings: "Their names they never tell me; but I see very well that there is in Heaven so great a difference between one angel and another, and between these and the others, that I cannot explain it."[125]

As mentioned earlier regarding the archangel who was assigned as guardian to **St. Frances of Rome** (1384-1440), this archangel appeared with the Saint's deceased son, Evangelista. The boy spoke of the wonders of Heaven and his happiness and revealed: "There are nine choirs of angels in Heaven, and the higher orders of angelic spirits instruct in the divine mysteries the less exalted intelligences."[126] The young boy also revealed: "My abode is with God; my companions are the Angels . . . If you wish to know my place, my mother, learn that God, of His great goodness, has appointed it in the second choir of angels, and the first hierarchy of archangels."[127]

Sr. Consolata Betrone (1903-1936) tells us that "In Heaven, every choir of angels attends to the fulfillment of its own office, without envying or desiring the office of another."

40. The First Angelic Hierarchy—Seraphim, Cherubim, Thrones

Tradition, as well as the opinions of theologians and the Doctors of the Church, agree that these three choirs are closest to the throne of God and are occupied with adoration and with singing the praises of God. As early as the time of **St. Cyril of Jerusalem** (315-386) and **St. John Chrysostom** (347-407), the Seraphim and Cherubim were ranked highest in the heavenly order.

41. The Seraphim

The Seraphim, strangely enough, are known to have six pairs of wings, as mentioned in Scripture. We first learn of this choir and its description in the book of *Isaias*: "In the year that king Ozias died, I saw the Lord sitting upon a throne, high and elevated: and his train filled the temple. Upon it stood the seraphims: the one had six wings and the other had six wings: with two they covered his face, and with two they covered his feet, and with two they flew. And they cried one to another, and said: Holy, holy, holy, the Lord God of hosts, all the earth is full of his glory." (*Is.* 6:1-3). So powerful and so vehement was the love expressed by this thrice holy cry that **Isaias** goes on to report, "the lintels of the doors were moved at the voice of him that cried, and the house was filled with smoke." (*Is.* 6:4).

As soon as Isaias bemoaned the fact that he was a man "of unclean lips" dwelling among people with unclean lips, "One of the seraphim flew to me and in his hand was a live coal which he had taken with the tongs off the altar. And he touched my mouth and said: 'Behold this hath touched thy lips and thy iniquities shall be taken away and thy sin shall be cleansed.' " (*Is.* 6:5-7). This fiery cleansing of Isaias seems in keeping with one of the attributes of the Seraphim, since the word seraphim means "having a fiery love" or "carriers of warmth." It also means the power to purify by means of lightning and the flame.

While all good angels love God exceedingly, the love of the Seraphim is said to be beyond compare. They are called "the princes of pure love" according to the great **St. Denis** (d. 258), who mentions eight properties of this love that are represented by fire. Among these properties is that "seraphic love signifies intense love, which is ever burning and consuming." He mentions that fire is in constant motion, just as the Seraphim are incessantly intent on God alone. Since fire is intensely hot, the love of the Seraphim is a burning love. Fire never loses its light, just as seraphic love abides in its fullness. "Fire not only penetrates what is combustible, but permeates throughout; and seraphic love plunges, loses and engulfs itself in the abyss of the Divinity by a glorious transformation. Fire communicates warmth and purifies; the Seraphim carry love and light into all the choirs of the other angels."

St. Gregory the Great agrees with St. Thomas Aquinas (1225-1274) when he writes: "We must simply say with Dionysius that the higher angels are never sent out for external earthly ministry." But, maybe exceptions are made? Perhaps St. Thomas Aquinas was unaware of the vision of **St. Francis of Assisi** (1181-1226) who died almost 50 years before him. In this vision (described earlier; see #19), St. Francis saw a being having six wings who imprinted on his body the Wounds of Jesus.

Perhaps an angel of extraordinary power and position was deputed to this task, since it was the first instance of a human receiving the glorious wounds.

Some of the popes have recognized the lofty position of the Seraphim and the Cherubim in their loving exaltation of the Blessed Virgin. **Pope Pius XI** (1857-1939) wrote in his encyclical *Lux Veritatis,* "The Blessed Virgin is the Mother of God; therefore, she is far more excellent than all the Angels, even the Seraphim and Cherubim." **Pope Pius XII** (1876-1958) agreed with his predecessor when he wrote in *Fulgens Corona*, "with the exception of God Himself, she is higher than all; by nature more beautiful, more graceful and more holy than the

Cherubim and Seraphim themselves and the whole host of angels."

42. The Cherubim

Just as an intense love is attributed to the Seraphim, light and admirable knowledge are the possession of the Cherubim. They are not only described as learned in the divine science of Heaven, but **St. Gregory** affirms that they have the very fullness of it. The name cherubim signifies the "power to know and to see God," to "receive the greatest gifts of His light," to "contemplate the divine splendor." They are also called the doctors of the science of the Saints. According to **Henri-Marie Boudon,** the Archdeacon of Evreux, "Divine light imparts to them admirable knowledge, and the holy effulgence with which they are replenished is reflected in abundant streams upon the other hierarchies."[128]

The first time we learn of the Cherubim in Holy Scripture is in *Genesis*: "And he cast out Adam; and placed before the paradise of pleasure cherubims, and a flaming sword, turning every way, to keep the way of the tree of life." (*Gen.* 3:24). The next time we hear of the Cherubim is in the book of *Exodus*. In giving instructions for the building of the Ark of the Covenant, it was ordered: "Thou shalt make also two cherubims of beaten gold, on the two sides of the oracle. Let one cherub be on the one side, and the other on the other. Let them cover both sides of the propitiatory, spreading their wings, and covering the oracle, and let them look one towards the other, their faces being turned towards the propitiatory wherewith the ark is to be covered." (*Ex.* 25:18-20). Next we read of a vision of **Ezechiel:**

> And I saw and behold in the firmament that was over the heads of the cherubim, there appeared over them as it were the sapphire stone, as the appearance of the likeness of a throne . . . And the glory of the Lord was lifted up from above the cherub . . . and the house was filled with the cloud, and the court was

> filled with the brightness of the glory of the Lord. And the sound of the wings of the cherubims was heard even to the outward court as the voice of God Almighty speaking. (*Ezech.* 10:1-5).

Cherubim are mentioned frequently throughout *Ezechiel* (especially in Chapters 1 and 10) and throughout the Old Testament, more specifically with regard to the Ark of the Covenant. One of their number is also mentioned in the *Autobiography* of **St. Teresa of Avila** (1515-1582). The Saint writes about her vision and what is called her Transverberation (piercing of her heart) in this manner:

> It was our Lord's will that I should see the angel in this wise. He was not large, but small of stature, and most beautiful—his face burning, as if he were one of the highest angels, who seem to be all of fire: they must be those whom we call cherubim . . . I saw in his hand a long spear of gold, and at the iron's point there seemed to be a little fire. He appeared to me to be thrusting it at times into my heart and to pierce my very entrails; when he drew it out, he seemed to draw them out also, and to leave me all on fire with a great love of God.[129]

The Saint's spiritual director and confessor, the Dominican Domingo Bañez, in examining the writings of the Saint, gave his own identification of the angel when he wrote in the margin of her manuscript: "It seems, rather, those that are called seraphims." This opinion prevailed for many years in various translations, but was eventually restored to the identification given by the Saint—that the angel belonged to the choir known as Cherubim. This is perhaps correct since the Saint does not mention the angel having six wings, with which the Seraphim are usually adorned, according to the visions of Isaias and St. Francis.

43. The Thrones

The angelic Thrones bear a comparison to the thrones of earth because, just as material thrones are raised above the ground, so are these celestial thrones exalted to a most sublime height, into a close vicinity to the glory and majesty of God. As **Archdeacon Boudon** relates: "Like kings sometimes cause themselves to be borne in their royal chair, so also God in a certain manner conveys His Spirit by these angels, and communicates it to the lesser angels and to men; as kings give judgment upon their thrones, so also it is from the midst of these thrones that God pronounces His decrees . . . it is there that His Divine judgments and counsels are manifested to other angels and to man."[130]

It is also stated that the main characteristics of those who belong to the order of thrones are submission and peace. For this reason, it is reported that they are patrons of true repose of soul and tranquil peace of heart. It is said that God rests on them and imparts His Spirit to them, which they pass on to angels and to mankind. Dionysius teaches that thrones carry warmth and an outpouring of wisdom and that they, like servants, are ever attentive to the will of God. He continues that they "dwell in fullest power, immovably and perfectly established in the Most High."[131]

44. The Second Angelic Hierarchy—Dominations, Virtues, Powers

This second hierarchy of angels is more especially devoted to the management of human affairs. **St. Paul**, in his epistle to the *Ephesians*, writes that God raised up Christ from the dead and set Him on His right hand in the heavenly places, "Above all principality, and power, and virtue, and dominion, and every name that is named, not only in this world but also in that which is to come." (*Eph.* 1:20, 21). And again, in his epistle to the *Colossians* St. Paul writes, "For in Him were all things created in heaven and on earth, visible and invisible, whether thrones, or dominations, or principalities, or powers: all things were created by him and in him." (*Col.* 1:16).

45. The Dominations

It is said that the Dominations (or Dominions) communicate the commands of God and make known to us His holy will. **Archdeacon Boudon** writes that it is "the special office of these spirits of light to make known to us the commands of God; they are, so to say, the secretaries of state of the great King Jesus."[132] Boudon also writes that "they will teach you to become masters of yourselves and of all things, raising you above all created beings by an intimate union with the Creator."[133]

St. Dionysius the Areopagite (first century) tells us that the Dominations "reject empty appearances, that they return completely to the true Lord, and share as far as it can [be done] in that everlasting and divine source of all dominion." Dionysius continues:

> The name given to the holy Dominations means, I think, a certain unbounded elevation to that which is above, freedom from all that is terrestrial, and from all inward inclination to the bondage of discord, a liberal superiority to harsh tyranny, freedom from degrading servility and from what is low, because they are untouched by any inconsistency. They are true lords, perpetually aspiring to true lordship and to the source of all lordship . . . They do not turn toward vain shadows, but wholly give themselves to that true authority, forever one with the godlike source of lordship.[134]

It is also reported that the main virtue of these heavenly spirits is their zeal for the maintenance of God's authority.

46. The Virtues

To this choir, which is mentioned by St. Paul (*Eph.* 1:21), has been confided the duty of enforcing the orders issued by the

Dominations. To them is attributed a great strength. **St. Gregory the Great** (540-604) is of the opinion that it is through the instrumentality of the Virtues that God ordinarily performs most of His miracles. It is also believed that God governs the seasons, the visible heavens and the elements through these angels, who also possess a keen intelligence. **Dionysius** writes that "the name indicates that they have an equal order with the divine Dominions and Powers. They are so placed that they can perceive God in an harmonious and unconfused way and indicate the ordered nature of the celestial and intellectual authority, purification, illumination and perfection." Dionysius continues that "the name of the holy Virtues signifies a certain powerful and unshakable courage welling forth into all their Godlike energies . . . and flowing forth providentially to those below it, filling them abundantly with virtue."[135]

47. The Powers

It is written that the Powers have, as it were, a kind of masculine and unshakable courage in all their activities. They look to that transcendent power which is the source of all power. It is also said that they are assigned to fight evil and defeat the plans of Satan.

Concerning the Powers, **Archdeacon Boudon** writes: "When we see storms gathering either in the Church or in the state, machinations to resist those who are working for the glory of God, extraordinary conspiracies to defeat some great good which is being planned for some diocese, city or country, then it is that we ought to perform frequent devotions in honor of these powers of Heaven, that they may overturn and destroy all the might and miserable plotting of Hell."[136]

48. The Third Angelic Hierarchy—Principalities, Archangels, Angels

According to **Archdeacon Henri Marie Boudon**, "This last hierarchy is specially engaged in the care of men, of kingdoms, and provinces, and of other things which peculiarly regard the good of men."[137]

49. The Principalities

The duties of the Principalities seem to be executive, in regard to the visible world of men. As **St. Thomas** relates: "The execution of the angelic ministrations consists in announcing divine matters . . . leadership belongs to the Principalities."[138] They are also commissioned to watch diligently over the welfare of kingdoms, states and those who govern. We are told that the Principalities could be invoked for the transformation of our souls. Since man is naturally weakened by sin, he is in need of support, which this glorious choir of angels is eager to perform. It is also believed that it is this choir that assists in guarding countries, and that the Principalities are charged with making announcements to mankind.

That it is recorded the Principalities have been given by God a certain influence over the Archangels and Angels and that they communicate to them the orders of Divine Providence. According to **St. Gregory the Great,** they are the princes of the heavenly spirits of the two lesser orders of their hierarchy, the Angels and Archangels. **Dionysius** writes that "The name of celestial Principalities signifies their Godlike princeliness and authoritativeness in an order which is holy and most fitting to the princely powers, and that they are wholly turned towards the Prince of princes, and lead others in princely fashion."[139] Finally, we read in the *Epistle to Diognetus*, which was written between the time of the Apostles and that of Constantine, that the unknown writer knew of this particular choir. He wrote that God did not send an "Angel or Principality, or one of those in charge of earthly things, or one entrusted with the administration of heavenly things, to save us from our sins. No, He sent the Designer and Architect of the universe in person."[140]

50. The Archangels

The first time we read the word archangel is in **St. Paul's** first letter to the *Thessalonians*, where he writes: "For the Lord himself shall come down from heaven with commandment, and with the voice of an archangel, and with the trumpet of God: and the dead who are in Christ, shall rise first." (*1 Thess.* 4:15). **St. Jude** also mentions the word archangel in his epistle. "When Michael the Archangel, disputing with the devil, contended about the body of Moses . . ." (*Jude* 1:9).

Besides St. Michael, this choir includes the archangels St. Gabriel, St. Raphael and at least four other members, since St. Raphael revealed to Tobias that he was one of seven who stand before the throne of God. **Boudon** gives the name Uriel to another of the Archangels, but since the name appears in the apocryphal book of *Enoch* and fourth book of *Esdras* (4 *Esdras* 4:1), the Church does not recognize it. The names of angels not found in the canonical books of the Bible were rejected under Pope Zachary in 745 and were again rejected in a synod held at Aix-la-Chapelle in 789.

Boudon tells us that "The Archangels make the Divine will known in such as are of great moment; and both the Angels and archangels are informed and enlightened therein by the Principalities, who represent in a special manner the empire and sovereignty of God."[141] It is believed that they are given as guardians to great personages, such as the Holy Father, Cardinals and others who have special work to do for the glory of God upon earth. One of these great personages was **St. Frances of Rome** (1384-1440), who, as described earlier, received an archangel as her guardian when he appeared with her deceased son, Evangelista.[142] After her husband's death, Frances founded in Rome the congregation of the Oblates of Mary, which adopted the Rule of St. Benedict.

It is the Archangels who also—with the Principalities and the Angels—watch over empires, provinces, towns and villages and are entrusted with their care.[143] An admirable devotion practiced by **Fr. Peter Faber** (one of the original Jesuits) was to greet the angels who were in charge of the various villages through which he traveled. It is said that **St. Francis Xavier** (1506-1552), when going to the Indies, paid his respects to the holy archangels who had charge of the area.

51. The Angels

It is needless to report that the Angels, who appear to be of the lowest order of heavenly beings, are mentioned throughout Scripture, in both the Old and the New Testaments, as well as throughout the histories of the Saints. These angels manifest the Divine will in ordinary matters. It is believed that guardian angels are members of this last choir. As **Boudon** reports, the "loving charity of these blessed spirits toward men is so exceedingly great and so admirable, that we shall never be able to make any adequate return either of gratitude or homage." He also writes that angels "are stars whose celestial influences we feel more often because they are nearer to us, watching over the good of each one . . . with an ineffable love and care."[144] It is said that they "mirror in a very particular way the goodness of God toward men and that they are ever ready to go wherever the will of God sends them. They have a true sense of values and they know that to serve God in any capacity is a very great honor."[145]

It is recommended by devout souls that we honor not only our own guardian angel, but also those who care for members of our families and friends. If one of us had the opportunity of meeting and conversing with members of royalty, we would consider it a rare privilege. We are unaware that around us are angels, the princes of Heaven, with whom we can converse at any time. We should also pay honor to the host of guardian angels who attend each Holy Mass with their charges and those heavenly princes who prostrate in adoration before the altar during the Holy Sacrifice, as well as those who keep Our Lord company in empty churches.

* * *

It has been noted that "Although the doctrine regarding the choirs of angels has been received in the Church with extraordinary unanimity, no proposition touching the angelic hierarchies is binding on our faith."[146]

52. The Archangel Michael— Who Is He?

His name, from the Hebrew *Mikha'el*—meaning "Who is like God?"—was the war cry of the good angels in the battle fought in Heaven against the rebellious angels, whose leader became Satan, and his followers, devils. Michael, the great warrior of that battle, is mentioned five times in Scripture. In the Old Testament, his name appears three times in the book of *Daniel.* When **Daniel** prayed that God would permit the Jews to return to Jerusalem, the Archangel Gabriel appeared to Daniel and said: "the prince [angel] of the kingdom of the Persians resisted me one and twenty days: and behold Michael, one of the chief princes, came to help me . . ." (*Dan.* 10:13). At the end of the tenth chapter, Gabriel repeats:

"But I will tell thee what is set down in the scripture of truth: and none is my helper in all these things, but Michael your prince." (*Dan.* 10:21).

Again in the book of *Daniel,* we read that the archangel shall defend the people at the time of the Antichrist: "Michael shall rise up, the great prince, who standeth for the children of thy people: and a time shall come such as never was from the time that nations began even until that time. And at that time shall thy people be saved, every one that shall be found written in the book." (*Dan.* 12:1).

In the New Testament the archangel is mentioned briefly in the epistle of **St. Jude**, as pointed out earlier (cf. *Jude* 1:9). But we learn more about Michael in *The Apocalypse* where we are told of his strength and his military victory against Satan and his followers: "And there was a great battle in heaven; Michael and his angels fought with the dragon, and the dragon fought and his angels: And they prevailed not, neither was their place found any more in heaven. And that great dragon was cast out, that old serpent, who is called the devil and Satan." (*Apoc.* 12:7-9).

Because of this vision, the Archangel Michael has always been known as the great defender of the Church and the archenemy of the devil. It was in this capacity that St. Michael was called upon by **Pope Leo XIII** to protect the people of the Church after he mystically heard the terrifying threats of the devil. (See #117.) As a result of this experience that took place on October 13, 1884, the Pope composed the prayer that was recited after all Low Masses throughout the world:

> St. Michael the Archangel, defend us in battle, be our safeguard against the wickedness and snares of the devil. May God rebuke him, we humbly pray, and do thou, O Prince of the Heavenly Host, by the power of God, cast into Hell Satan and the other evil spirits who prowl about the world for the ruin of souls. Amen.

This prayer, accompanied by three *Hail Marys* and other prayers, is recited after Low Masses in the traditional Latin Mass. It is still regarded as the most popular prayer ever to the archangel.

St. Thomas Aquinas writes of this archangel: "Michael is the breath of the Redeemer's spirit, who will, at the end of the world, combat and destroy Antichrist, as he did Lucifer in the beginning." According to many Doctors of the Church, it was the Archangel Michael who performed many services in Scripture for which his name is not mentioned. Regarded as the guardian angel of the Israelites, it is believed that St. Michael was the angel mentioned in the book of *Exodus:* "And the angel of God, who went before the camp of Israel, removing, went behind them: and together with him, the pillar of the cloud." (*Ex.* 14:19). And again in *Exodus* we read: "Behold I will send my angel, who shall go before thee, and keep thee in thy journey, and bring thee into the place that I have prepared. Take notice of him, and hear his voice, and do not think him one to be contemned: for he will not forgive when thou hast sinned, and my name is in him." (*Ex.* 23:20-21). In the same chapter of *Exodus* we find this passage: "And my angel shall go before thee, and shall bring thee in unto the Amorrhite, and the Hethite . . . whom I will destroy." (*Ex.* 23:23).

It is believed that St. Michael stood in the way against Balaam, as described in the book of *Numbers*: "And an angel of the Lord stood in the way against Balaam, who sat on the ass, and had two servants with him. (*Num.* 22:22). St. Michael is also thought to have slain the army of the Assyrians: "And it came to pass that night, that an angel of the Lord came, and slew in the camp of the Assyrians a hundred and eighty-five thousand." (*4 Kgs.* 19:35).

Because of these exploits, Christian tradition gives to St. Michael four offices: 1) to fight against Satan; 2) to rescue the souls of the faithful from the power of the devil, especially at the hour of death; 3) to attend the dying and accompany them to judgment; 4) to be the champion of God's people, the Israelites in the Old Law, the Christians in the New Testament, and to serve as the Patron of the Church, as he served the order of knights during the Middle Ages.

53. Is Michael the Leader of All the Angels? To Which Rank Does He Belong?

The question arises: To which of the angelic choirs does Michael belong? **St. Thomas Aquinas** in his *Summa Theologica* writes emphatically that St. Michael belongs to the third choir and the second to last of the ranks, that is, the Archangels.

There is, however, some opposition to this declaration of St. Thomas. Because of St. Michael's varied activities, it is thought by **St. Basil the Great** (329-379) and many of the Greek Fathers that St. Michael is the leader, or prince, of all the Angels, even of the choir of Seraphim, which is the rank closest to God. After all, the archangel is known as "the great prince" in the book of Daniel. (*Dan.* 12:1). Even the Archangel Gabriel, while in conversation with the prophet Daniel, describes St. Michael as "one of the chief princes." (*Dan.* 10:13). And again, Gabriel calls the archangel "Michael, your prince." (*Dan.* 10:21). And since the Church calls St. Michael "Prince of the Heavenly Hosts" in the prayer of Pope Leo XIII, and "Michael, the prince of the heavenly hosts" in the Intercessions of the feast of the three archangels (September 29), it would seem that he may be the very highest of all the Angels; after all, he was the leader of the Angels against the rebellious spirits: "And there was a great battle in heaven, Michael and his angels fought with the dragon and the dragon fought and his angels." (*Apoc.* 12:7). This was a celestial event, while other activities of the archangel have been for the benefit of man. Because of these ministrations to man, it would seem that St. Michael does belong, as St. Thomas Aquinas asserts, to the third choir, which includes the Principalities, Archangels and the Angels, all of whom are engaged in the care of men, and those things which relate to the welfare of men.

So, to which choir does the archangel belong? This is a question whose answer remains a mystery that will be happily revealed to us in Heaven.

54. The Early Veneration of St. Michael

Since this archangel was the champion of the Israelites, it would seem natural for him to be regarded as the defender of the Christian people as well, but instead, several of the early martyrs were adopted as military patrons. St. Michael, for reasons not given, was accepted in early times, not so much as a warrior, but as a healer. Medicinal springs, at Phrygia, Chairotopa and Colossae, where many reportedly were cured, were said to have been established by this archangel. At Colossae a group of pagans attempted to destroy the shrine by directing a stream against it, but the archangel prevented this when he suddenly appeared. He gave a new bed to the stream and, it is said, forever sanctified the waters. The Greeks claim that this apparition took place about the middle of the first century A.D. They even celebrated a feast on September 6 in commemoration of the event.

Sanctuaries were dedicated to the archangel as early as the first century.

55. The Feast of St. Michael

To St. Michael is given the distinction of being the first angel to be commemorated by a liturgical feast. Observed on September 29, this feast was instituted to commemorate the consecration in the year 530 of a church near Rome. For a time the feast was combined with a commemoration of the Guardian Angels, with separate feasts for St. Gabriel on March 24 and St. Raphael on October 24. These two feasts were suppressed and the joint feast of the three archangels was instituted, to be observed on September 29 in the new liturgical calendar (1970); but wherever the traditional ("Tridentine") calendar is still used in the Church, the three Archangels are still venerated on the three separate feast days.

56. St. Michael in Art

This archangel is usually represented as an angelic warrior, while striking a victorious pose, fully armed, with a helmet, sword and a shield that often bears the Latin inscription: *Quis ut Deus*?—"Who is like God?" He stands over a dragon, or Satan, whom he sometimes pierces with a lance. And often he is depicted holding a pair of scales in which he weighs the souls of the departed.

57. The Archangel Michael and the Saints

St. Michael is venerated in France as the patron saint of mariners. The archangel appeared in 708 to **St. Aubert,** the bishop of Avranches, and requested that a shrine be built on what is now known as **Mont-Saint-Michel**, overlooking the Atlantic Ocean. The first shrine was later replaced by the now famous church, which is completely surrounded by water at high tide but is accessible by land when the tide recedes.

Thomas of Celano, a companion and biographer of **St. Francis of Assisi** (1181-1226), writes of the Saint's devotion to the Archangel Michael. St. Francis ". . . often said that the blessed Michael should be honored more especially than the rest of the angels, in as much as he has the office of presenting souls to God." The Saint also kept a fast of forty days in honor of St. Michael between the feast of the Assumption and his feast (September 29). He also advised that "Everyone should offer to God, to honor so great a prince, some praise or some special gift."[147]

Because he was known as a warrior, it seems appropriate that this archangel would appear to **St. Joan of Arc** (1412-1431), the "Maid of Orleans," to counsel and prepare her for her military career. We learn that St. Joan, while only thirteen and a half years of age, began hearing voices—or as she sometimes called them, her "counsel." At first just a simple voice, it was soon accompanied by a "great light." She came to know the voices as being those of St. Michael, who was sometimes accompanied by other angels, and St. Margaret (of Antioch) and St. Catherine (of Alexandria), all of whom urged her to help the cause of France against the English invaders. At her trial, when asked about the voices and how she knew them to be those of the archangel and the Saints, she testified, "I saw them with these very eyes, as well as I see you."

It seems that the Saint was guided throughout her military career by her voices. When she began the first campaign, the heir to the French throne offered her a sword, but she begged that a search be made in the chapel of St. Catherine-de-Fierbois for a sword that was buried behind the altar. It was found exactly where the voices had indicated. It was also the voices that informed her that she would be wounded and later taken captive by the English.

When **St. Paul of the Cross** (1694-1775) was overseeing the building of a house for the members of his Passionist Order, many difficulties developed, including the ill will of some who did all they could to prevent the completion of the work. The boldest among them one night went so far as to plan the burning and demolition of the work already completed. They were about to torch the building when a great beam of light fell upon them from on high, and in the midst was an angel with a sword in his hand. From the angel's attitude, they realized this mighty being meant to guard the new building and would harm those who attempted to resist him. In an instant, all fled the area and no further difficulty was encountered. This angel was identified as the Archangel Michael, who visibly appeared at times to defend the new congregation and its blessed founder.[148]

58. The Archangel Gabriel—Who Is He?

The name Gabriel, from the Hebrew, means "Man of God" or "Strength of God." The first mention of this archangel's name in Scripture appears in the book of *Daniel* when Daniel had a vision of a ram and a goat that has significance in the coming of the Antichrist. **Daniel** writes: "And it came to pass when I Daniel saw the vision and sought the meaning, that behold there stood before me, as it were, the appearance of a man. And I heard the voice of a man between Ulai: and he called, and said: Gabriel, make this man to understand the vision. And he came and stood near where I stood: and when he was come, I fell on my face trembling." (*Dan.* 8:15-17). In the next chapter, Daniel is given other information, and he writes: "And as I was yet speaking in prayer, behold the man Gabriel, whom I had seen in the vision at the beginning, flying swiftly, touched me at the time of the evening sacrifice. And he instructed me, and spoke to me and said: O Daniel, I am now come forth to teach thee, and that thou mightest understand." (*Dan.* 9:21-22).

When next we read of St. Gabriel in Scripture, he appeared to **Zachary,** "standing on the right side of the altar of incense." (*Luke* 1:11). After being informed that his elderly wife Elizabeth would bear a son, Zachary questioned the announcement: "Whereby shall I know this? For I am an old man, and my wife is advanced in years." To this the angel answered, "I am Gabriel, who stand before God; and am sent to speak to thee, and to bring thee these good tidings." (*Luke* 1:18-19).

The most wonderful and extraordinarily happy assignment that could have been given to an angel of God was given to Gabriel when he appeared to the **Blessed Virgin Mary** to announce that she was chosen to be the Mother of God. "And in the sixth month, the angel Gabriel was sent from God into a city of Galilee, called Nazareth, to a virgin espoused to a man whose name was Joseph, of the house of David; and the virgin's name was Mary." (*Luke* 1:26-27). After addressing the Holy Virgin with, "Hail, full of grace, the Lord is with thee: blessed art thou among women," the angel said to her, "Behold, thou shalt conceive in thy womb, and shalt bring forth a son; and thou shalt call his name Jesus." (*Luke* 1:31). We recall this happy event and the words of the Archangel Gabriel each time we recite the words of the *Hail Mary*.

Just as St. Michael is thought to have performed other duties in Scripture, although he is not specifically mentioned, so too the Archangel Gabriel, although not mentioned by name, is believed to have been the angel who performed services for the newborn Jesus and the Holy Family.

Was Gabriel the angel who appeared to the shepherds? "And behold an angel of the Lord stood by them, and the brightness of God shone round about them; and they feared with a great fear. And the angel said to them: Fear not, for behold, I bring you good tidings of great joy, that shall be to all the people: For, this day, is born to you a Saviour, who is Christ the Lord, in the city of David." (*Luke* 2:9-11).

Since the Angel Gabriel was present at the conception of Jesus, could it be that he continued to make other announcements, such as telling **St. Joseph** in a dream to take Mary as his wife? Was Gabriel the angel who "appeared in sleep to Joseph, saying: Arise, and take the child and his mother, and fly into Egypt: and be there until I shall tell thee. For it will come to pass that Herod will seek the child to destroy him"? (*Matt.* 2:13). After Herod's death, was Gabriel the angel who "appeared in sleep to Joseph in Egypt, saying: Arise, and take the child and his mother and go into the land of Israel. For they are dead that sought the life of the child"? (*Matt.* 2:19-20).

Because of the many messages delivered by this angel, he has been appropriately named the patron of messengers. **Ven. Mary of Agreda's** interesting description of the Archangel Gabriel, given earlier, is well worth repeating here. The Venerable writes in *The Mystical City of God* that at the Incarnation, the Archangel Gabriel was accompanied "by many thousands of the most beautiful angels in visible forms." The archangel, when making the pronouncement that the humble Mary was to be the Mother of God, is said to have appeared in this manner:

> The appearance of the great prince and legate was that of a most handsome youth of rarest beauty; his face emitted resplendent rays of light, his bearing was grave and majestic, his advance measured, his motions composed, his words weighty and powerful, his whole presence displayed a pleasing, kindly gravity and more of godlike qualities than all the other angels until then seen in visible form by the heavenly Mistress. He wore a diadem of exquisite splendor and his vestments glowed in various colors full of refulgent beauty. Encased on his breast, he bore a most beautiful cross, disclosing the mystery of the Incarnation, which He had come to announce.[149]

59. The Archangel Gabriel and the Saints

Père Lamy (1855-1931), a mystic and visionary of heavenly subjects and angels, writes of St. Gabriel that he "is taller by a head than the other angels. It is by this that I recognize at once a spirit of a higher choir." The holy cleric also adds, "The Archangel Gabriel has his hair well cut and wavy."[150] Another time, the holy cleric wrote: "The Blessed Virgin had been kind enough to put me under the protection of the holy Archangel Gabriel, to make me over to him, and with my bad sight that protection has been very useful to me." This protection was wonderfully demonstrated one day when the priest, because of his poor eyesight, was walking along a country road with his head leaning forward to protect his eyes from the sun's glare. Suddenly a bicycle rider was almost upon him. As the holy mystic wrote: "I should have been knocked down in one turn of the wheel, but the holy Archangel Gabriel seized the bicycle by the two wheels and put it neatly on one side. He lifted the bicycle and the rider and put them both down on the grass that fringes the road. Weight is nothing to an archangel."

Evidently the archangel was visible to the cyclist, because Père Lamy said, "I saw the cyclist standing open-mouthed, looking at the angel and at me. I had a mad impulse to laugh, seeing the face of the poor boy . . . I went my way from them (after thanking the archangel) . . . and I saw another cyclist coming on full speed. The first shouted like a madman, 'There are two of them! There are two of them!'" The second cyclist did not see the vision, but the first apparently told of it, since the mystic writes: "The talk of the railway man and his comrade on the apparition has given rise to various versions. They spoke about it in the country pubs. They asked me questions about it and I pretended not to understand."[151]

60. The Archangel Raphael—Who Is He?

His name meaning "God Heals" or the "Divine Healer," the Archangel Raphael is mentioned in Scripture in only one book, that of *Tobias*. And it is as a healer, guide, matchmaker and exorcist that Raphael accomplished the mission given him by God.

The events began when the young Tobias was sent to a distant city by his blind father, who was also named Tobias, to collect money that was owed to him by a man named Gabelus. Before setting out, Tobias looked about for a traveling companion, and as Scripture reveals: "Tobias going forth found a beautiful young man, standing girded, and as it were ready to walk. And not knowing that he was an angel of God, he saluted him and said: From whence art thou, good young man?" (*Tob.* 5:5-6). The angel's answer was: "Of the children of Israel."

After assuring Tobias that he knew the way to Rages, in the country of the Medes, the angel agreed to serve as a guide. Taking the young man to meet his blind father, Tobias introduced them. During a brief exchange, the young man told the elder Tobias, "Be of good courage, thy cure from God is at hand." (*Tob.* 5:13). Since Tobias was an only child his mother was very fearful that he would not return safely to them, but the elder Tobias, not knowing that the young man was an angel, comforted his wife by telling her: "Weep not; our son will arrive thither safe, and will return safe to us, and thy eyes shall see him. For I believe that the good angel of God doth accompany him, and doth order all things well that are done about him so that he shall return to us with joy." (*Tob.* 5:26-27).

Accompanied by the family dog, Tobias and Raphael set out and spent the first night by the river Tigris. When Tobias went to the water to wash his feet, "behold a monstrous fish came up to devour him." (*Tob.* 6:2). Tobias, very much afraid, called to Raphael for help, but on the angel's advice and being inspired with confidence, Tobias grabbed the fish by the gill and brought it ashore. Raphael then instructed him, "Take out the entrails of this fish, and lay up his heart, and his gall, and his liver for thee: for these are necessary for useful medicines." (*Tob.* 6:5). He then explained the cures that could be obtained by the application of these parts. When Tobias asked where they should stay during the second night, the angel answered, "Here is one whose name is Raguel, a near kinsman of thy tribe, and he hath a daughter named Sara . . . Ask her therefore of her father, and he will give her thee to wife." (*Tob.* 6:11, 13).

At this advice from the archangel, Tobias asked Sara's father for her hand in marriage, which was granted. However, despite her good character, Sara was plagued by an evil spirit. In order to defeat this devil, Tobias heeded St. Raphael's advice regarding the useful parts of the fish he had caught. On his wedding night, Tobias "took out of his bag part of the [fish's] liver and laid it upon burning coals. Then the angel Raphael took the devil and bound him in the desert of upper Egypt." (*Tob.* 8:2, 3). Because of this help from St. Raphael, Sara was no longer bothered by the demon, and the young couple's wedding was celebrated with several weeks of feasting and rejoicing. Then, because he was newly married, Tobias asked Raphael to journey alone to Rages to obtain the money owed to the elder Tobias. Taking four of Raguel's servants and two camels, Raphael journeyed to the city of the Medes and, with the note written by the elder Tobias, received the money from Gabelus.

Upon his return to the house of Raguel, the angel, together with the younger Tobias and his wife Sara, began the journey back to the parents of Tobias in Ninive. During the journey, the angel made certain that Tobias still had the gall of the fish and instructed him: "As soon as thou shalt come into thy house, forthwith adore the Lord thy God: and giving thanks to him, go to thy father, and kiss him. And immediately anoint his eyes with this gall of the fish, which thou carriest with thee. For be assured that his eyes shall be presently opened, and thy father shall see the light of heaven, and shall rejoice in the sight of thee." (*Tob.* 4:7-8).

Upon their arrival, there followed a touching and typical scene since the dog that had accompanied them on their journey showed his delight at returning home: "Then the dog, which had been with them in the way, ran before, and coming as if he had brought the news, shewed his joy by his fawning and wagging his tail." (*Tob.* 11:9).

Just as the healer, the Archangel Raphael, had instructed, Tobias first thanked God, then kissed his father and, "taking of the gall of the fish, anointed his father's eyes . . . and a white skin began to come out of his eyes, like the skin of an egg. And Tobias took hold of it and drew it from his eyes, and immediately he recovered his sight." (*Tob.* 13:15).

While the father and son were wondering how to reward Raphael for his many services, he identified himself by saying, "I am the angel Raphael, one of the seven who stand before the

Lord. And when they had heard these things, they were troubled, and being seized with fear they fell upon the ground on their faces." (*Tob.* 12:15-16). The angel then said to them, "Peace be to you, fear not. For when I was with you, I was there by the will of God: bless ye him, and sing praises to him. I seemed indeed to eat and to drink with you: but I use an invisible meat and drink, which cannot be seen by men. It is time therefore that I return to him that sent me: but bless ye God, and publish all his wonderful works. And when he had said these things, he was taken from their sight, and they could see him no more." (*Tob.* 12:17-21). Tobias and his father remained prostrate for three hours, blessing God, and when they recovered, they spoke of the archangel with wonderment.

61. The Archangel Raphael and the Saints

Since the Archangel Raphael served as a guide for Tobias and is regarded as the patron of travelers, his services were called upon by **St. Anthony Mary Claret** (1807-1870) during his visit to Marseilles, a city with which he was unfamiliar, while he was awaiting passage on a ship to Rome. In answer to the Saint's prayer, a young man presented himself at his room and offered his services as a guide. The young man accompanied St. Anthony Mary wherever he needed to go, but always left his side at meal time, only to reappear at the end of the meal. On the day of the Saint's departure, the young guide accompanied him to the port, saw him safely aboard the ship and promptly disappeared. The Saint's biographer reports, "Assuredly it was the Archangel Saint Raphael, whom Blessed Anthony invoked at the beginning of his itinerary."[152]

62. All Three Archangels Together

Ven. Anne Catherine Emmerich (1770-1824), a mystic and visionary, once saw in Heaven a dome that was surrounded by three of the nine angelic choirs and four great, luminous angels veiled with their wings, who moved constantly around them. The three archangels, Michael, Gabriel and Raphael, "stood severally over a part of the dome." Gabriel and Raphael were wearing "long, white robes like priests'. Michael wore a helmet with a crest of rays, and his body seemed encased in armor and girt with cords, his robe descending to the knees like a fringed apron. In one hand he held a long staff surmounted by a cross, under which floated the standard of the Lamb; in the other was a flaming sword."[153]

Père Lamy (1855-1931), when referring to angels of a higher choir, wrote:

> What is very beautiful about them are the gold plates of irregular shapes set like mosaic all over the upper part of their bodies. These plates glitter in every direction, with a constant coming and going of light. They get light from God . . . Those gold plates are perpetually moving; you could call them as many suns.
>
> The sleeves of their tunics go down to the forearm; the tunic goes down to the knees, the lower half of the body being dressed in a sort of short skirt. They are like athletes. Their garments are of white, but a white that has nothing earthly about it. I cannot describe it because it is [in] no way comparable to our color of white. It is a white much gentler to the eye. But these holy personages are wrapped in a light so different from our own that everything after it looks dark. When you see fifty angels together, you are filled with wonder . . . They have imprinted on their faces their goodwill toward man.[154]

Père Lamy tells of a favor received at the hands of one or more of the Archangels in the late summer of 1923 when he should have been bitten by countless bees. His poor eyesight is what put him in jeopardy. He says that he was

> coming back from a little turn in the woods. I was facing the chapel where there are two swarms of bees. I

had gathered some flowers and parsnip tops. Lost in my thought, I had forgotten the bees, and startled by their buzzing, I waved the flowers about and that gathered them all together. I made for the lawn to get into the chapel, but I was followed by countless bees, when I distinctly heard these words, "Don't sting, don't sting, our Queen would not be pleased! He must go back home with his ass, and as he would go alone, we should be obliged to go with him in human guise." My idea is that it was the voice of the holy archangel. I think I recognized it. When we got to the vestibule, all the bees held back. I thanked the three archangels.[155]

63. Other Archangels

Since the Archangel Raphael revealed himself to **Tobias** with the words, "I am Raphael, one of the seven who stand before the Lord" (*Tob.* 12:16), and since Michael and Gabriel are identified also as archangels, many have wondered about the identity of the other four archangels mentioned by Raphael. The four remaining angels "who stand before the Lord" are said to have the names Uriel, Raguel, Sariel and Jeremiel, but these names are taken from apocryphal works, which are frowned upon and not accepted by the Catholic Church. The true identity of these four archangels will probably be known to us only in Heaven.

64. Guardian Angels— How Do We Know We Have Them?

We know we have a guardian angel from the teachings of the Church herself, based both on the Old and New Testaments and Tradition, and from the writings of the Doctors of the Church. We have an assurance from the mouth of Jesus, who stated: "See that you despise not one of these little ones: for I say to you, that their angels always see the face of my Father who is in heaven." (*Matt.* 18:10). Scripture adds: "For he hath given his angels charge over thee; to keep thee in all thy ways." (*Ps.* 90:11). And in the book of *Exodus* we learn that in addition to our guardians, the good Lord often assigns other angels to help in particular situations. In giving certain rules to the children of Israel, God told them: "Behold I will send my angel, who shall go before thee, and keep thee in thy journey, and bring thee into the place that I have prepared. Take notice of him, and hear his voice, and do not think him one to be contemned: for he will not forgive when thou hast sinned, and my name is in him. But if thou wilt hear his voice, and do all that I speak, I will be an enemy to thy enemies, and will afflict them that afflict thee." (*Ex.* 23:20-22).

In the *Acts of the Apostles* **St. Paul** had a vision of his guardian angel, who appeared and prophesied when the ship on which the Saint was sailing as a prisoner was caught in a terrible tempest that lasted for days. Scripture relates that afterward, Paul spoke to those on board in this way: "And now I exhort you to be of good cheer. For there shall be no loss of any man's life among you, but only of the ship. For an angel of God, whose I am, and whom I serve, stood by me this night, saying: Fear not, Paul, thou must be brought before Caesar; and behold, God hath given thee all of them that sail with thee." (*Acts* 27:22-24). On board were "two hundred threescore and sixteen souls." (*Acts* 27:37). The ship finally ran aground; "the forepart indeed, sticking fast, remained unmoveable: but the hinder part was broken with the violence of the sea." (*Acts* 27:41). The strongest on board were permitted to swim ashore, "and the rest, some they carried on boards, and some on those things that belonged to the ship. And so it came to pass that every soul got safe to land." (*Acts* 27:44). Just as St. Paul's guardian angel had prophesied, all who had been on board were saved. The only casualty was the ship.

The *Catechism of the Catholic Church* states: "From infancy to death human life is surrounded by their [angels'] watchful care and intercession." (#336). **St. Basil the Great** (329-379), a Doctor of the Church, writes: "That each one of the faithful has an angel who directs his life as a pedagogue and a shepherd nobody can deny, remembering the words of Our Lord: 'See that you despise not one of these little ones: for I say to you, that their angels always see the face of my Father who is in heaven.'" (*Matt.* 18:10). This saint adds, "Beside each stands an angel as protector and shepherd leading him to life."[156]

The Bible represents the Angels not only as our guardians, but also as actually interceding for us and offering our prayers to God. St. Raphael the Archangel addressed these words to **Tobias:** "When thou didst pray with tears, and didst bury the dead, and didst leave thy dinner, and hide the dead by day in thy house, and bury them by night, I offered thy prayer to the Lord." (*Tob.* 12:12). **St. Paul** in writing about the guardians explains, "Are they not all ministering spirits, sent to minister for them, who shall receive the inheritance of salvation?" (*Heb.* 1:14).

St. Ambrose (340-397) cites his belief by remarking: "We should pray to the angels who are given to us as guardians." **St. Francis de Sales** (1567-1622) was so mindful of guardian angels that he adopted the practice of pausing momentarily before delivering his sermons to pray that the guardian angels of the congregation would soften the hearts of their charges to hear his words with benefit. Also, this saint recommended that "Since God often sends us inspirations by means of His angels, we should frequently return our aspirations to Him by means of the same messengers."[157] An authority on this subject, **Fr. Suarez**, S.J., writes that "Even though Scripture does not affirm explicitly the existence of guardian angels, nor has the Church defined this truth, it is nevertheless universally admitted, and it is so firmly based upon Scripture as interpreted by the Fathers, that its denial would be a very great rashness and practically an error."[158]

65. What Are the Ways Guardian Angels Assist Their Charges?

In the little booklet, *The Guardian Angels—Our Heavenly Companions*, the anonymous author lists seven special offices rendered each of us by our holy guardian angels: 1.) They preserve us from many unknown dangers to soul and body. 2.) They defend us against the temptations of the evil spirits. 3.) They inspire us with holy thoughts and prompt us to deeds of virtue in the Divine service. 4.) They warn us of spiritual dangers and admonish us when we have sinned. 5.) They unite with us in prayer and offer our prayers to God. 6.) They defend us at the hour of death against the last attacks of our spiritual foes. 7.) They console the souls languishing in Purgatory and then conduct them to Heaven when their faults have been fully expiated.[159]

St. Margaret Mary Alacoque (1647-1690) confirms that guardian angels console their charges in Purgatory. Having mystically visited Purgatory on a number of occasions, she witnessed souls raising their hands to Heaven and imploring mercy. All the while their guardian angels were at their side consoling and encouraging them.

This saint gives us another example of the services rendered by guardian angels in her letter to Mother de Saumaise, dated July, 1688. St. Margaret Mary, who was a member of the Visitation Order and the visionary of the Sacred Heart devotion, wrote about a vision she experienced in which the Sacred Heart once again was shown to her and in which the Blessed Virgin gave various counsels. She writes that she was taken during this vision to a very spacious and beautiful place where she saw a throne of fire which supported the Sacred Heart. From this throne "shot forth flames so luminous and glowing that the whole place was lighted up and warmed by them." Present, in addition to the Blessed Virgin Mary, were St. Francis de Sales and St. Claude de la Colombière. "The Daughters of the Visitation were there with their guardian angels beside them, each one holding a heart in his hand." Apparently the hearts were those of their charges. After various thoughts were exchanged,

> all the guardian angels drew near to present Him with what they held in their hands. As soon as these hearts touched the sacred Wound, they became beautiful and

> shone like stars. Some of them did not shine as brightly as others. The names of several remained written in letters of gold in the Sacred Heart, into which some of those I speak of eagerly disappeared and were buried with mutual pleasure . . . These were the hearts of those who had labored the most to make Him known and loved . . .[160]

The story is told that **St. Gregory of Tours** (538-594), while still a child, was much concerned because his father was seriously ill. One night, after fervent prayers, he had a dream in which his guardian angel instructed him to "write the name of Jesus on a small wooden chip and lay it on your father's pillow." The next morning Gregory related the dream to his mother, who instructed him to do exactly as the angel had suggested. Needless to report, the father quickly regained his health. Some years later the father was again bedridden. Once again, Gregory prayed for his father, but this time the cure was different. The angel instructed him in a dream to use the liver of a fish. This, of course, is reminiscent of the miracle worked by the Archangel Raphael in favor of the father of Tobias. Once again the Saint's father was restored to health and vigor.

A very busy guardian angel was that of **St. Gemma Galgani** (1878-1903), who remained visible to her most of the time. She tells us that he "would kneel beside her, reciting vocal prayers, such as the Psalms alternately, and ejaculatory prayers or aspirations." But in addition, he "comforted her during her illnesses; he cured her wounds after her first mystical scourging, and above all protected her in the dreadful fights she had to undergo against Satan." One evening, after having been beaten cruelly by the devil, the poor girl could not move. The angel enabled her to get up from the floor and to lie down on her bed, and he then stood watching by her bedside.[161]

The Saint's angel even gave some advice that we might also heed. This is perhaps the only time that an angel dictated words of advice. These are the sentences: "Remember, my daughter, that he who really loves Jesus speaks little and endures all. I order you from Jesus, never to say your opinion if you are not asked to; never uphold your opinion, but at once give it up. When you commit a fault, accuse yourself without waiting to be questioned. And finally, remember to watch your eyes and think that the mortified eye will see the beauty of Heaven."[162]

That angels are messengers of God is a fact that is not disputed. angels also act as messengers for some people, as demonstrated in the lives of **St. Gemma Galgani** (1878-1903) and **Bl. Padre Pio** (1887-1968). As related before, St. Gemma sent letters to her spiritual director by way of her guardian angel; but in Padre Pio's case, the holy priest communicated not only with his own guardian angel, but also with the angels of those he had accepted under his spiritual care—his spiritual children. Once when Padre Alessio saw Padre Pio reciting the Holy Rosary, he approached him and was asked, "Didn't you see all those guardian angels going backward and forward from my spiritual children, bringing messages from them?"[163]

Sometimes at night, while Bl. Padre Pio was reciting the Rosary, he was heard to say aloud such expressions as, "Tell her I will pray for her," or, "Tell him I will knock at the heart of Jesus for this grace." All who heard him speak this way were convinced he was speaking with the guardian angels of his spiritual children.[164]

Since our guardian angels are always eager to help us, we are advised by **St. Jean-Marie-Baptiste Vianney** (1786-1859) to "Hide behind your good angel when you find it impossible to pray, and charge him to pray in your stead." **St. John Bosco** (1815-1888) recommends, "When tempted, invoke your angel. He is more eager to help you than you are to be helped! Ignore the devil and do not be afraid of him: he trembles and flees at your guardian angel's sight."

The devil is conquered by Our Blessed Mother Mary under the title of the "Immaculate Conception," since she has never been touched by the stain of Original Sin.

St. Thomas Aquinas never again experienced temptations of the flesh after angels tied an invisible cord tightly around his waist. *(Picture from an old booklet on the Angelic Warfare Confraternity.)*

While St. Veronica Giuliani is deep in prayer, her guardian angel happily remains in the kitchen, preparing the meal for which St. Veronica is responsible.

St. Rita of Cascia, "Saint of the Impossible," received a thorn wound in her brow from Our Lord, who honored her by asking her to share in His Passion. In this depiction, an angel is given the task of placing a crown of thorns on St. Rita's head.

Bl. Angela of Foligno receives Holy Communion from the hands of an angel. Adoring Our Lord in the Blessed Sacrament, Bl. Angela barely seems to notice the angel.

The Angel Guardian of Portugal, who appeared to the three children of Fatima, brought them Holy Communion and taught them the famous Fatima prayers of reparation.

A childlike angel woke St. Catherine Labouré from sleep and led her to the chapel where she was to see the Blessed Mother. The angel's voice became deep and commanding when he announced the entrance of the Queen of Angels.

St. Michael the Archangel as guardian of the Church in China.

St. Francis de Sales and his companion kneel and pray to the guardian angel of the Chablais region of France before entering it. Thousands of conversions from Calvinism resulted from St. Francis' apostolate there.

Guardian angels remain by their charges throughout life, guarding them from danger and pointing the way to salvation.

Angels are often depicted with musical instruments, highlighting one of their chief joys, which is to praise God. This angel plays the lute.

While the Blessed Mother intercedes with her Son for the souls in Purgatory, the angels pull the purified souls out of the fire and lead them to Heaven. The Child Jesus holds two brown scapulars.

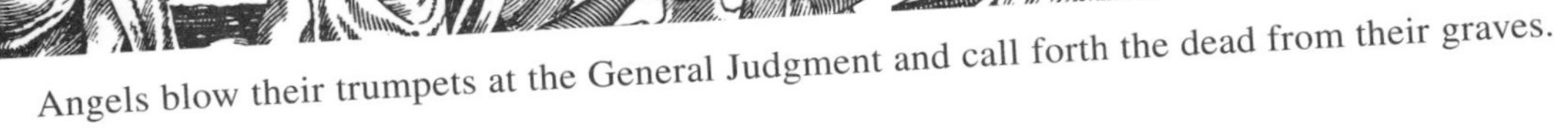

Angels blow their trumpets at the General Judgment and call forth the dead from their graves.

The Angels adore and praise the Holy Trinity in this highly stylized painting of the Throne of God. Two angels kneel before the mysterious unity of God the Father, Son and Holy Spirit.

66. The Blessed Mother Tells Us How Angels Assist Us

In the book *The Mystical City of God*, the Blessed Virgin tells the **Ven. Mary of Agreda** and us to "show thyself thankful for the favor which God vouchsafed thee in appointing angels to assist thee, teach thee and guide thee through tribulations and sorrows." The Blessed Virgin strongly exhorted Ven. Mary of Agreda to "live attentive to the calls, urgings and inspirations with which these angels seek to rouse thee, move and excite thee to the recollection of the Most High and to the exercise of all the virtues."[165]

67. When Is the Guardian Angel Appointed?

St. Thomas Aquinas is of the following opinion: "As long as the child is in the mother's womb, it is not entirely separate . . . And therefore it can be said with some degree of probability that the angel who guards the mother guards the child while in the womb. But at its birth, when it becomes separate from the mother, an angel guardian is appointed to it."[166] **St. Jerome** agrees with this when he writes: "Great is the dignity of souls for each one to have an angel assigned to guard it from the moment it is born."[167] However, **St. Anselm** has added that "Every soul is committed to an angel when it is united with the body."[168] St. Anselm was obviously of the opinion that the guardian angel is assigned before birth.

68. Are Those Born into Non-Christian Religions Given Guardian Angels?

St. Jerome and **St. John Chrysostom** share the opinion that *every* person, from the moment he is born into this world, has a guardian angel. On the other hand, **St. Basil the Great** and **St. Cyril of Alexandria** both limit the angelic ministry to faithful Christians. However, it is the opinion of the majority of theologians that guardian angels are given to *all* men. Suarez agrees with these theologians and the Doctors of the Church who maintain that the just as well as the sinner, the faithful and the unbeliever—the baptized as well as the unbaptized—all have angel guardians.

69. Do Angels Grieve for the Sinner? Do Angels Have Emotions?

We are told by **St. Thomas Aquinas** that "Where there is grief and sorrow, there is not perfect happiness" and that "the Angels are perfectly happy, therefore they have no cause for grief . . . Angels do not grieve, either for sins or for the pains inflicted on men."[169] While this might be true for the most part, some others have written of the Angels' "joy" or "sorrow" regarding events on earth, especially **Pope Leo XIII** (1878-1903), who wrote about the Angels' involvement in happenings mentioned in the New Testament. He wrote in his encyclical *Augustissimae Virginis Mariae:* "The Angels revealed each of these mysteries in due time; they played a great part in them; they were constantly present at them with countenances indicative of joy, now of sorrow, now of triumphant exultation."

One wonders if the Angels might not feel some degree of sorrow when their charges commit serious sin. One can imagine that they hang their heads in shame and disappointment. Since they are ever solicituous for our spiritual welfare, would our angels be somewhat apprehensive when we venture into sinful situations and temptations? What could have been the condition of the Angels while the martyrs suffered? Was the angel who comforted Our Lord in the Garden saddened at His distress? Certainly the situation called for genuine grief. Did the angel who comforted Jesus after the temptations of the devil feel concerned for Our Lord during the trial and then relieved at the departure of the evil spirit? Would an angel be pleased if his charge, after the Particular Judgment, is sentenced to Hell? We are told that our guardians visit their charges in Purgatory. One can only imagine their joy when they accompany the souls to Heaven. While angels might not grieve, as St. Thomas writes, many visions of the Saints testify that they certainly feel some emotions.

The guardian angel of **St. Gregory of Tours** (538-594) was certainly not pleased each time he gave a blow to the Saint to rouse him whenever he fell asleep during prayer time. Similar incidents of this kind are mentioned often in the lives of the Saints when their guardian angels also admonished them for small faults, such as distractions or not applying themselves to the times of meditation and prayer.

The guardian of **St. Frances of Rome** (1384-1440) was so displeased when the Saint committed the slightest fault that he disappeared; whereas at other times he was always visible to her. (See #16.)

It is reported that **St. Catherine of Siena** (1347-1380) was also favored with the visible presence of her guardian angel and that once, while praying in the church, she turned her head to gratify her curiosity. The disapproving look given by her angel was so severe that for several days she was inconsolable and performed severe penances in atonement. **Bl. Veronica of Binasco** (1445-1497) relates a similar experience. She tells us that "once when prompted by curiosity, I happened during the time of Mass to look at one of the sisters who was kneeling near the altar; the angel of God who is constantly beside me rebuked me with such severity that I almost fainted with terror. How threateningly he looked at me."[170] She too performed penances for that fault.

St. Gemma Galgani (1878-1903) was a stigmatist who was favored with the almost constant appearance of her angel. Her biographer writes, "When Gemma proved somewhat faulty, her angel was hard with her, either with reproaching words or remaining silent, or showing her a severe countenance, and even sometimes inflicting on her a punishment."[171] Gemma relates that once, after a fault, "I looked up and saw my guardian angel glaring at me." Another time he said to her, "Are you not ashamed to commit faults in my presence?" To this she added, "He darted at me such severe looks."

St. Antony of Egypt (St. Anthony of the Desert) (251-356) tells us what our spiritual progress means to both the Angels and the Saints: "I tell you truly, my beloved, that our carelessness and our humiliation and our turning aside from the way are not a loss to us only, but they are a weariness for the Angels and for all the Saints in Christ Jesus. Our humiliation gives grief to them all, and our salvation gives joy and refreshment to them all."

It would seem from these experiences of the Saints that angels do have some sort of "emotions," even though, as Thomas of Aquinas relates above, they experience continual happiness. It seems, however, that they experience something corresponding to anger and displeasure when it concerns the good of our souls and our advancement in the spiritual life.

70. From which Angelic Choir Are Guardian Angels Appointed?

Many theologians and Doctors of the Church agree that while guardian angels are usually taken from the last choir, that of angels, they can also be taken from the choirs of Archangels and Principalities, since all these angels are closest to the human order in God's Providence. Once again we turn to **St. Thomas Aquinas**, who tells us that, "Although men are equal in nature, still inequality exists among them according as Divine Providence orders some to the greater, and others to the lesser things . . . Thus it is a greater office to guard one man than another."[172]

St. Dionysius (c. 545) states that it is probable that "the greater angels are appointed to keep those chosen by God for the higher degree of glory," and that for the others, "the guardianship of men is attributed to the angels who belong to the lowest order."[173] **St. Thomas Aquinas** agrees that "such guardianship belongs to the lowest order of the Angels," but he quickly adds that even "Angels of the lowest order can coerce the demons and work miracles."

St. Thomas Aquinas continues: ". . . an angel is appointed to each man to guard him; and such guardianship belongs to the lowest order of the Angels, whose place it is, according to Gregory, to announce the 'lesser things,' for it seems to be the least of the angelic offices to procure what concerns the salvation of only one man."[174] It is the opinion of some theologians that a person is continually being given angels of a higher order as he advances in the spiritual life, while either retaining his original guardian, or receiving a replacement for the original guardian. It is also their opinion that a young man, on becoming a priest, is given an angel of a higher order, while, in many cases, retaining his original angel guardian.

St. Joseph of Cupertino (1603-1663) was a conventual friar minor who lived most of his life at Assisi. He is regarded as one of the most extraordinary ecstatics who ever lived. Honored with many heavenly visions, he was likewise familiar with the Angels, who often appeared in visible form to bring him heavenly comfort. Sister Catherine of Cantu, a tertiary, once saw St. Joseph of Cupertino enter Assisi accompanied by two angels, while another nun, Sister Cecilia Nobili of Nocera, was spiritually informed that the Saint's guardian angel was of a higher angelic choir than the angels of ordinary men. The Saint had such a great reverence for his guardian angel that he never entered his cell without inviting the angel to enter first.[175] St. Joseph of Cupertino is known for his amazing levitations that were witnessed by many trustworthy people as well as by many members of his community.

Ven. Anne Catherine Emmerich (1774-1824), who had many visions of angels, seems to agree when she reports, "I have often seen a man receive a higher and more powerful guardian when called to great things . . ."[176]

As noted before, **St. Frances of Rome** received an archangel as her visible guardian when she was about to found a new order.

71. Saints' Visions of Guardian Angels

That each person has a guardian angel is also demonstrated in the lives of the Saints, who have thankfully left us accounts of their visions and experiences. Perhaps the earliest account is that of **St. Hilary** (476-558) that was written by Paul, one of his disciples. Butler tells us that the facts can be believed without a doubt since it is a "substantially faithful record." The Saint's history reports that as a lad of twelve he was impressed with one of St. Paul's epistles, so much so that he soon left home, crossed the Apennines and built a hermitage beside the river Ronco. When disciples became attracted to his way of life, he built an abbey where his followers practiced praise, prayer and manual labor. It is reported that he was always visibly protected by his guardian angel in times of danger, particularly when Theodoric the Goth threatened to destroy him and the abbey because of the Saint's refusal to pay him tribute. The conqueror, however, became favorably impressed with the Saint, begged for his prayers and gave him territory for the enlargement of his abbey. The Saint died at the age of eighty-two.[177]

St. Bernard (1090-1153) remarked, "How happy you would be if you could see how the guardian angels hasten to join those who sing the Psalms and the reverential bearing they maintain next to those who pray and meditate. They go back and forth between God and us, bearing our sighs to the throne of God."[178]

St. Francis of Assisi (1181-1226) was very devoted to the Angels, who, he remarked, "walk with us in the midst of the shadow of death." According to the Saint's companion and biographer, Thomas of Celano, St. Francis often taught "that their presence must not be offended, and that we must not presume to do before them what we would not do before men, because in choir we sing in the sight of the Angels . . . and that they are our companions who are everywhere with us."[179]

An unusual vision is reported in the biography of **St. Mary Magdalene de' Pazzi** (1566-1607) regarding not only her own guardian angel, but the guardian angels of her companions in religion. In her vision the Saint entered a beautiful garden where the guardian angels of the nuns were weaving crowns of flowers. Each garland was different, according to the virtues that each soul possessed. Some crowns were white, others red, and others were of different colors. Each crown was bound by threads of gold, this precious metal representing the virtue of love.

Jesus explained to the Saint: "If those souls do not have charity, their angels will never be able to make up their chaplets; without love, those flowers will indeed serve as ornaments in Paradise, but they cannot be formed into a crown." Some of the angels were hurrying with their work; others worked more slowly, according to the longer or shorter life of each religious. After learning this, the Saint remarked, "I saw my angel, who was working very swiftly and had already finished more than half. However, I desire neither life nor death, but only that the will of God be fulfilled in me and with me."[180]

We have the word of **St. Humilitas** (1226-1310)—wife, mother, religious and foundress—who wrote in one of her treatises that she lived in constant communion with two heavenly beings, "one of whom was her guardian angel and the other was a celestial spirit sent to her when she was thirty years of age, to guide and advise her in the difficult work with which she was entrusted."[181]

All during her brief life, **St. Germaine Cousin** (1579-1601) was badly mistreated by her family, and in particular by her stepmother, who had the child sleep under a staircase on the outside of the home. Her only occupation was to shepherd the family's sheep, and in this chore Germaine made good use of her guardian angel, especially when it was time for Holy Mass. As soon as she heard the bell summoning the faithful, she would plant her crook in the ground and commend the care of her flock to her guardian angel before hurrying off to church. It is reported that never once did she find on her return that a sheep strayed or had fallen prey to the wolves who lurked in the nearby forest. Many other marvels are reported of this little saint before she died at the age of twenty-two. She is numbered among the Incorruptibles.[182]

Père Lamy (1855-1931), who had numerous visions of angels, admits, "I often see them, and they do all sorts of kindnesses for me." The holy priest was so familiar with his guardian angel that, "sometimes when it is going to be bad weather, my good angel comes and tells me, 'If you are going out [do such and such],' and I arrange things accordingly. Other times he says when I am getting ready to go out, 'You are too tired,' and I stay in. I see them [the angels] in the chapel, in my room, in the street. Still, not every day . . . They send me their light, and I am comforted whilst there is need."[183]

Bl. Faustina Kowalska (1905-1938), who received the visions that produced the Divine Mercy devotion, saw her guardian angel a number of times, particularly one day when she was traveling from Cracow to Warsaw. She writes in her *Diary*, "I saw my guardian angel, who accompanied me throughout the journey as far as Warsaw. He disappeared when we entered the convent gate . . . When we took our seats for the return journey from Warsaw to Cracow, I once again saw my guardian angel at my side. He was absorbed in prayer and in contemplating God, and I followed him with my thoughts. When we arrived at the convent entrance, he disappeared."[184]

One who always relied on her guardian angel to help her in her everyday work was **Bl. Mary Fortunata Viti** (1827-1922), a lay sister of the Benedictine Order. She was always intent on serving her sisters and never complained when she was overburdened, as she often was. One day when she was mending an unusual amount of clothing, two sisters brought her a second basket of clothing to be mended. With perfect serenity she accepted the work and told the sisters, "With the assistance of my guardian angel I will finish it all." With childlike simplicity she would address the angel, "Holy Guardian Angel, come and help me, for I do not know how I will get through."[185] The Beata, at night, when she was caring for the sick, would commend her charges to the care of her guardian angel, who, as the accounts relate, "would many times lend his assistance in an extraordinary manner." Perhaps, like Bl. Mary Fortunata, we could rely on our guardian angels when we are overburdened with work or when we are concerned for the sick.

72. Will Our Guardian Angels Stay with Us in Heaven?

Many spiritual writers are of the opinion that our angels remain with us in Heaven. One writer reports: "They are not separated from us after our death, but remain with us in Heaven, not, however, to help us to attain salvation, since that has already been obtained." The author bases this on **St. Thomas Aquinas** (1225-1274), who wrote: "After the Day of Judgment, men will not be led any more to salvation by the ministry of the Angels, yet those who are already saved will be enlightened through the angelic ministry." The Angelic Doctor continues: "As to the execution of the angelic offices, it will to a certain degree remain after the Day of Judgment, and to a certain degree will cease. It will cease accordingly as their offices are directed towards leading others to their end, but it will remain accordingly as it agrees with the attainment of the end. Thus also the various ranks of soldiers have different duties to perform in battle and in triumph."[186]

73. The Feast of the Guardian Angels

Beginning like many other feasts as a local observance, the Feast of the Holy Guardian Angels was observed in various locations before it was placed in the Roman calendar. Among the earliest petitions from particular churches for a feast to be allowed as a supplement to the Breviary was a request from Cordova in 1579. Approval was received in February, 1582 for the special Breviary office of the Guardian Angels. The feast was still observed locally until Pope Paul V (1602-1621) placed it among the feasts of the general calendar. We read: "Paul V gave an impetus to the veneration of guardian angels by the authorization of a feast and proper office in their honor."[187]

The feast was given further importance by Pope Clement X (1670-1676) when he ordered the feast to be kept by the whole Church on October 2. This date is still reserved for the observance of the Feast of the Guardian Angels. In the proper office in the Roman Breviary and in the Mass of the Holy Guardian Angels, their threefold office is remembered in extracts taken from Sacred Scripture: they praise God, they act as His messengers and they watch over mortal men.

74. Something Told Me Not To . . .

How many times have we heard the phrase, "Something told me not to," or have said it ourselves? Could the "something" have been our guardian angel who warned us of impending danger? How often have we narrowly missed being involved in a traffic accident or a dangerous situation? How many times, when we were thoroughly lost, did we somehow find our way? Could an angel have directed us? When a friend one has not seen in years suddenly comes to mind, is it our angel telling us the friend might be in need of prayers? What of a departed soul one has almost forgotten? Is it our angel who reminds us of the soul who might need only a few prayers to escape Purgatory? When our minds drift away during Holy Mass, is it our guardian angels who nudge us into recollection?

All of us have had an experience that seemed to have been unusual and which we cannot explain. Could it have been a warning, an inspiration, a holy thought, a comforting thought, a direction, a remembrance given by our angels? Angels speak without words, but convey their messages, as it were, with inspirations.

May we be more atuned to the workings of our angels and thank them for their love, their attention, their many favors and their prayers.

75. Counsels Given by the Blessed Mother with regard to Guardian Angels

After each episode in the life of the Virgin Mary in **Ven. Mary of Agreda's** *The Mystical City of God*, a section is given entitled, "Instruction given to me by the Queen of Heaven." In one of these instructions, the Blessed Mother suggests "three different points":

> The first is that thou, by incessant praise and acknowledgment, show thyself thankful for the favor which God vouchsafed thee in appointing angels to assist thee, teach thee and guide thee through tribulations and sorrows . . .
>
> The second point is that thou, in every place and at all times, preserve love and reverence toward these holy spirits, as if thou didst see them with thy corporeal eyes, and that thou dare not do before them what thou wouldst not do in public.
>
> Let the third point be, that thou live attentive to the calls, urgings and inspirations, by which these angels seek to rouse thee, move and excite thee to the recollection of the Most High and to the exercise of all the virtues.[188]

76. Obligations We Owe Our Guardian Angels According to the Saints

An important lesson is given us by **Père Lamy** (1855-1931), mystic and visionary, who writes: "We do not give the Angels the importance they possess. We don't pray to them enough. They are very touched when we pray to them. There is great benefit in praying to the Angels. Our guardian angels—what do we do for them? A little scrap of prayer in the morning, a little scrap at night . . . Their mercy is so great towards us, and often we don't use it half enough. They look on us as needy little brothers. Their kindness towards us is extreme." The holy cleric adds:

> Nothing is so faithful as an angel . . . Our guardian angel very often saves us from accidents. We give him freedom over us, but what can the angel do when we are not in a state of grace? They want to help us, but are powerless. When we refuse respect to Our Lord, we send His servants packing; and among us Christians, how many are there who implore their help and protection? A little prayer, "Good evening, my good angel," and so on . . . that's all. When we pray to Our Lord, we serve the same Master, and that leaves them liberty of action over us. We don't resort enough to the holy Angels. They are there, but they are left alone. We don't turn to them sufficiently.[189]

St. Bernard (1090-1153), a Doctor of the Church, tells us that we owe our guardian angel profound *respect* for his presence, *gratitude* for all the benefits he confers upon us and *confidence* in his protection. The Saint likewise exhorted his spiritual sons: "In whatever place you may be, in whatever secret recess you may hide, think of your guardian angel. Never do in the presence of your angel what you would not do in my presence."[190]

The **Rev. Bruno Vercruysse, S.J.** in *New Practical Meditations,* elaborates on the three obligations we owe our angel as suggested by St. Bernard. First, we should show *respect* for his presence by acting in his sight, even when we are alone, as if we were in the company of some great person. Second, our *gratitude* for his charity should express itself in docility to his inspirations and in thanking him every night for what he has done for us. Third, we should demonstrate our *confidence* in him by consulting and invoking him in all our doubts and wants, with the conviction that this will never be done in vain.

— Part Two —
DEVILS

"Satan never gains so many cohorts as when, in his shrewdness, he spreads the rumor that he is long since dead."

—Archbishop Fulton Sheen

DEVILS

77. Does the Devil Really Exist?

Any consideration of the devil and his unholy activities must begin by proving that he exists, which we will attempt by first identifying him as Lucifer (Latin for "lightbearer" or "bringing light") since he first began as a pure spiritual being, endowed with supernatural grace. We can also call him by the Hebrew name, Satan ("adversary" or "accuser"), or demon (Greek *daimon*, or "spirit"), or by the Hebrew Beelzebub (*ba'al zebub*, "Lord of Flies"), or simply as the devil (Greek *diabolos*, the "slanderer" or "accuser"). In Sacred Scripture, he is also known as the "Evil One," the "Great Dragon" or the "Ancient Serpent."

How do we know he exists? If one believes that the Bible is the inspired word of God, there should be no doubt whatsoever, since Satan is mentioned numerous times in the Old Testament beginning with the book of *Genesis*, where he is identified as a serpent.[1] He is also mentioned under his various names in the books of *Leviticus*,[2] *Deuteronomy*,[3] *Judges*,[4] *Kings* [and *Samuel*],[5] *Paralipomenon*,[6] *Tobias*,[7] *Job*,[8] *Psalms*,[9] *Ecclesiasticus*,[10] *Wisdom*,[11] *Isaias*,[12] *Baruch*,[13] *Habacuc*,[14] *Zacharias*[15] and *Machabees*.[16]

In the New Testament, he is also mentioned countless times. In *Matthew* his name is given at least 22 times;[17] in *Mark*, 17 times;[18] in *Luke*, 15 times;[19] and in *John*, 11 times.[20] Following the Gospels the devil's name appears in the *Acts of the Apostles*,[21] in the epistle to the *Romans*,[22] in *1 Corinthians*,[23] *2 Corinthians*,[24] *Ephesians*,[25] *1 Thessalonians*,[26] *2 Thessalonians*,[27] *1 Timothy*,[28] *2 Timothy*,[29] *Hebrews*,[30] *James*,[31] *1 Peter*,[32] *1 John*,[33] *Jude*[34] and *The Apocalypse*.[35]

If the mention of the evil spirit's name in the Old and New Testaments is not enough, we can also add that the names of the devil were mentioned by Our Lord at least 20 times,[36] excluding the *repetition* of parables and statements of Our Lord as given by the four Evangelists. Then, we have in one sentence of *The Apocalypse* four different names of the devil: "And that great dragon was cast out, that old serpent, who is called the devil and Satan, who seduceth the whole world; and he was cast unto the earth, and his angels were thrown down with him." (*Apoc.* 12:9). Having acquired such a bad reputation, it is no wonder that the devil is depicted in art as an ugly creature with horns or as a creature horribly deformed.

For those who do not believe in Holy Scripture, the words of Our Lord Himself or the teachings of the Church, perhaps they will accept the experiences of the Saints, who not only saw the devils, but also experienced their rages in the form of physical abuse—attacks that were witnessed by others who gave sworn depositions. These experiences of the Saints will be described.

Does the devil really exist? Archbishop Fulton Sheen once warned that "Satan never gains so many cohorts as when, in his shrewdness, he spreads the rumor that he is long since dead."

78. Satan in Other Religions and Cultures

The devil by one name or another is mentioned in the history of most religions and in various cultures. The Manicheans, for instance, believed in a "Father of Grandeur" who was opposed by the "King of Darkness," whose kingdom, below the earth, exactly paralleled the higher realm of light. Evil was also recognized by the ancient religion of Iran, which promoted a life of purity, the conscientious fulfillment of all liturgical and moral precepts, and the positive renunciation of the devil and all demoniacal powers. Not only the Persians, but also the Babylonians and the Chaldeans recognized the devil and a dualism between the "forces" of darkness and light.

The Mohammedan school of theology professes a belief in one

God, omnipotent, omniscient, all merciful and the author of all good. Mohammed is recognized as his prophet. Their belief encompasses angels, a resurrection, a day of judgment and devils. Various kinds of demons figure in the Hindu tradition and are regarded as goblins, who take the form of animals and deformed humans. The Buddhist's Satan leads an army of demons depicted in Buddhist art as hideous monsters. It is especially interesting to note that Islamic folklore mentions desert spirits, who may be either benign or malicious. Among the latter is Iblis, an angel who rebelled against God and was driven out of Paradise. Prominent in the folklore of eastern European Judaism since the 17th century is a demon who takes possession of people and speaks through them, causing them to behave in a demented manner, while traditional Jewish literature contains numerous stories describing the exorcism of such spirits.

79. The Origin of Satan

The first authoritative teaching of the Church on this subject was given in the decrees of the Fourth Lateran Council (1215), in which it is taught that the devil and the other demons were created by God in a state of innocence and that they became evil by their own act.

According to many theologians, Lucifer before his fall was the foremost of all the Angels in Heaven. Some theologians believe that none of the Angels was higher in position, though a few others claim that one or two angels may have been his equal. Endowed with beauty, innocence, grace and power, he nevertheless eventually committed the sin of pride.

Two theories are suggested for his fall from grace. One theory is that he desired independence from God and equality with God, as Isaias points out when he reports: "And thou saidst in thy heart: I will ascend into heaven, I will exalt my throne above the stars of God, I will sit in the mountain of the covenant . . . I will ascend above the height of the clouds, I will be like the most High." (*Is.* 14:13-14).

It is generally regarded throughout history that it is the leader of rebels who very often covets the kingly throne and that it is the one who stands nearest the throne who is most open to temptations of ambition. However, it is to be wondered how Lucifer, with his superior intelligence, could possibly believe he could become the equal of God. This is a problem that has been debated by many theologians. **St. Thomas Aquinas**, however, admits that the first sin of Satan was that of pride, or spiritual lust.

In addition to wanting an equality with God or superiority over Him, another theory is suggested for his fall from grace: Theologians have speculated that the mystery of the Divine Incarnation was revealed to the Angels. Here they realized that the Son of God would assume an earthly nature lower than their own and yet that they would be told to adore Him. **St. Paul** relates, ". . . when he bringeth in the first begotten into the world, he saith: And let all the angels of God adore him." (*Heb.* 1:6). This is presented as a possible reason for the fall of Satan—the sin of pride in refusing to adore a God who assumed the lowly nature of man. The countless number of angels who were of a similar mind followed Lucifer in his prideful revolt and everlasting punishment.

But immediately before receiving their punishment for this sin, there was a heavenly battle which is related not in the first books of the Bible (as would be expected), but in its last chapter. Here we learn that: "there was a great battle in heaven, Michael and his angels fought with the dragon, and the dragon fought and his angels: And they prevailed not, neither was their place found any more in heaven. And that great dragon was cast out, that old serpent who is called the devil and Satan, who seduceth the whole world; and he was cast unto the earth, and his angels were thrown down with him." (*Apoc.* 12:7-9). As Jesus Himself tells us, "I saw Satan like lightning falling from heaven." (*Luke* 10:18). **St. John Damascene** states that "There was no repentance for the angels after their fall, just as there is no repentance for men after death."

80. Before Their Fall, Did the Devils Enjoy the Full Beatific Vision?

Two saints, **St. Ignatius of Antioch** (d. 110) and **St. Clement of Alexandria** (d. 211) speculated that, before the great test, the Angels *did not* experience the full beatific vision, but existed in a state wherein they knew God but did not benefit from the full impact of His magnificence. Moreover, since the Beatific Vision is the reward of the faithful whose loyalty to God has been tested during their earthly life, some have considered that the Angels, too, had to first prove their worthiness of this vision of God, which was done by having their loyalty tested during the great angelic test. After this test the prideful angels were cast into Hell, while the faithful angels were admitted to the full benefit of their reward, the Beatific Vision.

St. Thomas Aquinas was of the opinion that once in the possession of the Beatific Vision, a human soul or an angel can never be tempted to any evil whatsoever. In Heaven the Beatific Vision renders one completely, totally and perfectly satisfied and happy. The theory is advanced that if the demons before their fall had been admitted to the full vision of God, they could not have entertained the notion of being equal to or greater than God, since God's splendor would have negated any thought of rebellion. The matter has been settled in more recent times by **Pope Leo XIII** (1878-1903) in his encyclical, *Libertas*. The Pope wrote, "the infinitely perfect God, although supremely free, because of the supremacy of His intellect and of His essential goodness, nevertheless cannot choose evil; neither [can] the Angels and Saints who enjoy the Beatific Vision."

81. Satan's Authority and Influence

It appears that Satan holds a certain sovereignty over those who followed him in rebellion, since we often read such descriptions in Scripture as: "the Devil and his angels" (*Apoc.* 12:9), or "the dragon and his angels" (*Apoc.* 12:7), or again "Beelzebub, the prince of devils" (*Matt.* 9:34; *Mark* 3:22), or finally, "the prince of the power of this air." (*Eph.* 2:22). At first it might seem strange that the rebellious angels should obey one of their own, especially the one who led them into destruction. It might be suggested that a disorderly group of devils would develop into anarachy and division. But then it is believed that their fall did not impair their natural powers and that Lucifer still had the same power of influence among his brethren as he had before their fall—that his superior intelligence would make it clear to them that they could achieve more success and do more harm to souls by being organized and united, instead of being independent and divided. Lucifer, who was their superior in Heaven, was, and is now, their superior in Hell.

St. Thomas Aquinas is of the opinion that among the demons there is precedence. Just as there are choirs, or levels of the Angels in Heaven, so too are there levels among the devils. The Saint writes: "The demons are not equal in nature, and so among them there exists a natural precedence."[37]

The influence of Satan and his followers—often called "his angels"—extended over the minds of men and was the cause of the Fall of our first parents, who disobeyed God when they accepted the promise of Satan that "ye shall be as gods." (*Gen.* 3:5). His success in causing Adam and Eve to sin resulted in the first sin committed by man, the Original Sin, which closed Heaven to man until the death and Resurrection of Jesus. It likewise stained all of Eve's children, a blemish removed only through Baptism. The *Catechism of the Catholic Church* affirms: "Revelation gives us the certainty of faith that the whole of human history is marked by the original fault freely committed by our first parents."[38] (#390).

Since he was successful in luring our first parents to their fall, Satan has continued to tempt their children in order to involve them in his own ruin—an endeavor that has peopled Hell. His most ambitious attempt—which revealed that his pride, envy and audacity had reached their zenith—took place when he approached and tempted Jesus Himself. (*Matt.* 4:1-11).

However, the *Catechism of the Catholic Church* also reminds us that:

> The power of Satan is not infinite. He is only a creature, powerful from the fact that he is pure spirit, but still a creature. He cannot prevent the building up of God's reign. Although Satan may act in the world out of hatred for God and his kingdom in Christ Jesus, and although his action may cause grave injuries—of a spiritual nature and, indirectly, even of a physical nature—to each man and to society, *the action is permitted by divine providence* which with strength and gentleness guides human and cosmic history. It is a great mystery that providence should permit diabolical activity, but "we know that in everything God works for good with those who love him." (*Rom.* 8:28). (#395).

82. Satan's Attributes

Theologians agree that there is absolutely nothing favorable that can be said about him. For example, one writer states that the devil is one being of whom we can say, without offending charity, that he is a liar, a cheat, a thief, a destroyer of souls, a persecutor, a snake in the grass and a blasphemer.

Scripture adds its own criticisms and appraisals by describing him (in the Douay-Rheims Bible) as: "an accuser,"[39] "liar,"[40] "murderer,"[41] "betrayer,"[42] "roaring lion,"[43] "blasphemer"[44] and "seducer,"[45] among other names. He is also depicted in Scripture as being "deceitful,"[46] "thieving,"[47] "hypocritical,"[48] "jealous,"[49] "fierce,"[50] "troublesome,"[51] "vain,"[52] "violent"[53] and "wicked,"[54] among other such descriptions.

Our Lord also gives His appraisal of the devil. While speaking with the Jews of His time who claimed that God was their father, Our Lord replied: "You are of your father the devil, and the desires of your father you will do. He was a murderer from the beginning, and he stood not in the truth; because truth is not in him. When he speaketh a lie, he speaketh of his own, for he is a liar, and the father thereof." (*John* 8:41, 44).

The Church's holy and gifted writers have written a great deal about Satan and his wicked ways, his unholy attributes, his origin, his fall, his seduction of souls and all that pertains to him. The list of such writers is lengthy, but they include such luminaries as St. Augustine, St. Thomas Aquinas, Tertullian, St. Cyprian and St. Irenaeus. The subject has also been explored in many documents of the Church and was not neglected by the Council of Trent, which faults "that old serpent, the everlasting enemy of the human race, for stirring up not only new but also old dissensions concerning Original Sin and its remedy, and [with] which the Church of God is in our times disturbed." The Council of Trent likewise states that the evil spirit incurred the wrath and indignation of God, and that the devil is master of the empire of death and everlasting punishment.[55]

Likewise Vatican Council II reminds us that, in spite of this evil, it is Christ "who overthrows the devil's domain and wards off the manifold malice of vice . . . More than that, man is healed, ennobled and perfected for the glory of God, the shame of the demon, and the bliss of men."[56]

83. The Influence of Satan over the Human Race

We must consider that it is not only by Satan that men fall, but by their own weaknesses with regard to wealth, the flesh, ambition and the like. However, the devil, with his superior intelligence, knows these weaknesses and preys upon them so that only those men who are spiritually strong overcome.

According to Rev. Adolphe Tanquerey in his book, *The Spiritual Life: A Treatise on Ascetical and Mystical Theology*, "The devil can act directly on the body, on our exterior and interior senses and particularly on the imagination and the memory, as well as on the passions which reside in the sensitive appetite.

Thus, the devil acts indirectly on the will, soliciting its consent through the sensitive appetite."[57] We are told by Tanquerey that the devil can act upon the external senses of sight, hearing and touch when permitted by God, but more often he acts upon our interior senses: the imagination, certain passions and the memory. Tanquerey writes: "Distressing and besetting images flit through the imagination and remain there in spite of every effort to expel them . . . One appears to have become the prey of fits of anger, to the anguish of despair, to instinctive feelings of antipathy, and dangerous sentimentality."[58] Tanquerey adds that it is difficult at times to decide whether a severe case is one of our own origin or that of the devil. He writes: "In case of doubt, it will always be well to consult a Catholic physician, who can examine whether the phenomena are due to some morbid condition, and if they are, to prescribe the proper medical treatment." If the disturbance is not physical, then one can consult his confessor or another priest. Tanquerey notes that it is no easy matter to identify diabolical temptations,

> since our concupiscence itself may sufficiently account for the violence of temptation. It may be said, however, that when a temptation is sudden, violent, and protracted beyond measure, the devil is largely responsible for it. One can especially suspect his influence if the temptation casts the soul into deep and prolonged turmoil; if it excites a desire for the spectacular, for strange and conspicuous mortifications, and particularly if it induces a strong inclination to be silent about the whole affair with our confessors.[59]

Ralph Rath, in his book *The New Age*, writes that: "Ordinary temptations are thoughts and images the devil uses in attempting to turn Christians aside from doing God's will. Temptations are compulsive [urgent] in terms of strength, persistence and continuity. They may play upon a moral, spiritual or physical weakness, or a combination of these, and the temptations of the devil are carefully orchestrated to produce maximum effect."[60]

In his book, *The Devil: Does He Exist? And What Does He Do?* Father Delaporte of the Society of Mercy writes that an invisible enemy "sows in our imagination bad thoughts, he keeps them up, brings them back, in spite of our efforts to drive them away; he excites and stirs up our senses themselves; we feel ourselves interiorly harassed, incited, drawn away; it is like a discourse without words, but urgent and violent."[61] Father Delaporte notes that detestable thoughts pursue with greater fury those who devote themselves to practices of piety and that the devil often suggests troublesome thoughts even at the deathbed. The Rev. A. Poulain, S.J. notes that the devil's temptations "are sometimes of such violence that human passions are powerless to explain. The sufferer may feel himself at the end of his moral forces."

But then again, many place themselves in situations in which the devil exerts little effort in tempting them: by watching immoral movies, by reading immoral books or by fraternizing with people they know will influence them in unacceptable ways or by visiting places that would create a danger to their souls. For good reason does **St. Paul** warn us by suggesting ways in which we can combat successfully in this spiritual warfare: "Put you on the armour of God, that you may be able to stand against the deceits of the devil . . . to stand in all things perfect. Stand therefore, having your loins girt about with truth, and having on the breastplate of justice, and your feet shod with the preparation of the gospel of peace: In all things taking the shield of faith, wherewith you may be able to extinguish all the fiery darts of the most wicked one." (*Eph.* 6:11-16).

Vatican II warns and encourages us in the document, *Pastoral Constitution on the Church in the Modern World*, which states, "For a monumental struggle against the powers of darkness pervades the whole history of man. The battle was joined from the very origins of the world and will continue until the last day, as the Lord has attested. Caught in this conflict, man is obliged to wrestle constantly if he is to cling to what is good. Nor can he achieve his own integrity without valiant efforts and the help of God's grace."[62]

The *Catechism of the Council of Trent* notes that "There are many who, because they do not feel the assaults of demons against them, imagine that the whole matter is fictitious; nor is it surprising that such persons are not attacked by demons, to whom they have voluntarily surrendered themselves. They possess neither piety nor charity, nor any virtue worthy of a Christian; hence, they are entirely in the power of the devil, and there is no need of any temptation to overcome them, since their souls have already become his willing abode."[63] The complacency of many, it would therefore seem, is due to a laxity of conscience coupled with the weaknesses of the flesh and the desire to satisfy their fancies and their egos. It would be good to remember the familiar quotation: "The devil's deepest wile is to persuade us that he does not exist."

For others, however, the same *Catechism* soberly warns:

> But those who have dedicated themselves to God, leading a heavenly life upon earth, are the chief objects of the assaults of Satan. Against them he harbors bitterest hatred, laying snares for them each moment. Sacred Scripture is full of examples of holy men who, in spite of their firmness and resolution, were perverted by his violence or fraud. Adam, David, Solomon and others, whom it would be tedious to enumerate, experienced the violent and crafty cunning of demons, which neither human prudence nor human strength can overcome.[64]

To which we might add that the demons can be overcome by our resorting to prayer, penance, right living, the observance of the Commandments, the reception of the Sacraments and calling upon the grace of God.

We likewise learn that it is not only Satan by himself who tempts men, since sometimes a *host* of demons combine to attack an individual. We know this from Scripture when a possessed person, on being asked by Christ, "What is thy name?" replied: "My name is legion, for we are many." (*Mark* 5:9; *Luke* 8:30). In another passage Our Lord says of the devil, "He taketh with him seven other spirits more wicked than himself, and they enter in and dwell there." (*Matt.* 12:45).

Again, the *Catechism of the Council of Trent* reveals that the power of Satan and his devils is so restricted that without the permission of God, they could not have entered into the swine mentioned by the three Evangelists. (*Matt.* 8:30-32; *Mark* 5:11-13; *Luke* 8:32-33). Moreover, the devil is permitted to test humanity only by God's authority and control, and within the limits that God sets for him.

84. Do the Devils Know the Future?

We are told that Satan has a superior intelligence and natural powers. **St. Thomas Aquinas** quotes Dionysius as having written that "certain gifts were bestowed upon the demons which, we say, have not been changed at all, but remain entire and most brilliant. Now the knowledge of truth stands among those natural gifts, consequently there is some knowledge of truth in them."[65] In addition St. Thomas says that divine secrets are revealed to the devils only as is necessary and that this is done either by means of angels or "through some temporal workings of divine power, as Augustine says." The Saint makes clear that these secrets are revealed in a higher degree to the holy Angels, as would be expected.

St. John of the Cross (1542-1591), the Doctor of the Church who is known as the "Doctor of Mystical Theology," writes: "The devil can learn and foretell that a person's life will naturally last only a certain number of years. And he can determine many other events through such various ways that we would never finish recounting them all, nor could we even begin to explain many because of their intricacy and the devil's craftiness in inserting lies . . . Since his light is so vivid, he can easily deduce a particular effect from a specific cause. Yet the effect does not always materialize according to his deduction, since all causes depend upon God's will."[66]

The devil communicated a prophecy (with the permission of God) to **St. Anthony Mary Claret** (1807-1870) when a slip of paper mysteriously fell from this saint's Breviary. On the piece of brown colored paper was written, "They have named you Archbishop of Cuba. There you will work for your own, but I also will work for my own." The paper bore a signature in the form of three scratches. Recognizing the work of the devil, the Saint dismissed the prophecy and discarded the paper. But the announcement was repeated verbally on another occasion, and it was repeated again to a holy nun, whose virtue Fr. Claret recognized and appreciated.

This nun was one day praying in her cell when the demons, passing her door, were heard to say, "Now they wish to make him Archbishop of Cuba." The holy nun communicated this to Fr. Claret, who advised her to disregard it since it came from the "Father of Lies." Later on, however, the appointment became know by an authentic document. Fr. Claret had indeed been appointed archbishop of Santiago, Cuba, where he was to serve for six years with incredible virtue and distinction.

We know that the devil is devious in his temptations, and as we will learn later in the section about exorcisms, he might also reveal the sins of witnesses, or know of secrets, or predict the future. He can know sins or secrets by being a "silent witness" to them. Regarding the future, he might come close to knowing it by reasoning to a probable outcome of events based on known causes. But to know the future for certain he is not able, unless it is revealed to him by God. And the reason God would reveal the future to the devil is known to God alone.

85. How Many Devils Are There?

Just as we do not know the number of Angels in Heaven, neither do we know, even approximately, how many devils are in Hell or roaming the earth. There is a tradition that the world will not end until the number of saints in Heaven equals the number of the fallen angels.

We recall the incident in the Gospel of *Mark* when Our Lord was met by a possessed man who had been living in the tombs. On asking the unclean spirit, "What is thy name?" He received the answer, "My name is Legion, for we are many." Our Lord sent the unclean spirits into a herd of swine, who were subsequently hurled "violently" into the sea, "being about two thousand . . ." (*Mark* 5:9-13). Two thousand demons in one human being! One has to wonder then how many there are who are aggressively pursuing the souls of people now living on earth, and what of the number of those devils who are constantly tormenting the souls in Hell? **St. Thomas Aquinas** is of the opinion that "More Angels stood firm than sinned because sin is contrary to the natural inclination."[67] Thankfully, according to this saint, there are more good angels than bad, but no one except God knows the number of each.

Bl. Padre Pio (1887-1968), the stigmatic priest of our own time, once told a group of his admirers that "the number of devils active in the world is greater than that of all the human beings who have lived since Adam."[68] Another time, in his old age, while looking out his window at the great crowd in the square that had assembled for his blessing, he remarked to his fellow friars, "If all the devils that are here were to take bodily form, they would blot out the light of the sun!"[69]

Ven. Anne Catherine Emmerich (1774-1824) at an earlier date echoed the same opinion. While referring to the myriads of demons she had seen, she exclaimed, "Had they bodies, the air would be darkened."[70] And **St. Antony of the Desert** (251-356), who could see the devils, asserts that there are "swarms" of them in the air.

86. What Devils Look Like

One of the earliest instances of the devil appearing to a saint was reported by **St. Athanasius** in his biography of **St. Antony of Egypt** (251-356), who is also known as St. Antony of the Desert. St. Athanasius not only knew St. Antony and of his combats with demons, but he joined him a number of times in his desert exile. All we know of St. Antony today is what is told us by this holy bishop and Doctor of the Church.

We are told that Antony, at the age of eighteen, lost both his Christian parents. After arranging for his sister's security and her education, he gave away his own inheritance of 300 acres of fertile land, sold all he had, gave the proceeds to the poor and went into the Egyptian desert, seeking a closer union with God.

Antony's solitude was not destined to be a peaceful one. The devils, realizing the harm that would be done to their cause by Antony's future gathering of solitaries into a loosely knit community—which would eventually be the introduction of the monastic life to the Church—set about him with violence. Night and day they tempted and abused him, but seeing that he overcame all their efforts, they resorted to other measures. St. Athanasius writes that the demons produced fearful noises and tremblings, as though the Saint's pitiful abode were shaken by an earthquake. Then the devils began to appear as different beasts and reptiles. St. Athanasius writes:

> The demons appeared in the guise of beasts and creeping things, and the place was at once filled with the forms of lions, bears, leopards, bulls, serpents, asps, scorpions and wolves. And each moved according to its own likeness. The lion roared, ready to spring; the bull seemed thrusting with its horns; the serpent crept, yet reached him not; the wolf held itself as if ready to strike. And the noise of all the visions was terrible and their fury cruel. Antony addressed the beasts, "It is a sign of your helplessness that you have taken the shapes of brutes." Then

> looking up, Antony saw, as it were, the roof opening and a beam of light coming down to him. And the demons suddenly disappeared, and the soreness of his body ceased at once, and the building was again sound. . . . And a voice came to him: "I will always be thy helper, and I will make thee renowned everywhere."

St. Antony arose, prayed and was strengthened again in body.[71]

The devil not only appeared in the form of animals, but also as a comely woman, who came to tempt the Saint. Most artistic renderings of St. Antony have him in combat against fearful demons. St. Antony overcame all the attacks of the devils through fervent prayer, fought for a time against the Arian heresy, cured many people and died at the age of 105.

According to St. Paul, Satan often disguises himself as an Angel of light in order to seduce souls. (*2 Cor.* 11:14). **St. Martin of Tours** (316-397) received a vision of this kind, the story of which has been preserved for us by St. Sulpicius Severus (d. between 406-432). We are told that one day, when St. Martin was in his cell, he beheld in a dazzling light a young man clad in a royal garment, his head encircled by a diadem. Although greatly surprised, St. Martin remained silent. The apparition spoke in a pleasant voice: "Recognize him whom you see. I am Christ about to descend upon earth, but I wished first to show myself to you." When St. Martin did not reply, the apparition continued, "Martin, why do you hesitate to believe what you see? I am Christ." Under the inspiration of grace, St. Martin recognized his visitor and replied, "The Lord Jesus did not say that he would return in purple and with a crown. I will not recognize my Saviour unless I see Him as He suffered, with the stigmata and the Cross." The diabolic phantom then vanished, leaving behind an intolerable odor.[72]

St. Gregory the Great, in writing about the miracles of **St. Benedict** (480-550), reveals that Benedict was no stranger to the power, trickery and subtle insinuations of the enemy and was witness to the visible assaults of the devil. St. Gregory writes that in a monastery which Benedict had built, there was a monk who, instead of engaging in mental prayer following the recitation of the Divine Office, would habitually leave the choir and allow his thoughts to dwell on worldly and transitory matters. Despite the rebukes given by Pompeianus, the abbot, this monk would only correct himself for a day or two and then resume his careless behavior.

St. Gregory writes, "When the servant of God [St. Benedict] was informed, he said, 'I will come myself and reform him.' And when he was come to the same monastery, and the brethren, after the *Psalms* ended, at the accustomed time betook themselves to prayer, he perceived a little dark demon who pulled this monk out by the hem of his garment. Turning to Pompeianus and to Maurus, Benedict asked, 'See you not there who it is that draweth this monk out?' Who answered, 'No.' "

After two days of prayer, the monk Maurus was finally able to see the demon. The next day, when St. Benedict had finished his prayer, he went "out of the oratory and found the monk standing without, whom he forthwith struck with his abbatical staff, and from that time ever after, the monk was free from the wicked suggestions of the dark demon and remained constant at his prayers."[73] The devil, coward that he was, afraid that he too might be beaten with the staff, immediately fled and from then on "dared no more to take command of his thoughts," leaving the monk to his prayers.

The devil that appeared to **St. Dominic** (1170-1221) was neither on fire, nor did he have the slightest aspect of who he really was, since he appeared to the Saint as one of the friars. St. Dominic had given orders that all the brethren should retire to bed at a certain hour, so that they could rise with ease for Matins. For his part, he spent the night in church. There was, however, one of the friars in the church with head inclined as though rapt in prayer. The Saint gently bid him retire for the night as the others had done. The friar immediately obeyed. He returned, however, at the same hour on three consecutive nights. On the third night, the Saint could tolerate the disobedience no longer and with severity reproved him. Immediately the friar "gave a loud laugh, and, leaping high into the air, said, 'At last I have made you break the silence, and moved you to wrath!' But the Saint calmly replied, 'Not so, for I have power to dispense; neither is it blameworthy wrath when I utter reproofs unto the evil-doers.' And the demon, being so answered, was obliged to flee."[74]

We also learn of the time two of the brethren were traveling toward Bologna to attend a chapter when they were met along the way by a stranger, who joined them and began to ask questions about the business to be conducted. He was told that the Dominican Order was making plans to send the friars into other countries, England, Hungary, Greece and Germany. One of the friars mentioned, "It is said that we shall shortly be dispersed into all these provinces." On hearing this, the stranger uttered a loud cry of anguish and bellowed, "Your Order is my confusion." The stranger then "leapt into the air, and so disappeared." The friars realized that it was the voice of the demon, "who was thus compelled to bear witness to the power which the servants of God exercised against him."[75]

The devil is an inventor of disguises, as demonstrated in the lifetime of **St. Colette** (1381-1447), the reformer of the Poor Clare Order and the foundress of that branch known as the Colettines. During her girlhood in Corbie she had seen the devil, and later he tormented her at Besançon and appeared to her as a roaring black lion, although sometimes he came "in loathsome human guise." The lion often appeared and tormented her when she was about to make her Confession. At other times, the devil took the form of various animals and reptiles, and sometimes of cats. One day while in the confessional, St. Colette was telling her confessor, Father Pierre de Vaux, of Satan's latest pranks, when she suddenly thought that if the priest could see the lion he would better understand what she was experiencing. The lion was always visible to her, and she could hear him clearly, but when her prayer was answered, and the snarling black lion was made manifest for a moment to Father Pierre, he promptly fainted.[76]

For a time the demons, followed by lesser devils, appeared to St. Colette in horrible forms. Then loathsome reptiles crowded around her. They came as "huge serpents that threatened to coil themselves about her body. Vipers, lizards, worms and other ugly, crawling creatures" filled her cell. "Bats and repulsive-looking birds, even wolves and other wild beasts would invade the enclosure and rush at her." These she dismissed with her crucifix or holy water.[77] Another time, the demon assumed the appearance of a huge dragon.[78] The evil spirits tormented her in every monastery in which she lodged, but she faced them with courage and fearlessness as she advanced higher in the spiritual realm.

St. Teresa of Avila (1515-1582), the Discalced Carmelite nun who was also the first woman to be made a Doctor of the Church, described in her *Autobiography* some of the devils who appeared to her. On some occasions her sisters were witnesses to what was taking place and they assisted the Saint through the use of holy water, which was instrumental in dispersing the evil spirits. St. Teresa writes,

> Once when I was in an oratory, the devil appeared on my left hand in an abominable form; as he spoke to me, I paid particular attention to his mouth, which was horrible. Out of his body there seemed to be coming a great flame which was intensely bright and cast no shadow. He told me in a horrible way that I had indeed escaped out of his hands but he would get hold of me still. I was very much afraid and made the Sign of the Cross, whereupon he disappeared, but immediately returned again. This happened twice running, and I did not know what to do. But there was some Holy Water there, so I flung some in the direction of the apparition, and it never came back.[79]

St. Teresa writes that on another occasion, when she was suffering bitterly,

> The Lord evidently meant me to realize that this was the work of the devil, for I saw beside me a dark hideous devil, snarling as if in despair . . . One night, too, I thought the devils were stifling me, and when the nuns had sprinkled a great deal of Holy Water about, I saw a huge crowd of them running away as quickly as though they were about to fling themselves down a steep place. So often have these accursed creatures tormented me and so little am I afraid of them, now that I see they cannot stir unless the Lord allows them to.[80]

Again the Saint tells us of another occasion when the devil appeared: "Once, when I was about to communicate, I saw two devils of most hideous aspect. Their horns seemed to be around the poor priest's throat; and when I saw my Lord . . . in the hands of such a man . . . I knew for a certainty that those hands had offended Him and realized that here was a soul in mortal sin."[81]

One of the most unusual of the devil's appearances to **St. Joseph of Cupertino** (1603-1663) took place when that saint was praying one night before the tomb of St. Francis of Assisi. When the door to the basilica was opened violently, St. Joseph instinctively turned to watch as a man entered who walked more noisily than what would be considered normal. The Saint noticed that, as he approached, the lamps went out one by one. Finally, when all the lamps were extinguished and the intruder stood at his side in the darkness, the man suddenly threw St. Joseph to the floor and attempted to strangle him. After the Saint invoked St. Francis, he saw St. Francis leave his tomb and relight the lamps with a small candle. When the lamps were all lit, the devil suddenly vanished.[82]

The preceding took place after the death of **St. Francis of**

Assisi (1181-1226), but St. Francis, while alive, had several experiences of his own. A companion of the Saint and one who knew him well—Thomas of Celano—gives us several examples of his confrontation with the devil, including the present story involving one of the brothers. It seems that this brother, instead of submitting himself to the vicar of St. Francis, decided to accept another brother as his superior. The Saint gently corrected his follower, who threw himself at the feet of the priest St. Francis had chosen for him. The Saint then revealed to one of his companions: "I saw a devil on the back of that disobedient brother, clutching him by the neck. Subdued by such a one sitting on his back, he had spurned the curb of obedience and was following the pulling of the reins by his rider. And, when I prayed to the Lord for the brother, the devil suddenly left him in confusion."[83]

St. Margaret Mary Alacoque (1647-1690) wrote in her autobiography that, after experiencing a visit from Our Lord, she was visited by a demon. "For having presented himself to me under the appearance of a frightful Moor, his eyes flashing like two live coals and gnashing his teeth at me, he said, 'Accursed that thou art, I will capture thee, and, if once I have thee in my power, I will make thee feel what I can do; I will injure thee on every occasion.' " The Saint continues, "I nevertheless feared nothing, so great was the interior strength that I experienced . . . as I had by me a small crucifix to which my Sovereign Deliverer had given the power to drive from me all this infernal fury."[84]

The devil frequently appeared to **St. Gerard Majella** (1726-1755) as a massive dog, snarling and threatening to attack him. This was demonstrated when St. Gerard Majella was about to enter the Cathedral at Muro, when the demon rushed upon him in the form of a horrible mastiff, barking furiously and threatening to bite him. The demon vanished immediately when the Saint made the Sign of the Cross.

Several of St. Gerard's brethren were watching him one Sunday morning when he approached two young men who were standing at one side of the church. While standing before them

St. Gerard rebuked them with the words: "What are you doing here? This is not your place. In the name of God return to Hell." The two immediately disappeared. This occurrence is undeniable since the Saint's biographer states: "Several of our brethren were witnesses of it."

A man of Castelgrande named Francesco Mugnone was making a retreat at Caposele when Gerard approached him with the question, "Francesco, have you made a good Confession?" Francesco answered that he had. "No, it was not well made," said the Saint. "Look what you have behind you." Francesco, turning, saw at his side the demon under a horrible form. Thoroughly frightened, Francesco quickly made for the confessional.[85]

St. Gerard Majella was the special object of the devil's fury, almost as much, it would seem, as was St. Jean-Marie-Baptiste Vianney, the Curé of Ars. A perusal of St. Gerard's biographies would reveal the countless confrontations he had with demons, many of which were witnessed by his brothers in religion.

The devils that appeared to **St. Paul of the Cross** (1694-1775) sometimes took the form of cats that walked over his bed while he was trying to rest. Other times they appeared as enormous dogs or hateful-looking birds, or like a savage giant, tormenting and vexing him. One of his companions saw the devil in this last form when he went into the Saint's room to join him in prayer. At seeing the horrible vision, the poor religious in great terror said to St. Paul, "Father, do you see?" The Saint, accustomed to such visions, answered him: "Be quiet; don't be afraid; he's not come for you."[86]

St. Bernard (1090-1153) tells of a religious who was in his cell praying, when his sudden screams attracted the whole community. Thoroughly agitated, he took some moments before he was able to talk. Finally he explained, "My brethren, do not be astonished at seeing my mind disturbed. Two devils have appeared to me; their horrible appearance has put me out of my senses. What monstrosity! Rather all torments than again to endure the sight of them!"[87]

Father Paul of Moll (1824-1896), a Flemish Benedictine known as the "Wonder-worker of the Nineteenth Century," once told a friend, "I have just seen our Saviour, and immediately afterwards there filed past me a large troop of men on horseback, all clad in armor, like cavaliers of the Middle Ages: they were so many demons! When anything good happens, the devil at once interferes."[88] At other times the devil came as frightful animals.

Although the demons can appear in many frightful disguises, they have also been known to appear in more pleasing and celestial forms, even as the holy Mother of God. One such instance took place during the lifetime of **St. Peter Martyr** (1205-1252), who was only fifteen when he met St. Dominic and begged to be accepted into the Dominican Order.

Known as a celebrated preacher, St. Peter Martyr routinely engaged in disputes with heretics all over northern Italy. In one city, a prominent man had been won to heresy after he had visited a meeting of heretics. During the meeting, a vision of what seemed to be the Blessed Mother encouraged him to join the group. Determined to win the man back to the truth, St. Peter went to a meeting of the heretics. When the devil in the guise of the Blessed Mother appeared, the Saint held high a pyx in which he had placed a consecrated Host. After he addressed the false vision with the words, "If you are the Mother of God, adore your Son!" the devil left in dismay, to the astonishment of the heretics, many of whom were immediately converted.[89]

The demon donned the appearance of several heavenly personages when he showed himself to **St. Mary Magdalene de' Pazzi** (1566-1607), sometimes assuming the form of the Eternal Father, sometimes of Our Lord and at other times of the Holy Spirit or of one of the Saint's own angelic protectors. Her biographer quotes St. Ignatius Loyola as having said that the devil, in trying to transform himself into an angel of light, is betrayed by his serpent's tail. The disguises of the devil, as he appeared to St. Mary Magdalene, were ineffectual, since he betrayed himself, perhaps by the serpent's tail or in one way or another. At such times the Saint confronted him and ordered him: "By the power of God, depart from me and return to the torments of hell."[90] The Saint also saw the devils as poisonous vipers that covered her body and caused great pain by frequently biting her.

A mysterious snake appeared also to **St. Ignatius of Loyola** (1491-1556) "early in his progress" while he was in the hospital at Manresa. This vision took place "before he had experienced heavenly raptures," and it was often repeated. St. Ignatius found pleasure in looking upon it until he learned later what it really was. This vision first appeared as a luminous figure, which he could not perfectly distinguish. It was vague and formless, but it seemed to resemble a serpent "that had many points or centers, like eyes, from which issued a vivid light." One day, later in his spiritual life, when he was by the river Llobregat, he knelt before a cross that he frequently visited. While he was engaged in prayer, this luminous figure appeared to him, but being so near the cross, it assumed an unpleasant aspect and appeared to be without its usually bright color. At once the Saint realized that the vision was an illusion of the devil. But the devil, always persistent, appeared in the same manner again when St. Ignatius was at Manresa, as well as when he was in Paris and in Rome. Instead of the pleasant feeling he had experienced previously, St. Ignatius now had a painful impression from the vision. It is said that he thereafter sent the demon scurrying off "by striking at it and chasing it away with his staff."[91]

Teresa Helena Higginson (1844-1905), whose cause for beatification was introduced in 1935, was a teacher and a mystic who experienced many visions of Our Blessed Lady and of Our Lord, who appealed for the institution of a feast in honor of His Sacred Head as the Seat of Divine Wisdom. The devil, of course, tried every means to prevent this by stirring up confusion and presenting every kind of temptation. When, as Miss Higginson relates, "the temptations were at their height he came as an angel to comfort and console me." There were also other apparitions of the devil, who attempted to confuse her. According to Miss Higginson, "The devil came pretending to be Our Lord with the Blessed Sacrament, and he said that, God as he was, he could not resist my prayer in honor of the Seat of Divine Wisdom, and he said, 'Eat of the Bread of Life and drink of the refreshing fountain of my sacred heart.' Numerous devils were with him as angels, but the glaring splendor of his glory is so different from that of Our Lord's that I wondered at it."[92]

After offering a prayer to Our Lord, and being unable to reach for some holy water because of weakness, she writes: "I raised my left hand to remind Him, my Lord and my God, if it were He, that I was all His forever, and when I did this, that sham glory was turned into a cloud of sulphur or brimstone, which almost suffocated me, and he howled most fearfully and retired."[93] At other times he appeared in horrible forms and even very often as a man. Miss Higginson added, "I think he used the bodies of damned souls." She also adds, "Sometimes he would follow me about as a thing with a serpent's head, or a pig's head or a fox's head and tail, and a bird's wings and head with hooked bill. These appeared in church and out, but I appeared not to notice."[94] [Not that it detracts from Teresa Helena Higginson's personal sanctity, but Rome in June, 1938 denied a request for a feast in honor of the Sacred Head. —*Editor*, 1999.]

St. Stanislaus Kostka (1550-1568) was once tormented during an illness by a demon who appeared in the form of an angry dog that threatened to jump on him. The beast was finally driven off after he was confronted three times with the Sign of the Cross. The devil that invaded the house of **Bl. Anna Maria Taigi** (1769-1837) took frightful shapes like "wild animals out of the *Apocalypse*." Once, after a vision of the Blessed Mother, **St. Anthony Mary Claret** (1807-1870) saw "a formidable group of dragons who crept across the room, roaring and standing erect as though they were ready to swallow him."[95]

Apparitions of the devil were also experienced by **St. Elizabeth of Schönau** (1129-1164), who entered religious life at the age of twelve and advanced rapidly in spiritual matters, so that by the age of twenty-three she experienced heavenly manifestations. These, however, were mixed with numerous diabolical apparitions. On the advice of Abbot Hildelin, she recorded her visions on wax tablets, which were sent to her brother Egbert, a canon of Bonn, who also became a religious at Schönau. She reported that the devil frequently appeared in her cell as monks or priests who mocked and threatened her, but the most impressive apparition of the devil was the time he appeared as a great black bull, which dissolved into a black fire. From the midst of the fire emerged a herd of "loathsome goats." This period of trial is said to have lasted only a short time before her celestial visions once again returned. Having held the office of superior in her order for several years, she died at the age of only thirty-eight. The notes of St. Elizabeth, together with her oral explanations, were embodied by her brother Egbert into three books. The preface to these volumes contains her *Memoirs,* from which we derive all we know of this holy religious.[96]

We now advance to the Twentieth Century and consider apparitions of the devil as he made himself known closer to our own time.

The devil in the form of a cat often appeared to the great devotee of St. Joseph, **Bl. Brother André** of Montreal (Alfred Bessette) (1845-1937). This usually took place when the holy brother prepared a corpse for burial. After this act of mercy, he usually spent a sleepless night, being disturbed by strange sounds and the rattlings of objects caused by the large black cat. On being asked by one of his confreres about the cat, the holy man replied, "The devil does not like me to do these good works. He is trying to frighten me."[97]

Père Lamy (1885-1931) was a parish priest at Troyes, France, who experienced a number of mystical favors. As with many mystics, he too was annoyed by demons, who came to him in various forms, sometimes as a horse, a dog, a wolf. But the demons also assumed less terrifying aspects, as the good priest describes:

> Lucifer is tall, with quite a good-looking face, bony, bearded. He has fierce eyes, flashing; light hair, a fairly short, curly beard. He has the build of a very solid man of strong cut. He wears a white garment, a sort of antique peplum which comes halfway down his leg. Always climbing zig-zag the length of his body and his robe, through his beard, from the feet to the top of his head, are two kinds of flames, which seem to stick to him. One kind, the most numerous are black as burning pitch. The others are ordinary tongues of fire. It does not hinder his movements.

Sometimes appearing with Satan was the Blessed Virgin, who permitted the priest to see the devil in his sufferings, which deprived the evil spirit of any influence. The holy priest adds, "When I see him surrounded with flames, or rather, when the Blessed Virgin has the goodness to let me see his face surrounded with flames, I reckon the sufferings of Lucifer [to be] dreadful, dreadful."[98]

Sr. Josefa Menendez (1893-1923), whose cause for beatification was introduced in 1948, was favored with many mystical experiences and apparitions of the Sacred Heart. The devil was naturally determined to interrupt the progress of her soul by frequently visiting her. The devil first appeared to her as she was coming out of the chapel after having been to Confession. She was suddenly confronted by a huge black dog whose jaws sent forth flames. Standing in front of her, in order to prevent her passing, he tried to throw himself upon her. Although thoroughly frightened, Sr. Josefa held her rosary stretched out before her and went her way. Sometimes the devil appeared as a menacing hound that pursued her in the corridors, at other times as a serpent coiled in front of her. The apparitions finally took a human form, "more dreaded than any other." Eventually, the devil became bolder and not only appeared to her, but took hold of her, carrying her off to another area of the convent, where he physically tormented her. Her clothing was even set on fire, which left unmistakable scorch marks and wounds that took long to heal. These torments were witnessed by her companions and continued until the Blessed Mother intervened.

Later, by the will of God, she frequently visited Hell and suffered its pains. This was permitted so that she would purify her own soul, make reparation for the sins of others, and save countless souls. Once while in Hell, she reports that there were seven or eight people around her. She writes: "Their black bodies were unclothed, and I could see them only by the reflections of the fire. They were seated and were talking together. Their conversation dealt with ways of leading souls to ruin by means of instilling in them ambition, self-interest, the acquisition of wealth, sensuality and love of pleasure and other means. Finally, one of them added such horrible things that they can neither be written nor said. Then, as if engulfed in a whirl of smoke, they vanished."[99]

Bl. Padre Pio (1887-1968) was once beaten by invisible hands, as witnessed by Padres Evangelista and Agostino, who fell to their knees in prayer and continually sprinkled the room with Holy Water. After reacting to being struck repeatedly for fifteen minutes, the holy Padre came to himself and revealed that he "had been flogged by horrible men who looked like professional torturers." There were other times when he declared that the demons appeared to him in the form of various friends, colleagues, his confessor and superiors, even in the forms of the reigning pontiff and of Jesus, Mary, St. Francis and his Guardian Angel. At such times the holy Padre recognized the diabolical ruse by a certain feeling of apprehension and disgust, and to prove the true identity of the apparitions, he insisted that they utter words of praise to Jesus Christ—an order they refused.[100] Whereas diabolical visions gave Padre Pio an uneasy and unholy feeling, actual visions of holy persons gave him feelings of love, exhilaration and contentment.

Another time Padre Pio had a vision of naked women who "danced lasciviously in his room." Still another time the devil appeared as a black cat; and once, after a woman confessed her sins—which the Padre said were very grave ones—he was about to speak the words of absolution when "the woman sprang up, then gave a cavernous cry and disappeared." Padre Pio confessed to being frightened, and when he asked Padre Ignazio, who was outside the confessional, if he had seen a woman leave, Padre Ignazio declared that he had not.[101] This was yet another instance of the devil, the Father of Lies, using a disguise to hide his visitation.

Another description of demons is given us by **Sister Lucia of Fatima** in her memoirs entitled *Fatima in Lucia's Own Words*. She writes that Our Lady showed both her and her cousins Jacinta and Francisco "a great sea of fire which seemed to be under the earth. Plunged in this fire were demons and souls in human form, like transparent burning embers, all blackened or burnished bronze. . . . The demons could be distinguished by their terrifying and repellent likeness to frightful and unknown animals all black and transparent."[102]

After this frightful vision, Francisco had a horrifying experience. In *Fatima in Lucia's Own Words*, Sister Lucia tells that they were one day at a place called Pedreira, tending their sheep, when Francisco withdrew to a hollow among the rocks to pray, "as was his wont." After a considerable time, "we heard him shouting and crying out to us and to Our Lady. Distressed lest something might have happened to him, we ran in search of him, calling out his name. But it still took us some time before we could locate him. At last we came upon him trembling with fright, still on his knees, and so upset that he was unable to rise to his feet . . . In a voice half smothered with fright, he replied: 'It was one of those huge beasts that we saw in Hell. He was right here breathing out flames!' "[103] Sr. Lucia continues that Francisco "was anything but fearful. He'd go anywhere in the dark alone at night without the slightest hesitation." Neither was he afraid of snakes or small animals that children usually avoid.[104] Lucia continues, "I saw nothing, neither did Jacinta." The description of the devil as being a coward was confirmed in this instance, in which he succeeded in scaring a small child at prayer.

87. The Difference between Obsession and Possession

The two states of diabolical obsession and possession are often distinguished by saying that in cases of possession, the devil acts upon the body from within, while in cases of obsession, the devil annoys the body from without. *Obsession* takes the form of either violent and persistent temptations or an external form which affects the five senses. *Possession* is the presence of the devil in the body of the possessed. The devil does not unite with the body in the same manner as the soul does, nor does he enter into the soul itself. By being present in the body, he can act directly on the bodily members, causing all sorts of disturbing movements, often to the point of physical harm.

88. Obsession and Annoying Activities of the Devils

In this section we will enumerate the various antics and foul deeds performed by the demons to distract, annoy or disrupt the lives of the Saints. This they attempted by producing aggravations to the five senses.

They have assaulted the sense of **sight** by appearing in frightful forms, such as: armed men, repulsive animals, wolves, wild boars, toads, spiders, etc., all of which threatened to attack the Saints. (See #86.)

They have attacked the sense of **hearing** by uttering cries, blasphemies, obscene words, moanings, shrieks and noises of all kinds, such as those that afflicted the Curé of Ars and so many other saints. (See #90.)

They have assaulted the **sense of taste** by, for example, defiling in a horrible way everything that was to be eaten by Sister Veronica, a Capuchin nun.

They have afflicted the **sense of smell** with strong and unpleasant odors that were noticed not only by the saint involved, but by many others who were near the Saint and by those who might be in other areas of the building. Such an instance took place when St. Frances of Rome once thought a corpse in a state of full decomposition had been brought near and its matter applied to her face. Her garments retained the odor even after several washings. (See #91.)

Assaulting the sense of **touch** is a very frequent tool of the devil, when he afflicts the body with beatings, scratchings, biting and kickings, sometimes causing serious injuries. We are told that Ven. Agnes of Langeac was beaten twice a week for four years before her profession. Padre Pio suffered miserably at the hands of demons, as did many saints who will soon be identified. (See #89.)

The earliest report of such assaults is that given by St. Paul when he wrote: "And lest the greatness of the revelations should exalt me, there was given me a sting of my flesh, an angel of Satan to buffet me. For which thing thrice I besought the Lord, that it might depart from me." (*2 Cor.* 12:7-8).

Another early example of these attacks is that which we read about in the life of **St. Meinrad** (797-861). His history reveals that he retired to his hermitage on Mount Etzel, where he was subjected to a large band of black demons, whose number was impossible to count. They crowded around him and whispered terrible threats in his ears. They assumed frightful postures and hideous forms, while making such an uproar that it seemed as though the surrounding trees were affected. St. Meinrad is said to have remained calm throughout the experience and was even visited by an angel who comforted him and quickly dismissed the evil spirits, who never again troubled him.[105]

We read in the life of **St. Benedict** (480-550) about an annoyance that was also recorded in the *Acta Sanctorum* by the Bollandists. It is told that when St. Benedict first retired to the caves at Subiaco, a few miles from Rome, Satan knew full well the good that St. Benedict's Order would perform for the Church and attempted to distract the Saint. But this effort must be evaluated as a very feeble attempt. Satan, it is said, transformed himself into a blackbird that began to flutter around the hermit, sometimes approaching so near that the Saint could easily have caught it. Since the behavior of the bird was unusual, the Saint became immediately suspicious and made the Sign of the Cross. The Saint's suspicions were confirmed when the blackbird immediately disappeared.[106]

In the history of the Dominican **St. Peter of Verona** (1205-1252), we learn that vast crowds usually assembled to hear the Saint preach. One day, when the crowd was unusually large, so that the Saint had to preach out of doors, the devil, in the form of a black horse, galloped into the crowd, stomping many and frightening everyone. It is recorded that "The Saint simply made the Sign of the Cross, when the phantom vanished, and all the people saw it permeate the air like smoke."[107]

We learn of another form of annoyance used by the devil to distract a saint from prayer. One evening when **St. Colette** (1381-1447) was reading her prayerbook, an evil spirit blew out the lamp she was using. The Saint dutifully relit it, but again it was blown out. Once more she relit it, and it was again blown out, while the demon jeered at her and finally upset the lamp and spilled the oil over her book. The Saint, however, is said to have endured such antics with a serene and amiable disposition.[108]

St. Teresa of Avila (1515-1582) reports that on one particular day, "When I was at prayer, I saw beside me a devil, in a great fury, tearing some papers which he held in his hand. This brought me great comfort, for I thought it meant that what I had been praying for was granted me." Another time, the Saint was in the oratory, repeating some devotional prayers, "when actually the devil himself alighted on the book." This she surmised was to prevent her from finishing the prayers. The Saint writes: "I made the Sign of the Cross and he went away. I then began again and he came back. I think I began that prayer three times and not until I had sprinkled some Holy Water on him could I finish."[109]

St. Teresa writes in her *Autobiography* about her many experiences with devils and her visions of them. She recounts one experience "which gave me a bad fright."

> I was in a place where a certain person had died after leading for many years, as I knew, a very bad life. But for two years he had been ill and in some respects seemed to have mended his ways. He died without making his Confession, but in spite of all this, I did not myself think he would be damned. While his body was being wrapped in its shroud, I saw a great many devils taking hold of it and apparently playing with it and treating it roughly . . . they were dragging it about in turn with large hooks . . . During the whole of the funeral office, I saw no more devils, but afterwards, when the body was laid in the grave, there was such a crowd of them waiting there to take possession of it that I was beside myself at the sight . . . If they were taking possession like this of the unfortunate body, I reflected, what would they do with the soul?

The Saint gives this thoughtful consideration: "Would to God that this frightful thing which I saw could be seen by everyone who is leading an evil life! I think it would be a great incentive to amendment."[110]

St. Teresa also tells that once the devil was with her for five hours, "torturing me with such terrible pains and both inward and outward disquiet that I do not believe I could have endured them any longer." She continues that the sisters who were with her were terribly frightened, "and had no more idea of what to do for me than I had of how to help myself."[111] St. Teresa used holy water and prayer to combat the attacks and troubling activities of the spirits.

The recipient of numerous visions and accompanied for most of her life by the visible presence of an angel, **St. Frances of Rome** (1384-1440) was also annoyed by the activities of demons, who attempted on numerous occasions to interrupt her prayer life and her charity to the unfortunate. One particular bit of annoyance, but one which she accepted with great calmness, occurred when the devil grasped her head and lifted her by the hair as he suspended her over a cliff. The event occupied several minutes before she called upon the name of Jesus and was returned to safety. One can only imagine her gratitude for this deliverance, since she promptly cut off her beautiful hair and offered it as a token of thanksgiving to the One who had saved her.[112]

We tell in another section of this work about the painful attacks of the devil that were suffered by the Curé of Ars, **St. Jean-Marie-Baptiste Vianney** (1786-1859). In addition to these painful experiences, there were annoying activities which the Saint endured patiently. One such instance occurred on December 4, 1841, which was told by the holy Curé to Abbé Toccanier. The Curé revealed: "Last night the devil came into my room whilst I was reciting my Breviary. He was blowing hard, and seemed to vomit on the floor, I know not what, but it looked like either corn or some other grain. I told him: 'I am going over there to the Providence to tell them of your behavior, so that they may despise you!' " The Saint added that the demon stopped at once.

The cook of the Providence, Marie Filliat, was also annoyed by the activities of the devil. She related that on one occasion, "after thoroughly cleansing the saucepan, I filled it with water for the soup. I noticed little bits of meat in the water. Now the day was one of abstinence. I emptied the saucepan, rinsed it, and filled it once more with water. When the soup was ready to put on the table, I saw that there were bits of meat in it. M. le Curé, on being informed, told me, 'The devil has done this thing; serve the soup just as it is.' " Such cases of annoyance to this saint and those around him are numerous.

A pilgrimage to Rome influenced **St. Clement Mary Hofbauer** (1751-1820) to enter the Redemptorist Order. After his ordination he left his native Vienna for Warsaw, where he became the center of the spiritual and intellectual life of the city, preaching in both German and Polish. He founded several schools and other institutions for the young and spent as many as eighteen hours in the confessional, forgiving sins and directing consciences. He is known for the prodigious work he accomplished and for his untiring energy in serving the people of God.

His labors apparently infuriated the demons, who made several attempts to hinder his successes. Witnesses at the process of his beatification testified to these diabolical efforts. During the year 1801, while the Saint was preaching to a great crowd in his Warsaw church on the subject of Holy Communion, loud sounds like those of a suffocating child were heard, but no child could be found. Another time, before Holy Communion, deep murmurings were heard and then a voice shouting, "A child has been suffocated!" Soon this was followed by another voice, "A woman has just died in the crowd!" The people were in the grip of terror, but again the search for the victims was unsuccessful. Then, from throughout the church, cries were heard: "Fire! Fire! The church is burning!" Flames and smoke appeared, and even those outside the church saw the flames, but when the firemen arrived, neither smoke nor fire was visible. The whole event was attributed to diabolical influence.[113]

In the life of **St. Anthony of Padua** (1195-1231) we learn of a devilish illusion that took place at Brive, where he had established a little hermitage. Here he accepted postulants who wanted to imitate his love of poverty and solitude. On one occasion, when they were in great distress due to a lack of provisions, they applied for help from the people of a nearby village. One evening, some of his companions saw a band of ruffians destroying the field of one of the benefactors and hurried to notify the Saint. Very calmly St. Anthony replied, "Fear not. 'Tis but an artifice of the evil one to distract you." Wonderful to relate, the next morning the field was found untouched.[114]

A fierce effort of the devil to promote fear in the traveling companions of **St. Paul of the Cross** (1694-1775) took place on his journey to the city of Pisa, where he was invited by the Marquis of Montemar to preach to the troops. While St. Paul was traveling on the ship, *Royal Felucca*, a dreadful storm developed in the middle of the voyage. The ship was soon half full of water, which the sailors believed would cause them to sink. Nevertheless, they struck the sails and attempted to row to land, but soon they realized the futility of their efforts.

While the sailors stood as though anticipating the sinking of the vessel, St. Paul of the Cross stood upright on the poop deck with his arms extended and his crucifix in one hand. Addressing the terrified sailors, he said, "My children, fear nothing, trust in God and in the Blessed Virgin. This storm is caused by devils who are persecuting me." All on board watched as he then blessed the sea and called on Jesus, who had once calmed the sea and the winds for the frightened Apostles. Before St. Paul identified the storm as the work of the devil, the ship was a full five miles from land; but after his prayer, the ship was suddenly safe under the tower of Montenero. The unexpected arrival at land was regarded by all as a miracle, which they proclaimed with shouts of "A miracle—a miracle!"[115]

While **St. Anthony Mary Claret** (1807-1870) was preaching a mission in Sarreal, so many people gathered to hear him speak that the church was filled to capacity, with many being unable to enter. During one particularly fervent sermon, a great stone from the arch of the tower fell among the people. At once the Saint calmed the people, declaring that the demon wished to impede the fruit of the mission, but that God would not permit him to do any harm.

It is said that not a fragment of the stone touched anyone; in fact, the miracle "augmented the fervor and enthusiasm of the audience, and so the devil was defeated."[116]

The devil constantly hindered **St. Benedict's** (480-550) efforts to build the monastery at Monte Cassino. The demon was so enraged at the Saint's holy work that he pushed over a wall and crushed one of the monks to death. The monks immediately brought the dead man to St. Benedict, who restored him to life.

During the process for the beatification of **Brother André**

(Alfred Bessette) (1845-1937), the "devil's advocate" (Promoter of the Faith) asked Joseph Pichette, a layman and one of the brother's closest friends, if the brother had ever been vexed by the devil. The "devil's advocate" questioned M. Pichette specifically about an incident that had taken place during the enlarging of the presbytery in 1928. M. Pichette related that after he and Brother André had prayed in the crypt, they returned to the presbytery and passed a place where the workmen had removed the old flooring, leaving a hole about fifteen feet by ten feet wide and three feet deep. Along its edge lay a plank about a foot and a half wide. He continues:

> We stood on it [the plank] with our backs against the wall, while Brother André explained to me how the old and new constructions would be joined together. The Brother exclaimed, "How good God is!" He had not time to finish the phrase, when he left me suddenly, as though he wanted to fly over the gaping pit in front of us. He left me without any movement of jumping at all. Brother André landed on the opposite side, striking his head against the planking and remained there with his legs hanging down, while I ran to get assistance . . . For my part, this leap appeared to me to be a dozen feet, and I could not understand how a man could jump twelve feet.

The following year, when M. Pichette was at the Oratory, Brother André showed him a book, the life of Sister Mary Martha Chambon (her cause for beatification was opened in 1937), and one page in particular, which told that the devil had transported the sister in a similar fashion on numerous occasions. M. Pichette exclaimed, "So, at last I understood that the leap Brother André had made the year before must have been caused by the demon."[117]

Annoying is the proper description for the activities of the devils that took place during the lifetime of **Bl. Mary Fortunata Viti** (1827-1922). A number of these vexations are given by her biographer: for example, the time she was finishing some needed embroidery and lost the spool of thread. After searching diligently for it, she at last discovered it concealed neatly under her pillow. Another time, when she was sitting down at the distaff to complete some yarn, suddenly she "saw the tow, which had been prepared for spinning, tumbled about and thrown in all directions by some invisible hand." Still another time, when she was dressing in the morning, she discovered that one of her shoes was missing. It was later found in the infirmary. The devil not only attempted to try her patience by misplacing objects, but also by spoiling work she had done or by tearing that work into shreds.[118]

The most annoying of the devil's activities took place in the dining room. The sisters who worked in the kitchen often noticed that the Blessed would sometimes scarcely touch the food placed before her. When questioned about this, the holy nun, in simplicity and frankness, revealed that the very sight of the food nauseated her since the devil made it appear as though it were alive with maggots and disgusting vermin. We are told that Bl. Mary remained unruffled during such ordeals and in this way defeated the devil's purposes.[119] Her biographer assures us that:

> Sister Fortunata was at all times so simple and straightforward, so humble and docile, and possessed such a marked sense of the practical, that there can be no question here of figments of the imagination, of fabrications of the fancy, or of hysterical hallucinations.[120]

We know that **Bl. Padre Pio** (1887-1968) was often physically assaulted by the devil, but he was also tried by other annoying activities. We learn that for several years Padre Agostino exchanged letters with the stigmatic, but in 1912 he received a letter that was smeared with ink and difficult to read. The holy priest's guardian angel suggested to Padre Agostino that he place a crucifix on the smudged letters, which he did. Almost immediately they became clearer, so that he was able to read them.[121]

What we will consider next are pranks of the devil to demonstrate his displeasure with the promulgation of the dogma of the **Immaculate Conception** by Pope Pius IX. The events began to take place on the night of December 8, 1854, after a day of rejoicing and devotions in honor of the Immaculate Conception at the Motherhouse of the School Sisters of Notre Dame in Milwaukee.

When the candidates (the young girls just entering the convent) came into the dormitories, they found that water had been thrown on their beds. After putting everything in order, they slept throughout the night undisturbed and peacefully. However, "on the ensuing nights, grooves, formed in their pillows, were filled with water, while nothing else was wet. Sometimes the water was in their nightcaps, which nevertheless stood up stiff on their beds. At times a call bell in the apartment below was loudly rung. Articles left lying on a table in the dormitory moved from place to place, though no one was seen carrying them. Frequently the candidates received a violent box on the ear from an unseen hand.[122] On nights when these events did not take place, there were other disturbances, such as: "filthy water dropping from the ceiling, uncommon noises would awake them from their sleep, unpleasant odors filled their wardrobes and rooms, and clothing was found cut to pieces in such a way that it could no longer be worn."[123]

The Mother Superior knew from the very beginning that evil forces were the cause of the problems, but she realized that the Heavenly Queen, to whom the Order was dedicated, would protect them and present a remedy. The candidates, on the other hand, began to suffer from lack of sleep and ever increasing anxiety, while many thought they could not persevere in their vocations. Mother Caroline invited Bishop Henni to inspect the premises and to listen to individual reports. In the end the Bishop advised that the devil was endeavoring to destroy the candidature, which was then filled to capacity. He also warned, "Take heed lest there be among your number some medium through which he is at work."

This proved to be true when one of the candidates was found

to have concealed a difficulty from the sisters. It happened that the young lady in question had been promised in marriage, but had succeeded in fleeing the commitment by her entrance into the community. The rejected suitor took his revenge "by turning the powers of evil against the community." When the Bishop learned of this, he ordered her dismissal from the community. It was only then that peace was restored.

Those outside the community, on learning of the happenings, suggested that natural causes might have produced the events, but the answer was always that this was impossible, for vigilance committees were formed early, both among the candidates and the sisters. No one was ever permitted to linger behind when all were called to a common exercise. If some candidate became indisposed, two or three others were selected indiscriminately by the sisters in charge to wait upon her and remain with her until she was able to return to her duties. The possibility of trickery by one or more of the candidates was also rejected because "no one was permitted at any hour to go unaccompanied to the dormitories, the doors of which were kept locked, as were also those of all adjoining rooms. When bell-ringing began during the night, every bell known to be in the convent was locked in a room occupied by two of the sisters, who concealed the keys within. Trickery was at first suspected, but the disturbances were not caused by human agency."[124]

All the sisters who experienced the diabolical disturbances, in one way or another, expressed the same sentiment as did one of the sisters: "I have never regretted the experience—it did me good for a lifetime."[125]

89. Painful Activities of the Devils

The devil began his attacks on Christians immediately after the Resurrection. **St. Paul** writes, "Lest the greatness of the revelations should exalt me, there was given me a sting of my flesh, an angel of Satan to buffet me. For which thing thrice I besought the Lord, that it might depart from me." (*2 Cor.* 12:7-8).

St. Antony of the Desert (251-356) suffered pain at the hands of devils when he was only eighteen or twenty years of age. He distributed his inheritance among the poor and journeyed into the desert to seek perfection and to live an ascetical life. The devils became enraged at his decision and "tempted him day and night" with thoughts of the property he had given away and the luxury he had left behind. They suggested to him thoughts of money and fame and warned him that the attaining of virtue was difficult and might harm his health. When these and other temptations failed, they took to more serious and violent pursuits. St. Athanasius (d. 373), who was the Saint's first biographer, writes in the preface of his book: "I have hastened to write to your goodness what I myself know, for I saw him often, and what I was able to learn from himself; for I was his assistant for no little time."[126] St. Athanasius writes that St. Antony, early in his ascetical life, when he was about thirty-five years old,

> having asked one of his acquaintances to bring him bread from time to time, he entered one of the tombs; his friend closed the door of it on him, and he remained alone within. This the enemy would not endure, for he feared lest by degrees Antony should fill the desert with monks. Coming one night with a throng of demons, he so scourged the Saint that he lay on the ground speechless from the pain. For, he declared, the pain was so severe that blows from men could not have caused such agony. By God's providence, his friend came the next day bringing him bread, and when he opened the door and saw him lying on the ground as dead, he lifted him and took him to the village church and laid him on the ground. Many of his kin and the village people watched beside Antony as for one dead.

At about midnight St. Antony awoke, and seeing that everyone was asleep, he motioned for his friend, who lifted him up and, according to the Saint's wishes, carried him back to the tombs without waking anyone. After they arrived at the tomb, the door was again closed. St. Athanasius continues, "He could not stand because of the blows, but he prayed lying down." The devil, seeing that physical harm did not prevent Antony from praying, visited him that night in the form of different animals which roared and threatened harm. To this new attack, Antony responded: "If you had any power in you, it would have been enough that just one of you should come; but the Lord has taken your strength away, and that is why you try to frighten me, if possible, by your numbers. It is a sign of your helplessness that you have taken the shapes of brutes . . . our trust in the Lord is like a seal to us, and like a wall of safety."[127]

St. Antony endured many temptations. Especially mentioned was a vision of a comely woman and the appearance of phantom gold. But Antony overcame all temptations and performed many good works, including the healing and spiritual direction of his visitors, his struggles to combat the Arian heresy, and the organization of loosely knit communities which would eventually be the introduction of the monastic life in the Church. Most artistic renderings of St. Antony have him in combat against fearful demons who slash, beat and gnaw on his body. Despite these attacks and his many labors and penances, he died at the age of 105.

We read in a biography of **St. Dominic** (1170-1221) how careful the friars were in obeying every rule of the new order he founded. The following example of their obedience reveals the strength of some demons and their fury against those who are striving for holiness.

One night a friar was in the choir deep in prayer when he "was seized by an invisible hand and dragged violently about the church, so that he cried aloud for help." It is mentioned that these disturbances were very common in the beginning of the Dominican Order. "After hearing the cry, more than thirty brethren ran into the church to assist the sufferer, but in vain; they too were roughly handled, and like him, dragged and thrown about without pity." At length the friar Reginald arrived, took the first friar to the altar of St. Nicholas and dismissed the demon. It should be noted that the friars' vow of silence was still obeyed because, "in spite of the alarm and horror of the circumstances, not one of those present, who amounted in all to a considerable number, ventured to speak a single word, or so much as to utter a sound," except for the cry of the first friar who was attacked.[128]

It is revealed in the *Little Flowers of St. Francis* that **St. Francis of Assisi** (1181-1226) was once attacked by demons during prayer while his companions were sleeping. It is reported that "a great number of the fiercest devils came with very great noise and tumult, and they began to attack and persecute him. One took hold of him here, another there. One pulled him down, another up. One threatened him with one thing, another scolded him for something else. And so they strove to disturb his praying in different ways." After the Saint addressed the demons, they "seized him with great violence and fury and began to drag him around the church and to hurt him and persecute him much more than before." When this took place, the Saint cried out to the Lord, declaring that he was ready to endure every pain for love of Him. The report concludes: "The devils, having been humiliated and defeated by his endurance and patience, went away."[129] The Saint then left the church and wandered into a nearby forest where he surrendered himself to prayer and weeping.

We learn of another such confrontation with the devil from Thomas of Celano, St. Francis of Assisi's companion. He writes that the Saint was staying in Rome at the request of Cardinal Leo of the Holy Cross. St. Francis chose as a secluded place for prayer a tower that was divided by nine arched vaults that looked somewhat like small cells for hermits. During the first night, when he wanted to rest, "the devils came and made preparations for a hostile struggle . . . They beat him for a long time very severely and in the end left him as though half dead. After they had gone and he had recovered his breath, the Saint called his companion who was sleeping under one of the other arched vaults and said to him, 'Brother, I would like for you to stay near me because I am afraid to be alone. For the devils beat me a little while ago.' " Thomas of Celano continues, "The Saint was trembling and shaking in his members, like a person suffering a severe fever."[130]

Bl. Raymond of Capua, the confessor and biographer of **St. Catherine of Siena** (1347-1380), tells of some instances when the devils harassed this saint, but one event of particular note took place when they were returning to Siena. Bl. Raymond reports that the Saint was sitting on a donkey,

> and we were getting quite near the city when she was thrown from the saddle and fell headlong down a deep ravine. I called upon the Blessed Virgin, and then I saw Catherine laughing gaily as she lay there upon the ground, and she was saying that it was one of the 'Pickpocket's' [the devil's] blows. She got back on the donkey and we went on our way, but when we had gone about the distance of a bowshot, the evil spirit threw her again, and she finished up in the mud with the animal on top of her . . . I lifted her up out of the mud where she was lying spread-eagled under the donkey, and we urged her not to get on its back again because we were in any case quite close to the city, so she continued on foot between two of us. But the old enemy would not admit himself beaten, and he kept pulling her now one way, now another, and if we had not held on to her there is no knowing how many times she would have fallen down. And all the time she was laughing at him, treating him with contempt and mocking him.[131]

Bl. Christina of Stommeln (d. 1312) was attracted at a young age to the life of a "Beguine" (a woman who, with other laywomen, lived a devout life in adjoining homes). Her life was so remarkable that Butler counts it as one of the most extraordinary cases in hagiology and concedes that if her experiences had not been recorded by personal eyewitnesses and noted by Fr. Peter of Dacia, one would suspect the Blessed to be the victim of mental disease or hallucinations. The recipient of visions and ecstasies beginning at the age of ten, she also experienced dreadful assaults of the devil. Fr. Peter writes that once Christina was found up to her neck in mud in a pit without knowing how she got there. On three occasions, according to the parish priest, Fr. John of Cologne, Satan dragged her from bed and once took her to the roof of her house. Another time she was left bound to a tree in the garden. It was Fr. John himself, in the presence of her mother and others, who untied her. The devil also tormented her by fixing hot stones to her body, which people could see and touch.

Fr. Peter also gives a detailed account of repulsive incidents in which, on numerous occasions, Christina, her visitors, Fr. Peter himself and other Dominicans, clergy and lay people, were showered with filth which appeared out of nowhere. Various other forms of diabolic activity regularly took place, which included the demon's biting her with invisible teeth and tearing from her arms bits of flesh. The Blessed was abused by Satan for many years, but she survived to the age of 70 with a great reputation for sanctity. Pope St. Pius X confirmed the cultus in 1908. *Butler's Lives* notes that "the Holy See has recognized that the evidence touching the personal virtue of Blessed Christina justifies the continuation of her age-long local cultus."[132]

We are told that when demons first appeared to **St. Colette** (1381-1447), they did not touch her, but later they treated her so roughly that her body was badly bruised. Once she was treated so harshly that she was left half-dead on the floor of her cell.[133]

Such was also the case with **Ven. Mary of Jesus**, who is better known as Ven. Mary of Agreda (1602-1665). Early in her religious life, Our Lord, as a means of purifying His servant, chose as the furnace of tribulation, the attacks of Satan.

Her sicknesses became frequent and painful, to which were added terrible bodily sufferings inflicted by Satan, who also tempted her with vile words and images. She made rapid progress in virtue, but Satan became so enraged by her progress in the path of perfection that he continued his assaults on her body with more vigor than before, until her bones seemed about to be dislocated. At one point her life seemed in danger. These assaults were occasionally interrupted by visions of Our Blessed Mother and of Our Lord, which greatly inspired and encouraged her. Later, Mary of Agreda often bilocated to America, where she instructed the Indians in the Catholic Faith, a fact that was later confirmed beyond a doubt.[134]

Also treated harshly by the devils was **St. Catherine Tomàs** (1533-1574), who was so religious as a child that several convents offered to accept her. When she was twenty years old, she chose to join the canonesses of St. Augustine in their convent of St. Mary Magdalene at Palma. She quickly won the respect of all by her humility and sweetness. Favored with profound ecstasies after receiving Holy Communion, she also experienced severe temptations and assaults from demons that left her bruised and pained. Although the other nuns could not see the attackers, they could hear fearful shrieks and sounds.

The extent of these assaults is demonstrated by one instance in which the demons seized St. Catherine as she was walking to the refectory. Before the eyes of her companions, she was raised into the air and dropped into a cistern full of mud and water, from which she was pulled out with the greatest difficulty. (This is reminiscent of the experience of Bl. Christina of Stommeln, who was mentioned earlier.) Known as a saint during her lifetime, St. Catherine Tomàs died at the age of forty-one and was canonized in 1930.

St. Mary Magdalene de' Pazzi (1566-1607) was also physically harmed during the assaults of the demons, who at times took "the form of poisonous vipers that covered her flesh and caused her great pain by their biting." At other times the demons beat her "so fiercely that she seemed to be tortured with red-hot pincers and cut up limb by limb . . . so much so that she thought she must die."[135]

A contemporary and friend of **St. Ignatius Loyola** (1491-1556) writes that

> One night when Ignatius was sleeping, the devil tried to suffocate him. He tried to strangle him, grasping his throat as if by a hand so strong that Ignatius could not by any effort invoke the holy Name of Jesus. But when the devil strung the nerves of his soul and body to the utmost, repelling force by force, Ignatius broke out at last with the Name of Jesus; by which voice the attempt of the devil was repulsed. From this struggle, Ignatius (as we afterwards saw and noticed) was somewhat hoarse and without voice. I noticed that he was hoarse and I heard, if I am not mistaken, that this took place in the year 1541.[136]

The same biographer recorded another incident of an attack upon St. Ignatius. It took place when a young man named John Paul, who was for a long time the attendant of the Saint, was sleeping in a little room next to that of St. Ignatius. During the night he was awakened and heard the sound of blows, as if strong men were beating Ignatius, who groaned at each sound of attack. He immediately ran to Ignatius and found him sitting up in bed with the coverings pressed to his chest. When asked what was taking place, the Saint merely ordered him to return to his bed. John Paul did as he was told, but soon heard the sounds once again. This time, he found the Saint panting as if from a great physical fight.[137] It is said that St. Ignatius never saw the devils who tormented him, and that he was not in the least afraid of them.

Just as St. Ignatius Loyola was once strangled by the devil, a similar situation took place to the blind Carmelite lay brother, **John of St. Samson** (d. 1636). Not only was he frequently tempted and tormented by the devil, but he was also choked by the devil, who attempted to finish his effort by suffocating him. According to witnesses, the demons appeared in the form of frightful beasts who scratched him, while they were uttering chilling shrieks; the marks of many scratches and bruises would be plainly evident on his hands and face, as was testified by his contemporary, Father Matthew Pinault. Brother John would often make fun of the devils and mock them before sending them back to Hell to be punished by their ruler, "because they allowed themselves to be overcome by a mere nothing of a man."[138]

St. Margaret Mary Alacoque (1647-1690), the recipient of the Sacred Heart devotions, was not neglected by Satan, who frequently caused the Saint to fall and break what she was carrying. The Saint herself tells us, "Once when I was carrying a pan full of red-hot coals, he made me fall from the top to the bottom of a staircase without any of them being upset and without my sustaining the least injury; those who were present thought I must have broken my legs. But I felt my faithful guardian at my side, for I was often favored with his presence."[139]

While **St. Paul of the Cross** (1694-1775), the founder of the Passionist Order, traveled on errands of mercy or suffered from physical ailments, the devils attacked him so fiercely that bruises on his body were observed by his fellow religious. The devils, it seems, were also intent on interrupting his times of rest, so that he was often disturbed. One night, as he sat on his bed, he felt his head suddenly gripped by unseen hands. His head was then slammed against the wall with such violence that the infirmarian who slept in the next room was awakened. The next morning, when St. Paul's confessor asked how he felt, the Saint answered in words tinged with humor, "God does not suffer the operations of the devil to do one any great harm; but depend upon it, they do not do one any great good either."[140]

The devil that tormented **Bl. Anna Maria Taigi** (1769-1837) did so after she counseled the wayward brother of her friend, Msgr. Natali. The young man had flirted with suicide after a married woman with whom he had consorted died suddenly without the Sacraments of the Church. The night following his visit to Bl. Anna Maria's home, the devils physically tormented this holy housewife and then tried to strangle her. Msgr. Natali, who was present, was terrified at the sound of the infernal uproar. Bl. Anna Maria's counsels and prayers finally eventuated in the young man's conversion. Unfortunately, it came about only when the young man had contracted the plague and, seeing that he was soon to die, called for a priest. He confessed and died in the embrace of the Church. As Bl. Anna Maria had predicted, "God had seized him by the hair of his head."[141]

The torments she suffered because of this young man were not the only abuse she received at the hands of the demons. Since mild methods did not succeed in turning her from doing good, the devils took to more vicious methods. We are told that the devils began to howl like wild beasts, while animals "out of the *Apocalypse*" invaded her house. There were knocks on windows and doors. Furniture was overturned. All the while, Bl. Anna Maria was punched, kicked and beaten over the head and shoulders. Cadinal Pedicini reports: "They took her by the neck, rolled her underfoot, subjected her to frightful torments and tried to break down her purity by sensual apparitions."[142] Thankfully these occurrences took place at night while her children were asleep and unaware of what was going on, and before her husband, Domenico, had returned home from work.

Msgr. Natali, who lodged in a apartment upstairs from the Beata and her family, was witness to many of these diabolical activities. In his *Memoirs of Msgr. Natali*, the prelate gives details of these and other confrontations Bl. Anna Maria endured at the hands of the evil spirits, many of which he related during the Process of Anna Maria's beatification. Cardinal Pedicini, who was mentioned earlier, also testified at the Process to "having seen Anna many a time crying like a child as a result of the violent treatment she received." Other witnesses to these assaults besides Cardinal Pedicini and Msgr. Natali were three Cardinals, three Bishops, three marquises, an English lord, three religious, two duchesses, Anna's family, servants and neighbors.[143]

We read in the biography of the holy Curé of Ars, **St. Jean-**

Marie-Baptiste Vianney (1786-1859), of the many times he was awakened during the night by devils and their terrifying sounds. They were not content with just disturbing the few hours of sleep that he allowed himself each night, but by actually laying hands on the frail body of the priest, they also demonstrated their frustration over the many converts he was winning for the Church and the many souls who were being reconciled with their Redeemer. On more than one occasion the Saint felt a hand passing over his face or sensations as of rats scampering over his body. Occasionally the devil attempted to throw the Saint from his bed.

The holy Curé was often heard to say that when the assaults on his body were more numerous, they served as a good sign that there would be "a good haul of fish the next day." At other times he would say, "The devil gave me a good shaking last night, we shall have a great number of people tomorrow."[144] The Saint reports that, "He torments me in sundry ways. At times he seizes me by the feet and drags me about the room. It is because I convert souls to the good God."[145] More frightening activities of the devils were their noise makings, which were heard and witnessed by many parishioners. Descriptions of demonic noises can be found in another chapter of this book. (See #90.)

While **St. Anthony Mary Claret** (1807-1870) was staying for a time in Vich, he was not present one morning for breakfast. The people of the house, thinking he was ill, knocked on his door and asked if they could be of help to him. Not accustomed to hearing the Saint complain, they were surprised when he announced, "I have a severe pain in my side." The doctor and surgeon who were called examined the affliction and found a horrible wound in his side, "as if his flesh had been torn by the claws of a wild beast." The wound was so large that it exposed several ribs. St. Anthony Mary never mentioned what caused the wound, but everyone who saw it believed it to have been the work of the devil.

The doctors returned to examine their patient a few days later, noticed that gangrene was about to set in and advised a surgical operation the next day. But the next day when they arrived, their patient answered their knocks with a bright and smiling face. After St. Anthony Mary announced that the Blessed Mother had cured him during the night, the doctors insisted that they examine the wound. To their surprise they found nothing except clear, unblemished skin without the least trace of a scar! The doctors, amazed at their discovery, replied that the healing was not natural, while the others proclaimed it a miracle.[146]

Fr. Paul of Moll (1824-1896), the Flemish Benedictine known as the "Wonder-Worker of the Nineteenth Century," often suffered volleys of blows from the devil, who handled him roughly. The good priest once told a farmer, "The devil lifted me violently from my bed and threw me rudely on the floor." The farmer asked if he were not very frightened by these assaults. Father Paul replied, "What we ought to fear far more is the world where the devils swarm and where the devil reigns supreme."

Many of the assaults inflicted on **Teresa Helena Higginson** (1844-1905) were witnessed, while other attacks were heard from a room adjoining her bedroom. But she herself wrote of these attacks to her confessor. In one letter she wrote, "Whenever our dear good God accepted my poor prayers and little nothings in behalf of poor sinners, he, the devil, used to be infuriated and beat, drag and almost choke me." Another time she wrote that "the reason why the devil used to spit and throw that abominable filth of such awful stench at me was because at that time I resolved to mortify the senses more rigorously."[147]

One of Miss Higginson's friends, a fellow teacher and later a nun, Miss Susan Ryland, once shared rooms with her and witnessed many unusual happenings and attacks made upon this mystic. Miss Ryland tells that often there would be a knock at the door. When Teresa went to open it, she would receive a violent blow on the face from an unseen hand. When Miss Ryland answered the knock, no one was there. On one occasion Miss Higginson returned from having answered the door with a great swelling down one side of her face, which gradually developed into a horrible bruise.[148] There were many times when visitors heard Miss Higginson being thrown about her room, being dragged and her head being knocked violently against a door. At these times they would rush to her room, but she would always reply that it was the devil, who could do them no harm.

Sr. Josefa Menendez (1890-1923), whose cause for beatification has also been introduced, experienced many apparitions of the devil. Eventually he not only appeared to her, but often took hold of her, carrying her off to various parts of the convent, where he repeatedly beat her. Her clothing was even set on fire, which produced wounds that took a long time to heal. Her companions did not see the demon since we read that

> Showers of blows, administered by an invisible fist, fell upon her day and night, especially when she was in prayer. At other times she was violently snatched away from the chapel, or prevented from entering it. Under the very eyes of the superiors, she would suddenly disappear, and after a long search would be found thrown into some loft, or beneath heavy furniture, or in some unfrequented spot. These torments were witnessed by her companions and continued until the Blessed Mother intervened.[149]

Bl. Padre Pio (1887-1968) also frequently contested with the devil, beginning early in his monastic career. In a letter to Padre Agostino dated January 18, 1913, Padre Pio described a diabolical attack in which he heard a devilish noise, but saw nothing. But then a number of demons appeared "in the most abominable form." The Padre wrote, "They hurled themselves upon me, threw me on the floor, struck me violently, and threw pillows, books and chairs through the air and cursed me with exceedingly filthy words." A number of days later Padre Pio again wrote to Padre Agostino: "My body is all bruised because of the many blows that our enemies have rained upon me." Padre Pio even revealed that a number of times the demons snatched away his nightshirt and beat him unmercifully while he was naked and suffering terribly from the cold. He wrote, "Even after they left me, I remained nude for a long time, for I was powerless to move because of the cold. Those evil creatures would have thrown themselves all over me if sweet Jesus hadn't helped me."[150]

Padre Pio endured many attacks from demons, but we will quote just one more, which took place one night while he was praying for the success of an exorcism. The new superior, Padre Carmelo, and Padre Eusebio "heard a crash and, entering Padre Pio's room, found the old man on the floor in a pool of blood. His face was swollen and blood was pouring from his nose and from a deep cut above his eyebrows. There were no signs of forced entry, and nothing in the room was broken or disturbed. However, a pillow that was usually in Padre Pio's armchair was neatly tucked beneath the injured man's bleeding head." As Padre Eusebio went to ring for a doctor, Padre Carmelo asked Padre Pio who had placed the pillow under his head. Weakly, Padre Pio replied, "The Madonna."[151]

Yet another time the Blessed Lady revealed her solicitude for her beloved son. This time, while the devil was speaking through the mouth of a possessed girl, he admitted he had been "to see the old man I hate so much because he is a source of faith. I would have done more, only the White Lady stopped me."[152]

St. Nicholas of Tolentio (1245-1305) suffered such abuse that he was often left half dead. On one occasion he was assaulted so viciously that he was lame to the end of his life.[153] **St. Theodore of Alexandria** (fifth century) was often covered with wounds as the result of the devil's fury. Many other saints have been abused to one degree or another by evil spirits, including: **St. Margaret of Cortona** (1247-1297); **St. Veronica Giuliani** (1660-1727); **Ven. Anne Catherine Emmerich** (1774-1824); **St. Rose of Lima** (1586-1617); **St. Rita of Cascia** (d. 1457); and **Bl. Angela of Foligno** (d. 1309) among many, many others.

90. Noises and Shrieks of the Devils

When devils pester holy persons, they do not do it quietly. Loud noises, cries, shrieks and howls are used as devices to frighten the Saints into curtailing their penances or the good works they were performing for the Church. Oftentimes the devils cause a noisy disturbance to distract the Saints from their prayers or to vent their anger when a soul is snatched away from them and saved for Heaven. Such was the case during the lifetime of **St. Antony of the Desert** (251-356), one of the earliest saints known to be troubled in this manner. It was not only when the hermit was in solitary prayer that these noises were heard, but also when visitors sought him out on the barren hillsides of Kolsim. Few went away without hearing a confusion of terrifying sounds, like the noise of horses and weapons, or as some described it, like a city besieged by hostile armies. The holy hermit suffered not only from these noises, but also from physical attacks of the demons, which are mentioned elsewhere. (See #89.)

St. Antony was assisted in laying the foundation of the cenobitic life by **St. Pacomius** (292-348), who was the first to write its rule. It is said of St. Pacomius that the demons seemed bent on the total destruction of his cell, judging from the noises they produced. At other times they would set fire to his mat, just as they did to the bed of the holy Curé of Ars.

Another early solitary, **St. Hilarion** (d. 372), could not begin his prayers without hearing all about him the barking of invisible dogs, the bellowing of bulls, the hissing of serpents and other strange and terrifying noises. It is said that the possessed cried out in pain at his approach, and miracles followed him wherever he went.

Shrieks and loud howls were the devices used by demons to distract **St. Rita of Cascia** (1386-1457) while she was engaged in prayer and meditation. There was one occasion when a woman who had been possessed by the devil for many years was brought to St. Rita. Having pity for the woman, who had been tormented and cruelly mistreated by the demons, the Saint raised her eyes to Heaven and offered a prayer. Then making the Sign of the Cross on the woman's head, St. Rita immediately liberated the victim. The devil, on leaving the poor woman, is said to have uttered moans and frightful shrieks.[154]

St. Teresa of Avila (1515-1582), who had many encounters with the devil, tells us that many times her sisters heard the sound of heavy blows and voices. We are also told that the devils who viciously attacked **Bl. Anna Maria Taigi** (1769-1837) would howl like wild beasts while knocking on windows and doors and overturning furniture. **Bl. Mary Fortunata Viti** (1827-1922) heard the devil insulting her on many occasions. When her patience and tranquillity defeated him, she would hear the gnashing of teeth and a horrible, bestial growl.

One of the novices of **St. Mary Magdalene de' Pazzi** (1566-1607) recorded what the Saint experienced during the night hours while she was attempting to sleep. "Often during the night we heard someone going about in the dormitory, making a great noise, opening and closing windows, particularly the one that was near the bed of the Mother Mistress [St. Mary Magdalene] . . . And around her bed we heard someone making a din and thumping on the mattress. But she told us not to be afraid, that although it was the devil who was persecuting her, he could do no harm to us. Hence we had no fear, especially since she herself was with us."

Another time, while St. Mary Magdalene was talking in her sleep, one of her novices kept close watch and was listening as she spoke of "wanting to teach my little souls to love Love." The devil too was listening and made his presence known by suddenly opening the nearest window with a loud bang. He began to shake the bed violently and then, as the novice relates, "I was struck so roundly on one of my shoulders that I carried the mark of it for several days." The Saint, however, being jolted awake, reassured the novice not to be afraid, saying, "It is the devil who is chafing with envy. He hates me so much that, if he could, he would cut me to bits, because he does not want me to help my neighbor."[155]

The devil's taunts and abuses heaped upon **St. Paul of the Cross** (1694-1775) took various forms. The founder of the Passionist Order seemed to have been especially hated by the demons, who raged and discharged their fury on his person in order to give him no peace. According to one of his religious, "If the servant of God wished to take a little rest, especially during missions, the room was filled with devils, who woke him in terror by their hisses and other horrible noises, as if there were discharged several pieces of artillery."[156]

St. Anthony Mary Claret (1807-1870), known for his eloquence, his miracles and his mystical gifts, was once giving a mission in the Canary Islands in a church that was overflowing with people drawn by his saintly reputation. Suddenly, everyone was alarmed when subterranean noises were heard. These were followed by cries and howls like an army engaged in deadly combat. Descending the pulpit, the Saint said in a calm voice, "That is nothing. Be calm." As he ascended the pulpit and began the sermon, the devils, always obedient to his commands, remained silent. The people, for their part, felt themselves blessed to be so near a saint who demonstrated in a humble fashion his power over the enemy.[157]

Many times at night the clanking of chains alerted **Bl. André** (Alfred Bessette) (1845-1937) of approaching demons. This holy brother, who is known as the builder of the shrine of St. Joseph in Montreal, Canada, often said he had no fear of the devil and that he had "often beaten him, fighting body to body."[158] Often when he came from his visits to the dying, strange sounds were heard, especially one night when one of his friends was sleeping in a nearby room. The friend reported that he was "awakened by a deafening tumult, like the rattling of chains and the stamping of feet on the floor." Another time, after the brother returned from a wake, he heard a great deal of noise in the refectory: cups, saucers and glasses seemed to be crashing on the floor, but on investigation, everything was in order.[159] The devil seemed always enraged at the works of mercy performed by the holy brother.

In addition to frightful noises and disturbances that plagued **Bl. Mary Fortunata Viti** (1827-1922), a Benedictine lay sister, she also heard the devil speaking to her, calling her a fool, a dunce and similar names. The Blessed once confided to one of the sisters, "The horrible monster bothers me day and night; he is constantly heaping all kinds of derision and mockery upon me and maltreating me, in order to make me impatient; but I defend myself by invoking the Blessed Trinity." The confessor and spiritual director of the community, Msgr. Giovanni Pasqualitti, wrote: "With tears in her eyes, Sister Fortunata would tell me how the devil berated her with the most base and vile expressions. She could not see him, but she could hear his voice. Repeatedly, she perceived how he would order other devils to beat her and molest her in every way. But she did not despair." These insults became more frequent, more intense and more vulgar as the Blessed approached the end of her life. Many of these disturbances were apparently heard by the holy sister alone, since we are told that the sisters with whom she lived seldom knew of the terrible conflicts waged by the evil one, who was defeated by her humility and her obedience to her spiritual director.[160]

The devil attempted to interfere in **Teresa Helena Higginson's** (1844-1905) apostolate by attacking her physically as well as making his presence known by knockings and various noises that were heard by her frightened companions. As one of her companions, Kate Catterall, wrote,

> One night I heard a terrible noise against the wall of Miss Higginson's room nearest the landing which sounded like a loud clap of thunder and seemed as if it would shake the wall down, then a loud knocking as of furniture being broken to pieces on the floor in one

> corner of her room. We were all so terrified that I called out loudly for Miss Higginson, and after a short time she came to us looking deeply troubled. She told us not to be frightened, that it was the devil who had terrified us, that he had told her that he would let us know that he was there, but she did not think we should have heard him.

Kate Catterall continued explaining that another night, as she was in an adjoining room saying her night prayers,

> I distinctly heard blows given with great force, striking Miss Higginson, first on one side of the face and then on the other. I listened for a few seconds when her head was knocked several times on the floor of her room. . . . Then [there were] most terrible and piercing screams and sounds of someone being dragged across the room towards the door and struggling and pushing as if to get out, the screams continuing all the time and ending with a fiendish yell. Then everything seemed quiet and settled.[161]

Other times there were the banging on doors and the loud shaking of windows on a calm night when wind could not be blamed. There were also the moving of furniture when no one was in Miss Higginson's room, loud laughter, weird whisperings, rushing noises as if animals were scurring around, explosions and dreadful rumblings of thunder. In all, what took place with Miss Higginson was very much like that endured by the holy Curé of Ars, St. Jean-Marie-Baptiste Vianney.

91. Devils and Their Odors

If the Saints have been known to emit a heavenly fragrance, known as the odor of sanctity, it seems reasonable that the demons would have an opposing odor, one that is evil-smelling and very repulsive. We read of one such instance when the foul odor of demons was noticed in the life of **St. Teresa of Avila** (1515-1582). St. Teresa had used Holy Water to dismiss some demons. "The next persons to come in, two nuns who may safely be believed, for they would not tell a lie for anything, noticed a very bad smell, like brimstone. I could not detect it myself, but it had remained there long enough for them to have noticed it."[162]

St. Sulpicius Severus in his biography of **St. Martin of Tours** (316-397) tells of the demon who, in order to tempt the Saint, came dressed in royal magnificence and wearing a crown of gold. Declaring in a vain attitude that he was the King of Glory, the Son of God, the demon was nonetheless chased from the room by the Saint, who penetrated the disguise. But the demon retaliated by filling the room with such an unpleasant odor that St. Martin was likewise forced to flee.[163]

We also learn that the Company of Jesus, the Jesuits, during the lifetime of their founder, **St. Ignatius** (1491-1556), established a residence near the sanctuary of Our Lady of Loretto. The demons were enraged that much good was being performed by the priests and endeavored to interfere. The whole house is said to have been infested by these evil spirits, who often frightened the religious, sometimes physically abusing them and presenting illusions of the pleasures of the world to entice them to abandon their vocation. Not only were pleasant illusions presented, but unholy ones as well, with noises that caused many to become understandably frightened. The situation was so bad that the rector found it necessary to walk up and down the halls at night to comfort those who were being annoyed.

All the religious attempted to ignore these events, but one in particular, a Belgian novice, was visited by the devil in the disguise of a dark man clothed in green. When the novice resisted the devil's suggestion that he leave the Company, he made the Sign of the Cross, which caused the devil to become so infuriated that he withdrew, saying: "You won't listen to good advice." He then blew into the novice's face stinking smoke which infected the room and the hall in front of it for two days. "The fetid smell was plainly perceived by the deponent [person deposing] and many others." This event was told by Oliver Manareus, Rector of the College at Loreto, in a solemn deposition made "in the cold blood of mature age."[164]

The biography of **Bl. Mary Fortunata Viti** (1827-1922), a holy lay sister of the Benedictine Order, reveals many instances in which the devil attempted to disturb her prayers and her duties. Seeing that he could not succeed by his annoying activities, he tried inflicting on her a nauseous odor. This took place one day while she was on her way to the chapel to make a visit. Suddenly the passageway became intensely dark, as a dense fog filled the area. "The atmosphere became so acrid that she could scarcely breathe or proceed on her way. Recognizing the phenomenon as a phantom of the evil spirit, she reverently invoked the holy Name of Jesus and confidently made the Sign of the Cross. At once the illusion disappeared."[165]

92. Devils and Fire

We know that devils have expressed their displeasure with the holiness of certain saints and tried to cause confusion and interfere with their labors by setting either real fires or illusions of them. Such a specter took place in the lifetime of **St. Benedict** (480-550), the "father of Western monasticism," who founded the abbey on Monte Cassino. **St. Gregory the Great**, in writing about the miracles of St. Benedict, tells us that when St. Benedict first climbed to the top of Monte Cassino, where a magnificent monastery now stands, he destroyed the temple of Apollo, overthrew the altar, destroyed the idol and converted the temple into chapels of St. Martin and St. John. But the Saint knew that more had to be done to rid the place of the devil, and indicated a certain white marble slab where his fellow monks were to dig. Underneath, they found a bronze idol.

Since the location was near the kitchen, St. Gregory reports that the idol "was thrown into the kitchen for the time being." Another author states that it might have been thrown on top of the sweepings in the corner. St. Gregory continues that, after the next meal was completed and the refectory closed,

> Suddenly there seemed a flame to rise out of it, and, to the sight of all the monks, it appeared that all the kitchen was on fire. As they were casting on water to quench this fire, the man of God, hearing the tumult, came and perceiving that there appeared fire to the eyes of the brethren and not to his [own], he forthwith bowed his head in prayer, and calling upon those whom he saw deluded with an imaginary fire, he bade them sign their eyes that they might behold the kitchen and not those fantastical flames which the enemy had counterfeited.[166]

Another incident of this kind also took place in the lifetime of **St. Cuthbert** (d. 687), who had many mystical gifts, including those of prophecy and healing. We are told about St. Cuthbert by **St. Bede the Venerable** (672-735), who wrote about him in *The Ecclesiastical History of the English Nation.* St. Bede tells us that St. Cuthbert was one day preaching to a large number of people assembled in a certain village when he saw "in the spirit our old enemy coming to retard the work of salvation." To avert a disturbance St. Cuthbert warned the congregation: "Dearest brethren, as often as you hear the mysteries of the heavenly kingdom preached to you, you should listen with attentive heart and with watchful feelings, lest the devil, who has a thousand ways of harming you, prevent you by superfluous cares from hearing the word of salvation." As soon as St. Cuthbert said this, a house nearby caught fire, "so that flakes of fire seemed to fly through the air, and a storm of wind and thunder shook the sky." The people immediately rushed out to extinguish the fire, "yet with all their real water they could not put out the false flames until, at Cuthbert's prayer, the author of the deceit was put to flight and his fictitious fires dispersed along with him." Needless to relate, the people were astonished to see the house unharmed and they asked forgiveness "for their fickleness of mind."[167]

A strange, inexplicable fire was purposely set in the bedroom of the Curé of Ars, **St. Jean-Marie-Baptiste Vianney** (1786-1859), who was often besieged with noises that disturbed the few hours of sleep that were available to him each night. The gutteral voices and noises attributed to the demon were often heard by parishioners, but one event in particular caused a great deal of anxiety and strengthened their conviction that the holy Curé suffered the assaults of Satan.

This event took place in late February of 1857 at seven o'clock in the morning, when the Forty Hours Devotion was being observed in the church. While the Saint was hearing Confessions, a fire broke out in the rectory. The Rev. Alfred Monnin, a young missionary who was temporarily staying at the rectory, rushed to the Curé's room and at once noticed the mysterious character of the fire. He deposed that

> The bed, the canopy, the curtains of the bed, and everything near—everything had been consumed. The fire had only halted in front of the reliquary of St. Philomena, which had been placed on a chest of drawers. From that point it had drawn a line from top to bottom with geometrical accuracy, destroying everything on this side of the holy relic and sparing all on the other. As the fire had started without cause, so it died out in like manner, and it is very remarkable, and in some ways truly miraculous, that the flames had not spread from the heavy serge hangings to the floor of the upper story, which was very low, old, and very dry, and which would have blazed like straw.[168]

The Saint always took the fire and the demon's other rampages as signs of conversions that would take place on the following day. In fact, following the fire, there was an extraordinarily large influx of people into Ars who sought the Saint's confessional.

The noises and bodily attacks endured for thirty-five years, yet the Saint never saw his attacker. The noisy vexations were attested to by many reputable witnesses, who also saw the result of the demon's assault by fire. The burned bed, as well as the Saint's incorrupt body, can still be viewed by those who visit Ars.

St. Martin de Porres (1579-1639) was no stranger to the insidious workings of the devil. Always dismissed by the Saint in one way or another, the devil tried another tactic and visited St. Martin's cell during the silent hours of the night. By order of his superiors, Brother Fulano de Miranda was in the cell while the Saint was absorbed in heavenly contemplation. Suddenly there sounded a terrible noise, accompanied by a violent crash, amid cries and groans of invisible beings. This, of course, startled Brother Fulano, since no one but the two brothers was in the cell, but he soon remembered previous workings of the devil, who resented Brother Martin. Both religious were then subjected to fearful blows that came upon them in the darkness. But this was not all, for a flame flashed suddenly and exploded, filling the cell with fire and smoke. Everything seemed to be ablaze, including the furniture and other articles in the cell. But the fire was not contained, since it gradually worked its way to the adjoining rooms. Brother Fulano attempted to fight his way out of the cell amid flames and suffocating smoke, but Brother Martin remained kneeling, as though unaware of the devil's activities. The Saint calmly reassured Brother Fulano that they were perfectly safe and indicated that while the flames danced about the furniture, nothing had been destroyed. It was all a satanic illusion intended to terrify them and make them revert from their trust in God.

Brother Fulano promptly reported the incident to Father André de Lison, the master of novices, who commented, "Believe me . . . this humble brother is a great saint and one whom you should hold in real veneration. For I am persuaded that in the terrible events of the past night we have witnessed his extraordinary power over the demons, whom he has conquered on this and many other occasions by his invincible holiness—particularly his purity and faith."[169]

An apparition of fire is also noted in the biography of the Servant of God, **Teresa Helena Higginson** (1844-1905). In writing to her spiritual director about the devil's ill treatment, she notes:

> Sometimes he [the devil] cried as though some poor child were out upon the doorstep; sometimes he used to throw me completely out of bed, throw things at me that were in the room, and make awful noises, and I used to be afraid at first that the people of the house would hear. And several times when I awoke, I perceived a smell of something burning and the house being filled with smoke and brimstone; I thought surely the house was on fire. And other times I saw the whole bed and room full of flames and heard the crackling, and I am afraid in this case I proved a coward, for I was frightened more than I can tell at first, for there was no Holy Water: the devil threw something against the bottle and broke it . . . but I thought the house might really be burnt.[170]

The house was not harmed in the least, since the fire was just a phantasm of the devil. A witness to some of these activities of the devil was Susan Ryland, who lived in the same house. With reference to the above incident, she related in a letter to Father Powell that she smelled the thick smoke and often heard the violent attacks made on Miss Higginson by the devil, as well as the diabolical howls and shrieks, plus the thundering of animals in the house.

In her *Autobiography*, **St. Teresa of Avila** (1515-1582) also tells us about her experience with the devil and fire. She writes: "Once when I was in an oratory, he [the devil] appeared . . . Out of his body there seemed to be coming a great flame, which was intensely bright and cast no shadow."[171]

93. Satan and Lourdes

One year before the death of **St. Jean-Marie-Baptiste Vian-**

ney, the Curé of Ars (1786-1859) whose painful contacts with the devil are mentioned later, the Blessed Virgin appeared to **St. Bernadette Soubirous**, the first appearance taking place on February 11, 1858. The events at Lourdes are well known and need not be repeated here. What might be new to many are the false visions that took place soon after the last of St. Bernadette's eighteen visions. The devil, who had so recently been active at Ars, also became active at Lourdes in trying to discredit the visions of St. Bernadette. There were so many false visionaries cropping up—after the true visions were over—that the entire episode is known as an "infestation."

According to a reporter, J.-B. Estrade, who followed the events, the first alert as to demonic activity took place during one of Bernadette's visions when noises seemed to rise from the Gave River. There were sounds that seemed like a conversation taking place, also like the voices of a crowd in disagreement. Then one voice shouted, "Flee! Flee!" Bernadette revealed that the noises were quieted when the beautiful Lady in White looked toward the sounds with queenly authority.

Many authors, in writing about the events at Lourdes, neglect to mention the numerous recorded incidents of the false visionaries which demonstrate without question the activity of the demons, who instigated activities in front of the Grotto, in areas close by and even on the roads leading to Lourdes. Of the many "visionaries" we will mention only a few.

Msgr. Léon Cristiani remarks that in all the examples of these false visions, "They never occurred in the exact place where Bernadette had seen the Blessed Virgin and heard her name from her own mouth. Some invisible protection seemed to encircle the spot and also the person of Bernadette herself. Whereas she always remained completely 'natural,' that is, just what she was, very simple, very modest, very ignorant, but totally sincere and upright, other characteristics are to be found among these new visionaries."[172]

One of the first was Madeleine Cazaux, "forty-five years old, married, but of bad reputation and addicted to drink." She describes her "visions" in this way: "I saw something on the white stone, about the size of a ten-year-old girl: over her head she had a white veil, which fell to her shoulder, her hair was long and covered her breast. Every time the candle was moved the figure disappeared."[173] Another early "visionary" was Honorine Lacroix, over forty years old and a prostitute. Her description was almost similar to that of Madeleine Cazaux, except that the young girl in her vision was about four years of age with blue eyes and blond hair. The mayor of Lourdes, M. Lacadé, had a servant girl who was seized with convulsions as she was reciting the Rosary in front of the altar in the Grotto. Another woman was declared a false visionary when she was restrained from throwing herself in the Gave River .

In addition to the mayor and local clergy, who kept a record of these activities, Rev. L. J. M. Cros, S.J., after a thorough investigation, wrote a history of Our Lady of Lourdes in which he reported the facts concerning these false "visionaries." According to his report, many credible witnesses saw youthful "visionaries" at the Grotto who accepted the bouquets of flowers offered by pilgrims and plucked out of them all the lilies or roses, claiming, "The Virgin wants neither lilies nor roses." Other "visionaries" held rosaries, but not blessed ones. The priest reports, "They had a horror of rosaries which had been blessed, and wanted only new and unblessed rosaries. No object that had been blessed was returned by them if put into their hands." They held unblessed rosaries in front of their faces with the crucifix swinging at their eye level. These children would "run about in every direction, bent almost double, making strange faces and noises, like young dogs braying at their prey."[174] One evening another "visionary" cried out, "All of you are to recite a Rosary: the Lord is going to recite the Rosary," a thing unheard of, since Jesus would never say, "Pray for us sinners now and at the hour of our death" and other such petitions of the Rosary that pertain only to His children.

The Abbé Pène from a nearby village declared that a "visionary" of his parish told him of her experiences, but "I paid little attention, considering that it was nothing but a trick of the devil, designed to cast a shadow on the earlier appearances." Another religious, Brother Leobard, who was in charge of the Lourdes schools, declared: "The devil prompted the appearance of a host of visionaries, who indulged in the wildest extravagances. Yes, there is every reason to believe that many of them did see something, the evil one, in various guises."[175]

Another credible witness, Jean Domingieux, one day saw a "visionary" standing in front of the Grotto shouting to the crowd, "Bring out your rosaries. I shall bless them for you." Many in the crowd foolishly brought out their rosaries, which the "visionary" sprinkled with water from the Grotto.

The gamekeeper, Callet, reported: "One day I followed the visionary Barraou as far as the mill. He went into a bedroom and started climbing up the curtains of the bed, with hideous grimaces. He was grinding or gnashing his teeth, and his eyes had a wild look." Mme. Prat said: "Once I was present when Minino was having a vision: he was braying, and his face was so terrible that I could not bear to look at it."[176] One day, Canon Ribes, the director of the Grand Seminary of Tarbes, just north of Lourdes, visited Bernadette with his friend, another priest. They then went to the Grotto, where they found a young boy who was in the midst of a profound experience. Canon Ribes reports, "His features were contracted and repellent. My companion shouted to him: 'Get out of there! You are doing the devil's work!' The child, pretending not to hear, continued to move forward: 'Get out of there!' my companion thundered at him, 'Go, or the hand of God will strike you!' Immediately, the visionary extinguished his little candle, climbed over the barricade and disappeared."[177]

There were even two children from the village of Ossen who claimed to have visions. The Curé of Ségus, in reporting to ecclesiastical authorities, said that "For some considerable time they were, so to say, pursued and obsessed by the 'Vision.' They ran after her in the streets and into houses as if they were on a hunt. Their cries were often more like howls and their movements awkward and ungainly: more often than not, people were shocked by their disorderly and unseemly conduct. The parents, taking an innocent pride in the belief that their sons were seeing the Blessed Virgin, were partly responsible for failing to terminate these regrettable scenes."[178]

It seems that in almost all the cases mentioned above the "visionaries" were followed by crowds who were full of admiration, who marveled at what took place and who professed belief in the occurrences. Their approbation only encouraged others to fake celestial visions. Others who were shocked by many of the details of these false visions no longer believed even in the visions of Bernadette.

During the height of these activities, the Curé of Lourdes was obliged to preach a solemn sermon in which he appealed to the parents to prevent their children from participating in such activities. The Bishop of Tarbes, Msgr. Laurence, in attempting to ignore these happenings, thinking they would stop if not given Church recognition, was at last appealed to by M. Rouland, the Minister of Rites. The Bishop answered the appeal. In his letter he advanced the opinion that two of the boys, Lacaze and Pomies, were "suffering from an affliction of the nerves . . . and should they say or do unseemly things, they must be scolded and treated with severity."[179] He also forbade children under the age of fifteen from going to the Grotto and prohibited the others from communicating with the visionaries. After studying the matter carefully, the Bishop signed an order convoking a commission of enquiry into the Lourdes visions and mentioned only one name, that of Bernadette Soubirous. Fr. Cros, who had carefully studied the happenings, was convinced that Satan was behind them; for there was a similarity, a strategy in the false visions and their bizarre characteristics. "For Satan cannot fail to sign his own handiwork."

* * *

What frightens devils and drives them away

When the Saints were tempted or when suffering the various diabolical torments inflicted upon them, they used various means to force the devil to retreat. Here are some of the methods used by these courageous souls.

94. The Sign of the Cross

St. Martin de Porres (1579-1639) was one day climbing the stairs to the infirmary, carrying in one hand a brazier of burning coals and in the other some medical supplies, when halfway up the stairs a devilish monster appeared before him. The livid eyes and horrible form of the apparition easily betrayed the devil. When the Saint asked what he was doing there, the devil replied that he had hoped to destroy a human soul. St. Martin removed his belt and proceeded to drive the devil away with fierce blows, but was only successful in making the evil one retreat a short distance. He then took one of the burning coals and formed a huge Cross on the wall. The tempter fled at the sign of the Redemption. The Saint's biographer reports that on the following day Martin placed a wooden cross at the scene of the encounter, "and with his usual practical sense saw to it that a light was always burning on the staircase in the future."[180]

Apparitions and loud howls by the devil were often used to distract **St. Rita of Cascia** (1381-1457) while she was engaged in prayer and meditation. All of these attempts she quickly dismissed with the Sign of the Cross. On one occasion, a woman who had been possessed by the devil for many years was brought to St. Rita. Having pity for the woman, who had been tormented and cruelly mistreated by the demons, the Saint raised her eyes to Heaven and offered a prayer. Then making the Sign of the Cross on the woman's head, she immediately liberated the victim. The devil, on leaving the poor woman, is said to have uttered moans and frightful shrieks.[181]

Above: Our Lord commands, "Begone, Satan!" after the temptation in the desert, and the devil is forced to flee in shame.
Below: St. Benedict uses his abbatial staff to knock the demon out of a disobedient brother.

Top row, left: Until St. Benedict rebuked him, the devil sat on a stone needed for construction of Monte Cassino. *Top row, right:* The demon inhabiting an idol that had been cast into a stove causes the monks to see imaginary fire coming from the kitchen. *Remaining rows:* St. Benedict warns a monk that the devil is near; the monk is killed when the devil knocks a wall over on him. The brothers carry the dead monk to St. Benedict, who restores the brother to life.

In this startling depiction of two devils tempting St. Mary Magdalene de' Pazzi, evil masquerades as good. The two devils have only their cloven hooves and forked tails—visible from the rear—to give them away.

Souls experience severe torments as they are dragged into the fires of Hell in which they will burn for all eternity.

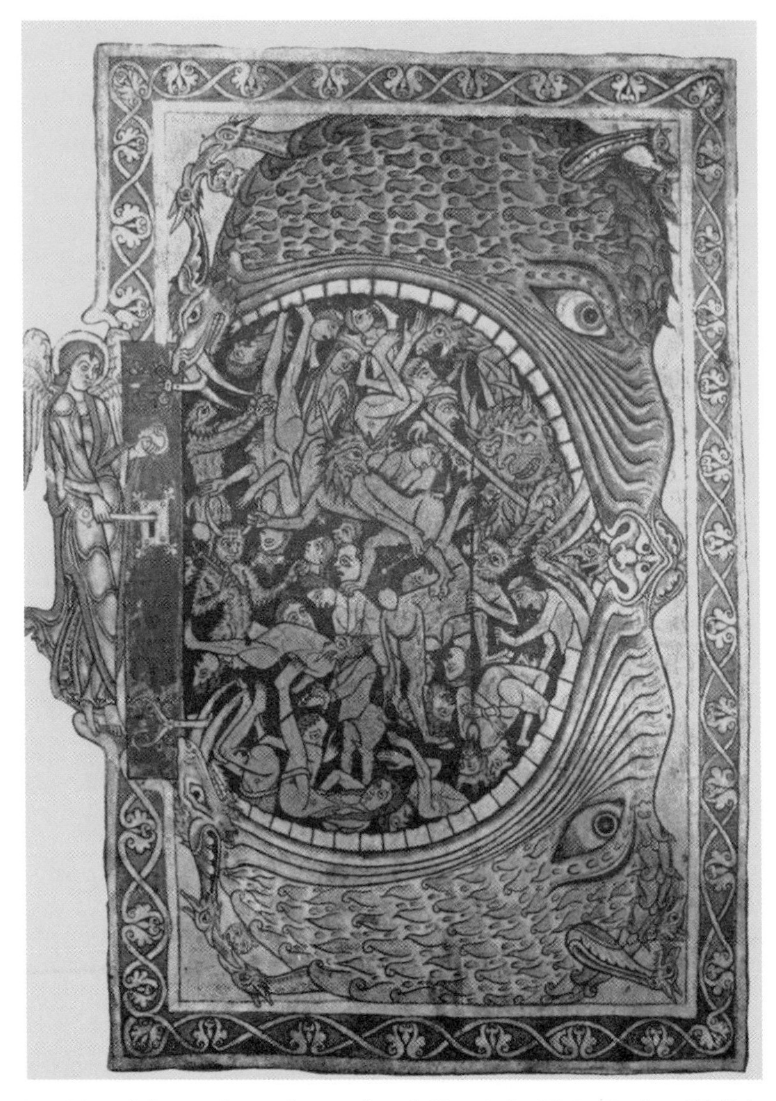

In this miniature from the medieval *Henri de Blois Psalter,* Hell is depicted as a cavernous mouth stuffed with unrepentant souls and malicious devils. The holy angel of God shuts the door and locks it, consigning the damned men and demons to a cramped, chaotic, dark and violent Hell for all eternity.

Art Resource: New York

This 13th-century French representation shows the inhabitants of Hell devouring each other in mutual hatred.

Although the red dragon described in chapter 12 of *The Apocalypse* attempted to devour the woman and her Child, he failed, for "her son was taken up to God and to his throne. And the woman fled into the wilderness, where she had a place prepared by God...." (*Apoc.* 12:5-6).

Angels surround the Blessed Virgin Mary, Queen of Angels, who, as the Immaculate Conception and Mother of the Saviour, triumphantly crushes the head of Satan.

St. Michael the Archangel is depicted holding a pair of scales in his hand while calmly subduing the devil, who is trying to tip the scale against one of the souls therein. In the sky above, good angels battle the bad angels, who are cast out of Heaven.

The Curé of Ars, **St. Jean-Marie-Baptiste Vianney** (1786-1859), was asked one time by his confessor how he repelled the attacks of the demons. The Saint replied, "I turn to God; I make the Sign of the Cross; I address a few contemptuous words to the devil." And then he added, "I have noticed, moreover, that the tumult is greater and the assaults more numerous if, on the following day, some big sinner is due to come to the confessional."

Bl. Mary Fortunata Viti (1827-1922), a humble lay sister of the Benedictine Order, often invoked the holy names of Jesus and Mary to dispel the demons. She was once heard to pray: "Accursed hellish serpent, depart from me forever, in the name of the Most Holy Trinity, and of the Immaculate Mother of God who crushed your rebellious head." At other times she invoked the name of Jesus and confidently made the Sign of the Cross. She once told her companion that she often defended herself by simply invoking the name of the Holy Trinity, which was most effective.

St. Alphonsus Liguori (1696-1787) had the following method of dismissing demons who were annoying him: With great authority he would make a great Sign of the Cross and then order the demons to prostrate themselves and to adore this sign of the Redemption. He would then add these words from Scripture: "That in the name of Jesus every knee should bow, of those that are in heaven, on earth, and under the earth." (*Phil.* 2:10). The Saint declared "that the devils have not the patience to endure such words and take to flight."[182]

95. The Holy Rosary

The Holy Rosary was used on two different occasions by **St. Paul of the Cross** (1694-1775) to free soldiers from the torments of the devil. In once instance a soldier was in his quarters when the devil started dragging him around. The Saint, who heard the noises and ran to investigate, immediately detected the devil and ordered him to leave, while placing the holy rosary around the soldier's neck. The frightened soldier confessed his sins that night and was enormously grateful for being delivered.[183]

Another soldier was already in the confessional when he was suddenly seized and dragged backward by an invisible power. Because he held tightly to the confessional, the confessional with the priest still in it was almost dragged along with the soldier. St. Paul was quickly notified and rushed to the scene where the witnesses, the penitent and the confessor were trembling with fear. After placing a rosary around the soldier's neck and after placing his own mantle over the soldier, the Saint took the penitent to the sacristy, where he heard his Confession and released him from his sins.[184]

Sr. Josefa Menendez (1890-1923) once saw the demon standing in front of her to prevent her passing, and he even tried to throw himself upon her. Although thoroughly frightened, Sr. Josefa held up her rosary stretched out before her and went her way.

We learn in the biography of the humble priest of Troyes, **Père Lamy** (1885-1931), that he was often granted visions of the Blessed Mother, many saints and angels, and even the devil himself. We know that the Blessed Virgin is mistress over the devil and that "He hates the priests, the representatives of Jesus Christ." The devil once told Père Lamy, "Give up praying and I will give up bothering you." The good priest also tells us that the recitation of the Holy Rosary is what "knocks Lucifer flat." He is the sworn enemy of the Rosary. This is the reason why many saints have told us to recite the Rosary often and to carry it with us.[185]

96. Holy Water

St. Teresa of Avila (1515-1582) also gives us advice on how to rid ourselves of the devil's annoyances: "From long experience I have learned that there is nothing like Holy Water to put devils to flight and prevent them from coming back again.

They also flee from the Cross, but return; so Holy Water must have great virtue."[186] This saint gives us an example of Holy Water's effectiveness. One night, she reports, "I thought the evil spirits would have suffocated me, and when the sisters threw much Holy Water about, I saw a great troop of them rush away as if tumbling over a precipice."[187] St. Teresa adds that she was tormented so often that later on she was little afraid of devils, "because I see they cannot stir without Our Lord's permission."

When **Bl. Anna Maria Taigi** (1769-1837) was being viciously attacked by the devil, Msgr. Natali, who lodged in an apartment upstairs in the Blessed's house, was one time awakened by the noise of the attack. He quickly threw on his stole, grabbed a bottle of Holy Water and rushed downstairs. He found Anna Maria on the floor covered with blood. After he sprinkled the room with the Holy Water, she was able to get up and resume her prayers.[188]

Tanquerey surmises that Holy Water makes the devil flee "because of the humiliation Satan must suffer at seeing himself baffled by such a simple device."[189]

97. Relics

The most important relic of all that would cause the greatest distress to the devil would be that of the True Cross—the instrument of our salvation. But other relics have also been effective.

We learn that **St. Lydwine of Schiedam** (1380-1433), in addition to her many frightful wounds, wore a rough belt of horse-hair as a penitential instrument. It usually encircled her body, but at her death it was found neatly folded on her bed near her shoulder. Jan Brugman, a lay brother of the Observance who was close to the Saint, tells that he was familiar with the cincture's perfume, and "I affirm, having made use of it in exorcism, that it revealed an irresistible power against demons."

Michel d'Esne reports, "As for me, I have taken it in my own hands and know by experience that devils have a great horror and fear of it."[190]

St. Jean-Marie-Baptiste Vianney, the Curé of Ars (1786-1859), was often called upon to perform exorcisms, which he accomplished in a short time with holy water or a blessing. But, according to Abbé Tailhades, the holy priest was also known to "always carry in his pocket a large silver reliquary containing several relics of the Passion and those of a few saints."[191]

St. Ignatius Loyola (1491-1556) was not in the least afraid of the demons who tormented him; in fact, it is said that the demons were afraid of him. During his lifetime, devils who were possessing people would cry out upon mention of the Saint's name, "Ignatius is my greatest enemy!" One of his biographers reports that "The devil is not to be believed when he speaks of himself, but he is trustworthy in what God forces him to say for the glory of His Saints." After the death of St. Ignatius, his followers experienced great power in dealing with the possessed by using pictures of the Saint or his relics.[192]

98. The Blessed Sacrament

In *The Mystical City of God,* Our Lady tells **Ven. Mary of Agreda** (1602-1665) that:

> Lucifer and his demons have such a fear of the most Holy Eucharist, that to approach it causes them more torments than to remain in Hell itself. Although they do enter churches in order to tempt souls, they enter them with aversion, forcing themselves to endure cruel pains in the hope of destroying a soul and drawing it into sin, especially in holy places and in the presence of the Holy Eucharist. Nothing except their furious hatred of the Lord and against souls could ever induce them to expose themselves to

> the torments of His real sacramental presence . . . Whenever He is carried through the streets [as in processions], they usually fly and disperse in all haste, and they would not dare to approach those that accompany Him, if by their long experience they did not know that they will induce some to forget the reverence due to their Lord.[193]

99. Warnings and Advice of St. Teresa of Avila

St. Teresa of Avila (1515-1582), in the *Interior Castle*, offers insight to us regarding the wiles of the devil:

> If the soul invariably followed the will of God, it is clear that it would not be lost. But the devil comes with his artful wiles and, under color of doing good, sets about undermining it in trivial ways, and involving it in practices which, so he gives it to understand, are not wrong; little by little he darkens its understanding, and weakens its will, and causes its self-love to increase, until in one way or another he begins to withdraw it from the love of God and to persuade it to indulge its own wishes . . . . there is no enclosure so strictly guarded that he cannot enter it, and no desert so solitary that he cannot visit it. And I would make one further remark—namely, that the reason the Lord permits this may possibly be so that He may observe the behavior of the soul which He wishes to set up as a light to others; for, if it is going to be a failure, it is better that it should be so at the outset than when it can do many souls harm.[194]

The Saint then gives her recommendations to the soul on how to combat against the temptations of the devil. The first recommendation is to practice humble and confident prayer to secure the help of God and His holy angels. As Tanquerey states, "Our prayer must be humble, for there is nothing that so quickly puts to flight this rebellious spirit, who, having revolted through pride, never knew the virtue of humility." St. Teresa also recommends that our prayer for God's help must be full of confidence, since God's own glory is bound up with our triumph.

Secondly, as exemplified in the previously mentioned events in the lives of the Saints, it is recommended that we use with all confidence the Sacraments and the Sacramentals of the Church. Among the Sacramentals, as we have noted, St. Teresa has suggested the frequent use of holy water. St. Teresa also recommends utter contempt of the devil. She reports: "So often have these accursed creatures tormented me and so little am I afraid of them, now that I see they cannot stir unless the Lord allows them to . . . Every time we pay little heed to them, they lose much of their power and the soul gains much more control over them."[195] She reports that the soul who suffers temptations should also resort to the intercession of St. Michael and his own guardian angel. Above all, such a one should appeal to the Blessed Virgin, who is always anxious to comfort and assist her distressed children in times of great danger.

100. Possession

When the proper Church authorities have determined beyond a reasonable doubt that the unusual activities and symptoms of a suspected possessed person are not attributable to mental distress, psycho-neurosis, nervous disorders or physical disease, possession by a demon is then considered. The Jesuit theologian, Louis Moden, suggests that one must have recourse to that "discernment of spirits which the Church has practiced throughout the centuries with spiritual care and a quiet tactfulness."[196] He likewise states that according to the doctrine of the discernment of spirits, anxiety, uneasiness and confusion are Satan's favorite weapons.[197]

As mentioned earlier, the devil, in taking possession of a person, enters the body, but he does not unite *with* the body in the same manner as the soul does, nor does he enter into the soul itself. As Tanquerey explains, he can indeed act directly on the bodily members and cause them to perform all sorts of motions, and indirectly he can move the faculties of the soul in so far as they depend for their operations upon the body.[198]

In a true possession, the victim might assume a gutteral voice, sometimes growling, ranting, screaming, baying, and if more than one demon is present, using distinctively different voices. He might moan, yelp helplessly or howl, as would a pack of beasts. The victim might even levitate and soar bodily about the room and perform feats of agility that are beyond the scope of nature. The victim might be thrown about and dragged, producing wounds and bruises. Before the exorcism begins, the victim, if brought into church, might probably scream, curse, laugh diabolically and blaspheme at the Holy Eucharist reserved in the Tabernacle. Holy Water sprinkled on him or a holy relic placed on him might cause a burning sensation, so that the victim screeches in pain, "You are burning me."

The victim might even froth at the mouth, spit, and vomit "unmentionable excrements," as did a poor victim at Piacenza in 1920. After her successful exorcism, "a little ball of salt pork, about the size of a nut, with seven horns, was found in the matter." The unusual aspect of the regurgitated matter in this case was that, when lifted up with a stick, it spread out as one piece of beautiful, colorful cloth.[199]

Terrible facial expressions, unusual strength, contortions and physical gymnastics might also be evident, as in the case of two boys at Illfurth, Germany, who were possessed between 1864 and 1869. It is reported that if the boys were sleeping on their backs, they would turn over and over at an incredible speed, like living tops.

The victim might also demonstrate a knowledge of foreign languages which were unknown to the possessed while in a normal state. He might also possess a knowledge not in keeping with his age, social condition or education and might even be aware of distant events and the hidden sins and secrets of those around him. Such was the case when Antoine Gay (1790-1871) was being exorcized. Dr. Pictet issued a medical certificate on November 12, 1843 which stated that, "During our first interview with Antoine Gay, that extraordinary thing which speaks through his mouth revealed the inmost secrets of our heart, told us the story of our life from the age of twelve onwards, giving details that are known only to God, our confessor and ourselves."[200]

During the exorcism of a young girl, Claire-Germaine Cèle of Natal, who was possessed in 1906 and 1907, another symptom of possession was noted when the demon would inflate her chest or stomach to enormous proportions. Her head sometimes appeared grotesquely swollen, with her cheeks inflated. Her neck would lengthen, and a goiter would appear. Most unusual of all is that a lump would sometimes form under the skin and travel throughout her body.

Tanquerey explains that there are two distinct states in a case of diabolical possession: the crisis and the period of calm. During the crisis the devil manifests his hatred and control over the body by imparting a feverish agitation, which produces contortions, outbursts of fury and blasphemous utterances, as previously mentioned. The victim loses consciousness and seems to lose all sense of what takes place within him. He retains no memory of what he says or does, or rather, of what the devil says or does *through* him. It is only at the beginning of the crisis that he is aware of the invasion of the evil one.[201] During the period of calm and quiet, it seems as though the devil has departed, although sometimes the victim develops a chronic infirmity, which doctors cannot diagnose or cure.

According to the *Roman Ritual,* in the section entitled *De Exorcizandis Obsessis a Daemonio,* which gives the Church's official pronouncement on the subject, there are three principal signs by which possession may be recognized, some of which have already been noted.

The *first sign* is that of speaking a language previously unknown to the subject. According to the *Roman Ritual*, it should be determined if such a language had been learned previously, or if the subject were reciting a few phrases that were memorized. It has also been noted that some subjects can translate perfectly a language previously unknown to them.

The *second indication* of possession is the knowledge of hidden matters. Once again the *Ritual* recommends that all care should be taken to learn if the subject was aware of distant and hidden matters by some natural means, such as a letter, or if perhaps the person had overheard these things. There might also be predictions of future events. A reasonable time should elapse to learn if the predictions take place as foretold. Vague predictions should not be considered.

The *third sign* according to the *Ritual* by which one may determine if the person is possessed is whether the subject exhibits a strength out of all proportion to his age and circumstances. Discounting the excitement caused by a nervous reaction in which energies are notably increased, this unnatural strength is such that many people are required to constrain the subject while he is struggling violently.[202]

It is comforting to note that possession does not usually afflict those who are practicing their religion—who are going to the Sacraments, wearing medals and using the Sacramentals—and especially those who are striving earnestly after perfection.[203]

101. The Devil and the Exorcist

The most successful exorcist of all, although that word is never used in Scripture, was Jesus Christ, who with only one command, dismissed the devils from possessed persons. Numerous examples of this are given,[204] with one spectacular exorcism being reported by three of the evangelists: *Matthew*, *Mark* and *Luke*.[205] This exorcism involved forcing a great many demons from one individual.

According to the Evangelists, Our Lord and His companions disembarked in the country of the Gerasens. Immediately there came to Him from out of the tombs a man with an unclean spirit. No man could hold him, it is said, not even with chains, since he burst them apart and broke the fetters in pieces. He spent his time among the monuments and in the mountains, crying and cutting himself with stones. But seeing Jesus in the distance, he ran and adored Him, saying in a loud voice: "What have I to do with thee, Jesus, the Son of the most high God? I adjure thee by God that thou torment me not." Jesus then asked,"What is thy name?" To this the voice answered, "My name is Legion, for we are many." The voice then petitioned Jesus to "send us into the swine [which were feeding nearby], that we may enter into them." After Jesus gave them leave, they entered the swine, "and the herd with great violence was carried headlong into the sea, being about two thousand, and were stifled in the sea." (*Mark* 5:1-13).

This question of Our Lord, "What is thy name?" is also recommended by the *Roman Ritual* to exorcists, since they must know with whom they are dealing: one demon or a legion. Names such as "Isabô," "Oripas," "Zolalethiel," "Isacaron" and "Asmodeus" might be heard coming from the possessed person. These names were actually given by demons during various exorcisms.

But first, before the exorcism even takes place, the *Ritual* recommends certain procedures and gives a number of wise counsels. (It is understood, of course, that no exorcism should be undertaken without the explicit permission of the local bishop, and then only by the priests he appoints.)

The first of these is that the exorcist should make a humble and sincere Confession, so that the devil may not be able to accuse him of sin. Earnest prayer and fasting should be part of the preparation, since Jesus Himself recommended it. One will remember that the Apostles, being unsuccessful in dismissing a devil, asked, "Why could not we cast him out?" To which Jesus replied, "This kind can go out by nothing, but by prayer and fasting." (*Mark* 9:27-28). The second counsel is that the possessed should be removed from the building in which the activities have occurred. A church or chapel is recommended. Another recommendation is that the exorcist should never be alone with the possessed. The witnesses, who should be few in number, should be serious and devout; if the possessed be a woman, the witnessing "matrons should be of tried prudence and virtue." The exorcist must not permit these witnesses to ask questions of the spirits, but should advise them to pray humbly and earnestly with him. Still another recommendation—but this one given to the exorcist by **St. Ignatius Loyola** and **St. Francis Xavier**—is that "showing a timid heart before the devil is strongly to be guarded against."

After recitation of the prescribed prayers, the exorcist should ask the energumen (the possessed person) a number of important questions and must do so authoritatively, because they are actually being addressed to the devil in the name of the Church of Jesus Christ. These questions should be limited to those recommended by the *Ritual*. He should ask about the number of spirits present and about the time and motives of their invasion. He also should ask what will be the time of their departure and the signs they will give at their leaving. The exorcist should also threaten to increase their torture in proportion to their resistance to leaving.

The exorcist should also redouble those prayers and activities that seem to irritate the possessing spirits. These should include invocations of the Holy Names of Jesus and Mary, making of the Sign of the Cross and sprinkling with Holy Water. He should force the possessed, if this is possible, to genuflect or bow before the Blessed Sacrament or the crucifix, or to reverence a holy relic. The exorcist is warned in the *Ritual* that he should be careful to avoid useless words, idle questions, and above all, attempts at humor. If the spirit should give sarcastic or ridiculous answers or speak at random, the exorcist should impose silence with authority and dignity.

The exorcist, in spite of his authority, should not commit the devil to go to a specific place, but he should leave this to Divine Justice. The exorcism should be conducted for several hours each day, even for days or months, until deliverance is effected, and the exorcist should allow himself proper times for rest. When the spirit or spirits finally leave the possessed person, the exorcist should beg God to forbid the devil ever to re-enter the body he has just left. The exorcist should thank God and exhort the person to avoid all sin in order not to fall again under the power of the devil.[206]

It is interesting to note that the Church officially established the office of exorcist in the third century, even though, of course, the Apostles themselves and all their disciples and followers in the priesthood performed the office of exorcist before that. And there is evidence that even in pre-Christian times professional "exorcists" existed among the ancient Babylonians, Egyptians and Greeks, showing that even the pagans recognized the existence of diabolical possession and made attempts to combat it. The Church's Sacrament of Baptism, as well as the blessing of Holy Oils and Holy Water, include exorcism prayers, asking God for protection from attacks of the devil.

Reference to exorcists can be found as early as the year 251 in the letters of Pope St. Cornelius (d. 253), but the first evidence of an *official rite* of exorcism dates from 1523. This was revised in 1614. But now there is a new 84-page rite, *De Exorcismis et Supplicationibus Quibusdam* (Of Exorcisms and Certain Supplications), approved by Pope John Paul II and issued in January 1999. The 1614 version, however, can still be used at the discretion of the exorcist. The issuance of the new rite is said to reaffirm the existence of the devil and the validity of exorcism, since the secular world in general seems to have relaxed its belief in all things spiritual.

102. The Earling, Iowa Case

It is said that no case of possession has been so thoroughly documented as was a case involving Anna Ecklund—the fictitious name that was given the energumen of the Earling, Iowa case for reasons of privacy. This exorcism began on September 1, 1928 when the possessed was 40 years of age. She was removed from her home and taken to Earling by train. It is said that during the journey she produced a great deal of difficulty for the train crew, who had been warned about her "fits." Upon her arrival, she was taken to the convent of the Franciscan Sisters where the nuns, two at a time, took turns in witnessing and helping whenever needed. Two priests were involved in the case, Fr. Joseph Steiger, the parish priest of Earling, and the exorcist, Rev.

Theophilus Riesinger, O.F.M. Cap., a man in his late 50's.

The possessed had been troubled by demons since the age of 14 and had already been examined by neurologists and psychiatrists, who pronounced her normal. Still, she was troubled by unbelievable lusts, so distasteful to her that she wanted to hang herself. When she married, her condition worsened and was so bad that each time she forced herself to go to Confession, she had an almost uncontrollable urge to strangle the confessor. Another symptom for this woman, who had only an eighth-grade education, was her understanding of foreign languages, especially Latin.

The Bishop had been alerted about Anna's condition as far back as 1902, the year in which the possession first took place. Since then, every pastor of her home town had added to the record, until the Bishop was forced to admit diabolical possession and authorized Fr. Theophilus to conduct the exorcism rites of the Church.

When the exorcist first encountered the woman, she was lying on a bed, her dress secured about her to prevent a repetition of an occurrence the day before. Around her the sisters were praying. This exorcism, which began in secret, became known when the howls and loud voices of the demons alerted people in the area. Soon every parish was petitioned to offer prayers for the success of the exorcism.

After the Sign of the Cross, the Litany of the Saints began. At this, the subject began to growl. It should be noted that never once throughout the long exorcism did her tongue or lips move when words came forth. It also became the practice for Anna to lapse into a coma each morning when the prayers began. She would regain consciousness only when the priest had finished for the day. She was also unaware of everything that had taken place.

At one point during the early part of the Litany, Anna actually rose in the air and seemed to attach herself to the ceiling. Fr. Theophilus restored order among the terrified nuns and ordered her to be brought down, which was accomplished with the greatest difficulty. The prayers of exorcism were met with roars, moaning, yelping and convulsive movements. Finally, Anna's body bloated, until two nursing sisters felt she would rupture. When the priest, according to the *Roman Ritual,* asked in the name of Jesus if there were one or more spirits involved, a voice answered, "There are many!"

In the presence of the Blessed Sacrament, which the exorcist wore in a pyx around his neck, the demons barked, howled mournfully, bellowed and moaned. The possessed woman began to froth at the mouth, to spit and vomit. It was finally learned, with great difficulty, that the first demon had been of the seraphic choir. When asked why the woman was possessed, the devil admitted that her own father, Jacob, had invited them to enter into her and that he, the father, was one of the possessing demons. Another demon was identified as none other than Judas Iscariot, the former Apostle. This admission was given with a "horribly prolonged moaning." Since the devil is the "Father of Lies," this identification might be pure symbolism, according to Fr. A. Poulain, S.J., who notes that the demons occasionally assume the names of historic characters. Another demon was identified as Mina, who had engaged in illicit contacts with the woman's father. She also admitted that she had been a Catholic and that she had killed four "little ones," although she did not give other details.

Then, noticing a different voice, the priest insisted on an identification. It was Jacob, the girl's father, who admitted that he had cursed Anna in her hearing and willed the devils in Hell to enter into her when she was fourteen because she repeatedly refused to commit incest with him. Jacob at times expressed his hatred of his daughter, growling and whining in torment.

Realizing that days were passing without success, the good priest, who had been praying from dawn to dusk, now began to pray day and night with only brief periods of rest. Prayers from the *Ritual* were repeated, sprinklings with Holy Water and blessings with the crucifix were made. All the while the demons pleaded to be left alone, explaining that while they were of Hell, they were not literally in it and that it was a tremendous relief to be able to roam the earth.

Father Theophilus' strategy worked, since the voices diminished somewhat. A period of calm was experienced. Then the good priest commanded that the demons give a sign of their leave-taking. It was nine o'clock in the evening, September 23, 1928. The possessed suddenly stood upright on the bed. The priest ordered the demons to depart as he called on the names of Almighty God, the Crucified Jesus, the Blessed Virgin and the Archangel Michael. Then came the moan of many voices which sounded as from a distance. Anna Ecklund collapsed upon the bed and fell into a deep slumber, but before doing so, she uttered a fervent, "God bless you." The nuns in the room began to weep, even though they detected a vile odor that filled the room. This the good priest identified as the parting sign.

The exorcism had lasted exactly 23 days. Anna returned home and lived in peace. Everyone who knew her protected her identity and the place of her residence so that she lived a trouble-free life in the arms of the Church. A summary of the exorcism was written and received the Imprimatur of the Most Reverend Joseph F. Busch, Bishop of St. Cloud, Minnesota, a thing unprecedented, since other exorcisms have been only mentioned and not made as public as was this of Earling, Iowa.[207]

103. Another Case of Possession

A book entitled *The Exorcist* by William Peter Blatty that was published in 1971 was based on a factual case. However, it did not involve a young girl, as depicted in the book and in the movie of the same name, but concerned a fourteen-year-old boy. The place was Mt. Ranier, Maryland, a suburb of Washington, D.C. The house where the family lived was demolished and is now a playground, but it retains the title "The Devil's Lot."

It was January of 1949 when the boy's bed started jumping in the night and dresser drawers inexplicably opened of their own accord. The parents at first thought the problem somehow involved the boy's favorite aunt in St. Louis who had recently died. When the activities continued and were accompanied by the boy's writhings and abnormal behavior, a Protestant minister was called to offer prayers of exorcism. Because he was unable to quiet the situation, a Catholic priest was called into the case.

The first exorcist was a 29-year-old priest who began the prayers according to the rite in the *Roman Ritual*, after receiving the permission of the Bishop, and after doctors had declared that the activities were not caused by physical or mental conditions. During one of the early sessions, while the priest was at the boy's bedside, the boy, although strapped to the bed, not only broke the straps, but somehow obtained a spring from his bed. With this he slashed the priest's arm from the shoulder to the wrist. Thoroughly shaken by this event, the priest ended the exorcism.

Scratches and welts that had been forming on the boy's body then began to spell out words, especially that of "Hell," and on one occasion, "Louis." Thinking that this was an indication that they should move to St. Louis, the home of the aunt who had died, the parents took the boy there and contacted the local Bishop. After permission was received from the Bishop, a 52-year-old Jesuit was assigned to the case. It was learned that the aunt had told the boy about her beliefs concerning the dead and had introduced him to the Ouija board as a means of contacting the departed. For several weeks the Jesuit was assisted by another priest and performed the exorcism in the company of several witnesses. Each night the priest wrote a summary of the details of what had taken place, which was in turn signed by the witnesses.

According to the *Roman Ritual*, the priest is allowed to ask the devil two questions. The first question asked was, "What is your name?" To this the devil answered, "Legion." When asked, "When will you leave?" the devil did not answer, but said that before he would leave, the boy had to say one special word, and he would not permit the boy to say it. During one of the first sessions, a Holy Water bottle flew across the room, and the bed on which one of the priests was leaning started to shake violently. It was said that the boy was able to spit with great force and accuracy from the bed to the opposite wall, one time hitting the priest in the eye. Writhings, screeches, curses and abusive language accompanied the Latin prayers of the priest.

The exorcism began in the rectory of the exorcist, then continued in a hospital, but was finally accomplished in the Alexian Brothers Hospital in St. Louis. During one of the sessions, a statue of St. Michael the Archangel was placed in the room. The final session took place when the devil, speaking through the boy, announced that St. Michael was in the room. Then a deep mature voice, unlike the snarlings of the devil, spoke through the boy: "I command you to leave in the name of '*Dominus.*'"

"*Dominus*," meaning "the Lord," was apparently the word the devil said he would not permit the boy to speak, but since the boy spoke the word through the power of the Archangel Michael, the devil was forced to leave. His departure was not done quietly, since a loud noise like an explosion filled the room and a bright light flared in the chapel. The boy later awoke peacefully, as from a deep sleep, and told of a dream he had had about a beautiful angel with a flaming sword. The boy, now delivered from the devil, returned to Maryland with his parents, and all three promptly converted to Catholicism. The identity of the boy was withheld. Now in his 60's, it is said that he has led an ordinary life, married and fathered a son, who is named Michael.

104. An Unusual Case from Long Ago

Another unusual case of possession took place in Italy in 1568. Although known with good reason as the "Father of Lies," the devil at times might also tell the truth in spite of himself. One such truthful statement was told when a person believed to be possessed was taken to the Church of St. Margaret in Todi, Italy. It was the usual practice in the area to take possessed persons to this church, where prayers of deliverance were offered in a crypt under the altar.

During the exorcism, the voice of the devil, speaking through the possessed, suddenly announced, "Here rests the body of **Bl. John the Almsgiver**!" At that time the titles "Blessed" or

"Saint" were given to anyone who local authorities believed merited them. Since there had always been a traditional belief that a very holy person had been buried in the church, but whose place of burial had been lost track of during the following two hundred years, a search of records was made, with the result that a marble tomb containing bones and bearing the identifying inscription was discovered. This revealed that the Blessed had died on the eighth day of June in the year 1330.

When an aged missal was found which bore the notice that "Blessed" John of Todi had been buried in the Church of St. Margaret in 1330, the Bishop of Todi accepted it as proof that the sanctity of John the Almsgiver had been recognized two hundred years earlier and that a cult had existed at that time. Because of the discovery, the Bishop had the relics suitably enshrined and exposed for the faithful on September 3, 1568. Later, a magnificent statue depicting the Blessed was erected in the church. Clad in a Benedictine habit, the figure has several bags slung over the shoulder, apparently representing alms for the poor. Bl. John the Almsgiver is also known as Bl. John of Todi and as Bl. John Rainuzzi (Raynutius). The remains of the Blessed might well have remained in obscurity had it not been for the announcement made by the demon during the exorcism of 1568.[208]

105. How Does a Person Become Possessed?

In one case, possession took place because of repeated sacrilegious Holy Communions. Possession could also be achieved by a malefice, or what is commonly called a "spell." It is well established that the devil acts through "sortileges," that is, through sorcery, witchery or enchantments. It could also occur upon following the bad advice of another, as it did with a woman who said a prayer to Mercury, a false god, on the advice of an old woman who claimed magical powers. It could also take place, as it did in the Earling, Iowa case, by an invitation in the form of a curse, in which one person invites the devil to occupy the body of another person who is despised. It could take place by relying on a Ouija board to communicate with the dead. And it can, indeed, be accomplished by a pact with the devil, the sale of one's soul for certain powers, such as what took place with Claire-Germaine Cèle, who made a pact with the devil after she had made sacrilegious Confessions and Communions.

Although many believe the possessed person is always primarily responsible for his condition, this is not necessarily the case. Certainly, cases of possession have been documented in which demons were able to enter a person because he engaged in habitual, gravely sinful acts or in occult activities. However, when demons work through sortileges, which some call "the devil's sacraments," a third party uses charms or spells to cause the possession of an innocent person. A demon may gain the strength to resist exorcism for a time if "supported" by malefice. One exorcist claims that "a devil who . . . may appear to have lost almost all his strength, will sometimes show signs of renewed vigor and, when questioned by the exorcist, will be obliged to admit that he owes his renewed strength to magic practices."

The cause of possession might also be completely mysterious: neither the fault of the possessed nor the result of sortilege. Perhaps God allows demons to possess people for somewhat the same reasons He allows them to physically beat certain saints: in order for the possessed person to gain merit and confound the devil by humbly bearing suffering, and to demonstrate clearly that demons do indeed exist. According to Cristiani, instances of possession are "proofs of the existence of a supernatural world in which so many persons no longer believe." He continues, "There have been historical records of souls who have used the suffering of possession to attain a high degree of sanctity.[209]

106. Saints as Exorcists

The biographies of the Saints contain countless incidents in which they exorcised the devil from people, but there were also instances in which they exorcised places. One of the first to exorcise the demons in a particular location was **St. Benedict** (480-547) when he first came upon Monte Cassino, which now supports the magnificent abbey with its superlative architectural and artistic works. The Mount had been capped by a temple of Apollo where pagan sacrifices were offered. When the Saint arrived there, he destroyed the temple, dedicated the whole place to the honor and glory of God, and built two chapels, one to St. Martin and another to St. John. St. Benedict then proceeded to convert the former adorers of Apollo. Pope St. Gregory the Great (540-604), in writing about St. Benedict, tell us that

> The old enemy, not bearing this silently, did present himself in the sight of the father, and with great cries complained of the violence he suffered, in so much that the brethren heard him, though they could see nothing. For, as the venerable father told his disciples, the wicked fiend represented himself to his sight all on fire and, with flaming mouth and flashing eyes, seemed to rage against him. And then, they all heard what he said, for first, he called him by name, and when the man of God would make him no answer, he fell to reviling him. And whereas before he cried, "Benedict, Benedict," and saw he could get no answer, then he cried, "Maledict ["cursed"], what hast thou to do with me, and why dost thou persecute me?"

St. Benedict, no doubt inspired, had his brethren dig in a certain place, where they found a brazen idol, which they then carelessly threw into the kitchen.[210] This same idol was mentioned in the incident involving an illusion of fire, recounted earlier. (See #92.)

Not just a particular place, but a whole city benefited from the sanctity of **St. Francis of Assisi** (1181-1226). Because the city of Arezzo was in the grip of civil war, the Saint stopped at a little place just outside the city. By the grace of God, he saw the devils rejoicing over the situation. Since St. Francis was unable to visit the city himself, he chose one of his brothers, Sylvester, "a man of God of worthy simplicity," to go in his place. The good brother was instructed to "Go before the gate of the city and, on the part of Almighty God, command the devils to leave the city as quickly as they can." Brother Sylvester did as he was told. While standing at the gate of the city, he prayed, "On the part of Almighty God and at the command of our father Francis, depart from here, all you devils." The result of the brother's obedience was that the city quickly resumed its serenity.[211]

In addition to places, many people also benefited from the holiness of the Saints, such as from the extraordinary exorcism performed by **St. Dominic** (1170-1221). While on a journey of some days, St. Dominic and his companions spent the night in a church, where they were discovered the next morning by a crowd of people. Since the Saint was well known, the people brought him the sick and infirm, imploring him to restore their health with his healing touch. Among those presented were some possessed persons, who were gathered together before him.

Cardinal Ranieri Capocci, who lived during the time of St. Dominic, reported in a sermon that the Saint "took a stole and fastened it on his shoulders, as if about to vest for Holy Mass; then, throwing it round the necks of the possessed, they were immediately delivered." Apparently St. Dominic surprised the demons before they were ready to plan a defense.[212]

Another time, while the Saint was preaching in the church of the nuns of St. Sixtus, a demon, speaking through a possessed woman in the congregation, interrupted the sermon by shouting, "Villain, these nuns were once all mine own, and thou hast robbed me of them all. This soul at least is mine, and thou shalt not take her from me, for we are seven in number that have her in our keeping." One can only imagine the reaction of the people, but St. Dominic, in a calm voice, ordered the demon to be quiet, and making the Sign of the Cross, "he delivered her from her tormentors in the presence of all the spectators." A few days later, the woman threw herself on her knees before the Saint and begged to be admitted to his order. She was placed in the convent of St. Sixtus, where St. Dominic gave her the name of

Amata, but she stayed only a little while before joining the Dominican Order at Bologna, where she died in the odor of sanctity.[213]

St. Joseph of Cupertino (1603-1663) had such an esteem for the vow of obedience that he credited it with his ability to terrify the devil and subject even irrational animals to his will. When his superiors petitioned him to exorcise evil spirits, he would command Satan to depart by saying, "Out of obedience I have come, therefore you must depart." It is said that the demons were so bewildered by his childlike obedience that they departed immediately. At other times, after praying the Litany of the Blessed Virgin, he would gently address the demon in this manner: "I have come, not to drive you from this body, but only to obey; if therefore you wish to leave, do so; but if not, do as you like; for me it is sufficient to have obeyed." The proud spirits, confronted by this obediently humble friar, departed without difficulty. Another time when confronted by a possessed person, St. Joseph of Cupertino was struck soundly in the face by the devil. Undaunted, the Saint presented the written command of his superior to the possessed and said, "Here, take it! O holy obedience." After St. Joseph prayed the Litany of Our Lady, the demon left the possessed person quickly and quietly.[214]

Another who also valued the vow of obedience when confronted by possessed persons was **St. Mary Magdalene de' Pazzi** (1566-1607). One day, the nun was called into the parlor to speak with a mother and her daughter, who was "possessed by evil spirits." In the course of the conversation, the demon gave evidence of his presence by "causing the girl to tremble, to foam at the mouth and to do other vulgar acts." St. Mary Magdalene called Fr. Augustine Campi and begged him to command the demon, in the Name of God, to leave the girl. The priest, however, turned the tables by telling the Saint: "I command you, under obedience, to exorcise the evil one." St. Mary Magdalene obeyed. Tracing over the possessed one the Sign of the Cross, she spoke with authority: "I command you in the name of God to leave this body." The devil was forced to depart as ordered and "never again did he dare molest the girl."[215]

The Curé of Ars, **St. Jean-Marie-Baptiste Vianney** (1786-1859), was not only troubled and attacked by the devil, he also had a great deal of control over them and performed a number of exorcisms. One such case is told by Jean Picard, the village farrier, and was witnessed by many others. It seems that a poor woman, raving and shrieking, was brought to the Saint from a considerable distance by her husband. After the Curé of Ars studied the situation, he declared that she must be taken to the Bishop of the diocese. The woman, now recovering her speech, and in words that frightened the witnesses, said, "If I had the power of Jesus Christ, I should plunge you all into Hell." After ordering her to be quiet, the Saint told some of the men to take her to the foot of the high altar.

Since her strength was unnaturally great, it required four men to carry her there. The Saint then placed his reliquary—containing relics of the Passion and some of the Saints—on the head of the possessed woman. Immediately, she became rigid as a corpse. In a few moments she stood up unassisted and walked about. She even blessed herself with Holy Water and fell on her knees in prayer. She was perfectly cured. According to the Saint's *Proces de l'Ordinaire*, we learn that she spent three days at Ars to "the edification of all the pilgrims."[216]

We are also told of another possessed woman, from the neighborhood of Clermont-Ferrand, who sang and danced the whole day in front of the church at Ars. Pierre Oriol, one of the men who served as the Curé of Ars' bodyguard, tells that they made her drink a few drops of Holy Water. Immediately, she began to rage and bite the walls of the church. Her son, who had accompanied her, stood by helplessly as a priest succeeded in leading her to a place between the presbytery and the church, where the Saint would have to pass. When the holy Curé approached the place where the woman stood, he blessed her. To the surprise of the witnesses, she immediately became calm. Her son revealed later that the woman had suffered from her possession for forty years and had never before shown herself either so furious or so calm.[217]

The holy Curé performed another "easy exorcism" on December 27, 1857. A young schoolmistress who demonstrated every symptom of diabolical possession was brought to the Saint by the vicar of Saint-Pierre of Avignon, and the superior of the Franciscan nuns of Orange. The case had previously been studied by the Archbishop of Avignon, who personally recommended that the woman be taken to the Curé of Ars.

Upon her arrival at Ars, she was taken to the sacristy, where the Saint was about to vest for Holy Mass. The woman immediately became agitated and attempted to leave, saying that there were too many people present. St. John Vianney made a sign for everyone to withdraw and then found himself alone with the possessed.

Those that left only heard sounds from the sacristy, but the Vicar of Avignon remained near the door and heard the Saint ask: "You absolutely insist on going out?"

"Yes," came the reply.

The Saint then asked, "And why?"

"Because I am with a man whom I do not like."

"So you do not like me?" the Saint said in a tone of irony.

A shrill "No" was the only reply of the demon who possessed the woman. It can be presumed that the Curé of Ars blessed her, because she immediately opened the door, weeping tears of joy. Looking back at the Saint, she said, "I fear lest he should come back." St. John reassured her. In fact, the demon never returned, and the woman was able to resume her teaching career at Orange.[218]

107. Are Exorcisms Performed Today?

First let us mention that "exorcism" is practiced in many religions throughout the world, as for instance, in Islam, where it is called *da'wah*. In Japan the Buddhist monks perform exorcisms, as do many witch doctors and faith healers in other countries. Among Protestants, exorcism is confined mostly to missionaries in areas where spirit-possession cults are common. Pentecostals also regularly pray for the expulsion of demons. In all such cases of supposed non-Catholic "exorcisms," however, it must be said that, in so far as they are successful, they are successful only through the power of Jesus Christ.

For an answer to the question of present-day exorcisms, we turn to John Cardinal O'Connor of New York. In an article in *Time Magazine* dated March 19, 1990, the author reports that the Cardinal's comments on this subject "became a headline grabber" when, during a sermon recounting the devil's threefold temptation of Jesus in the wilderness, the Cardinal revealed that two exorcisms had been performed in his archdiocese during the past year (1989-1990). The Cardinal added, "As far as we know, they have been successful."[219] The Cardinal also remarked that "diabolically instigated violence is on the rise," and he specifically mentioned heavy-metal rock music as helping to trap people, especially teenagers, into dabbling in dangerous Satanist practices.

Exactly how many Catholic exorcisms take place we do not know. Statistics are not kept, but one priest noted, "It's not a thing people talk about." The exorcist himself would not willingly reveal that an exorcism took place, and witnesses feel compelled to keep the matter secret.

However, in 1999, when commenting on the new 84-page rite of exorcism, *De Exorcismis et Supplicationibus Quibusdam* (Of Exorcisms and Certain Supplications), Father James LeBar, chief exorcist for the archdiocese of New York, revealed that in the past three years his team of five exorcists had freed 50 to 60 people from demonic possession across the nation. Many of those afflicted had suffered ten to twenty years.

Possession has been recognized by the Congregation for the Doctrine of the Faith, which has addressed the issue in the person of Joseph Cardinal Ratzinger. The Cardinal issued a document in 1984 on the current norms that should govern exorcisms. This came about when the Congregation was asked about the increasing number of assemblies formed to pray for liberation from the influence of demons. Such assemblies do not perform formal exorcisms as such, but are usually led by members of the laity, even when a priest is present.

The Cardinal quoted Canon 1172, which reads: "No one can legitimately perform exorcisms over the possessed unless he has obtained special and express permission from the local ordinary. Such permission is to be granted only to a priest endowed with piety, knowledge, prudence and integrity of life."[220]

The Cardinal writes that if assemblies conduct services for liberation from demons, they may not use the formula, or any part of it, which was set forth by Pope Leo XIII. The Cardinal continues that bishops should guard lest people should attempt to lead assemblies in which prayers are employed to obtain liberation from demons, "and in the course of which the demons are directly disturbed and an attempt is made to determine their identity."[221] This, the Cardinal relates, applies even to cases which, although they do not involve true diabolical possession, nevertheless manifest diabolical influences in some way.

The Cardinal makes it clear that these norms should not stop the faithful from praying as Jesus taught us, that they may be freed from evil influences. They should also remember the Tradition of the Church, which teaches about the influence in these matters of the Apostles, the Saints, and especially the Most Blessed Virgin Mary.

108. The Blessed Virgin's Role in Exorcisms

That great lover of the Blessed Mother, **St. Louis De Montfort** (1673-1716), tells us that the devil fears her, in a certain sense, more than he fears God Himself. He writes:

> Not that the anger, the hatred and the power of God are not infinitely greater [against the devil] than those of the Blessed Virgin, for the perfections of Mary are limited; but first, because Satan, being proud, suffers infinitely more from being beaten and punished by a little and humble handmaid of God, and her humility humbles him more than the divine power; and sec-

> ondly, because God has given Mary such great power against the devils that—as they have often been obliged to confess, in spite of themselves, by the mouths of the possessed—they fear one of her sighs for a soul more than the prayers of all the Saints, and one of her threats against them more than all other torments.[222]

St. Alphonsus de Liguori (1696-1787) says that **St. Alphonsus Rodriguez** (1533-1617), when he was troubled by the devil with impure thoughts, would ask for Our Lady's help. The devil once told St. Alphonsus Rodriguez: "Give up thy devotion to Mary, and I will cease to tempt thee."[223] St. Alphonsus de Liguori also writes that "The devil is not satisfied with a soul turning against Jesus Christ, unless it also turns from His Mother. Otherwise, the devil fears that the Mother will again, by her intercession, bring back her Son."[224]

St. Bonaventure writes that "men do not fear a powerful, hostile army as much as the powers of Hell fear the name and protection of Mary."[225] **St. Germanus** also writes, "Thou, O Lady, by the simple invocation of thy most powerful name, give security to thy servants against all the assaults of the enemy."[226] **St. Bridget** was once visited by Our Blessed Lady, who revealed that the enemy flies "even from the most abandoned sinners and who consequently are the farthest from God and fully possessed by the devil, if they only invoke her most powerful name with a true purpose of amendment." But at the same time, the Blessed Lady added that if the soul does not amend its life and obliterate its sins by sorrow, the devils almost immediately return and continue to possess it.[227]

The fear which the devil has for the Blessed Virgin was demonstrated in one exorcism when the priest, during the third session, told the devil, "That's enough! You are going to leave, for the Virgin Mary has ordered you to; it's not from me anymore, a little servant of God, but from the Virgin Mary." Turning to the altar of the Blessed Mother, the priest continued, "Come, Virgin Mary, make Satan depart . . . one little gesture from you, and the devil will go back to Hell."

The devil could endure this no longer and began stammering: "Madam . . . Madam . . . I am frightened, Madam . . . We can't say anything to you, Great Lady! It is forbidden to us . . . I'm frightened! I am frightened! She is coming! She is descending from the clouds! No, no! Leave me a little while longer! Just a little while, Madam!" Then turning to the priest, the devil snarled, "You don't frighten me!" Then quieter, "I'm afraid of her, the Great Lady, of her alone, for I can do nothing against her; her will prevails." Then, as though Our Lady had spoken to the devil, he answered simply: "I shall have to go! I shall have to! Yes, Madam." The possessed woman was then relieved of her sufferings.[228]

In a letter dated February, 1959, Fr. Berger-Bergès, a longtime exorcist, remarked about the devil's respect for the Blessed Virgin. The priest writes that "Many a time Satan has had to confess, 'SHE is the most powerful.' 'I can do nothing against you, Great Lady.' 'I can't manage anything, because of her. And something makes me say so . . . Something . . . that is, God.' " The priest also disclosed, "Never, never, has Satan been known to insult the Blessed Virgin."[229]

109. The Pope and Freemasonry

Membership in the fraternal organization of the Masons (founded in England in 1717) was forbidden by the Church as early as 1738 when Pope Clement XII announced its first condemnation. Since then, eight different popes, in 17 different pronouncements, and at least six different local Church councils, have condemned Freemasonry. Pope Leo XIII, in his encyclical *Humanum Genus (On Freemasonry)*, dated April 20, 1884, writes:

> As soon as the constitution and the spirit of the Masonic sect were clearly discovered by manifest signs of its action, by cases investigated, by the pub-

> lication of its laws and of its rites and commentaries, with the addition often of the personal testimony of those who were in the secret, this Apostolic See denounced the sect of the Freemasons and publicly declared its constitutions, as contrary to law and right, to be pernicious, no less to Christendom than to the State; and it forbade anyone to enter the society, under the penalties which the Church is wont to inflict upon exceptionally guilty persons.

In this encyclical, Pope Leo XIII goes on to describe Freemasonry as a dark conspiracy, as being pernicious, a monstrous doctrine, a power for evil and a contagious, fatal plague.

Membership in this cult has always been forbidden by the Church. For serious doctrinal and pastoral reasons, Catholics were forbidden to join the Freemasons under penalty of excommunication according to Church law before 1983. Now, membership is regarded as a "serious sin" (a "mortal sin"), which prohibits members from receiving the Holy Eucharist. This is contained in a pronouncement issued by the Sacred Congregation for the Doctrine of the Faith dated November 26, 1983, which was approved by Pope John Paul II. It reads as follows:

> The Church's negative position on Masonic associations . . . remains unaltered, since their principles have always been regarded as irreconcilable with the Church's doctrine. Hence, joining them remains prohibited by the Church. Catholics enrolled in Masonic associations are *involved in serious sin and may not approach Holy Communion.* Local ecclesiastical authorities do not have the faculty to pronounce a judgment on the nature of Masonic associations which might include a diminution of the above-mentioned judgment. [Emphasis added.]

To understand fully why the Church looks so unfavorably upon the Masonic sect, one is encouraged to read books such as

Behind the Lodge Door by Paul A. Fisher (TAN), *Christianity and American Freemasonry* by William J. Whalen (Ignatius Press), and *Freemasonry, Mankind's Hidden Enemy* by Bro. Charles Madden, O.F.M.Conv. (TAN). This last book gives the current official Catholic statements on the subject.

Ever since the Masonic Order was established and spread throughout Europe, "Its principles and basic rituals have embodied a naturalistic religion, active participation in which is incompatible with Christian faith and practice. Grand Orient Freemasonry, which developed in Latin countries, is atheistic, irreligious and anticlerical. In some places, Freemasonry has been regarded as subversive of the state; in Catholic quarters, it has been considered hostile to the Church and its doctrine."[230]

110. Satanism

Also known as devil worship, Satanism has been regarded as a gesture of extreme protest against God and organized religion. Satanic cults have been documented in Europe and America as far back as the 17th century, but earlier roots are said to be difficult to trace. In more recent times, the movement is thought to have been inspired by **Alastair Crowley**, the English Rosicrucian (d. 1947), whose writings inspired **Anton Szandor La Vey** (b. 1930) to found the "Church of Satan."

In La Vey's *Satanic Bible*, his followers are taught that indulgence should be practiced instead of abstinence, while revenge should be practiced instead of turning the other cheek, and that by committing so-called sins the person will experience physical, mental and emotional gratification. In other words, "the Satanist believes in the complete gratification of his ego." In the *Satanic Bible*, any relationship with God is deemed nonsense. "The Satanist need not bow his head to anyone and must find in himself all the resources necessary to create his own happiness on earth." Satanism professes a profound rebellion against religion in general and against Christianity in particular.[231] The Church of Satan has been registered in San Francisco as a legitimate religion, with tax exempt status.

In the United States and in many other countries, countless independent groups of Satanists are active and bear such names as: Order of the Black Ram, Werewolf Order, Worldwide Church of Satanic Liberation and Our Lady of Endor Coven, among many other titles. It is totally impossible to estimate the number of these groups, since they are more or less underground or secretive of their existence.

According to an article in the Vatican newspaper, *L'Osservatore Romano*,

> Satanism is defined as groups or movements which, whether they are isolated or more or less structured and organized, practice in some form the cult (e.g.: adoration, veneration, evocation) of that entity indicated in the Bible by the name of demon, devil or Satan. Such an entity is generally understood by the Satanists as a being, or metaphysical force, or a mysterious, innate element of a human being, or an unknown natural energy that is evoked by diverse proper names through the use of certain ritual practices.[232]

The principal satanic ceremony has traditionally centered on the "black mass," during which a consecrated Host, stolen from a Catholic church, is abused and desecrated. Animals might be slaughtered and corpses desecrated, there might be physical violence on minors, and often sexual perversion is present. Murders have also been reported to have taken place at "black masses," in which the murderers acted in the name of Satan. Often wearing black robes and sitting before pentagrams ringed with black candles, they pray to or adore Satan. The rite follows more or less that of the Catholic Mass, but instead of the name of God, the name of Satan is invoked, together with the names of various demons. Their corruption of the *Our Father* begins, "Our father who art in Hell . . ." Some groups follow Anton Szandor La Vey's book *The Satanic Rituals* during their exercises and read from his *Satanic Bible.*

Now and then we learn of satanic activities, such as when a

priest in Indianapolis was called to the home of a teenage devil worshiper because objects in the home kept moving inexplicably. Another priest began the ministry of warning parents and children that "Satanism is not a lark. It often means tragedy and death for the child and for others." This same priest became involved in this work when a 15-year-old student attempted suicide because he wanted to meet Satan.

The motivations which draw people to Satanism are many. Some people might have the idea of obtaining material advantages, even though such a gain would be detrimental to others. Other people might have a morbid attraction for what is fearful and gruesome, or they might feel that they could get a cure for various traumas. Some might desire to gratify sexual deviations or obtain mystical powers that would flatter their pride.

How do persons become involved in Satanism? According to the article in *L'Osservatore Romano*, a person can be introduced to Satanism by:

> frequenting esoteric, magical or occult circles, to the point of feeling satiated with their ideas and practices and the desire of pushing beyond to try new roads of knowledge; the participation in spiritualist seances, in order to evoke particular entities, during which it is easy to reach the point of evoking demonic spirits . . . having recourse to magicians in order to deal with problems of various types . . . with the aid of so-called black magic, which almost inevitably introduces them into the world of satanic rites carried out by individuals or more or less organized groups; the idolatrous attraction shown to some singers and rock groups, who are allowed, through the messages of their songs, to curse, to invite to suicide, homicide, violence, sexual perversion and the use of drugs.[233]

Satanism has been treated by the movie industry in movies such as *Rosemary's Baby* in which a woman had sexual relations with Satan and then produced a demon-child, which was initially cared for by a coven of well-dressed and seemingly respectable people. There is an old movie entitled *The Devil and Daniel Webster* in which a man contracts with the devil—for wealth in return for his immortal soul. Then there is the more recent "comedy" entitled *Bedazzled* with Dudley Moore, who sells his soul to the devil for seven favors, which he uses in an unsuccessful effort to attract the attention of a young lady. Another "comedy" is *Devil's Food* with Dabney Coleman, in which a woman sells her soul to the devil for the ability to eat all she wants without gaining weight. Both these last movies present the devils as likeable and seemingly harmless persons. In both movies the devils are tricked into cancelling the pacts. In reality, pacts with the devil are seldom cancelled and usually end in some sort of disaster for the individual entering into them. (Oddly, there was more or less a belief in the American movie industry that someone always dies or is killed during the production of movies that have the word "devil" as part of their title.)

But are contracts with the devil really possible? Fr. Delaporte stated that they are indeed possible and that they do indeed take place. But unlike in the stories in the movies previously mentioned, if someone contracts with the devil, he is indeed playing with fire. The devils are definitely not congenial, likeable entities. Fr. Delaporte further states that by virtue of such a contract, the devil "grants to man a certain share of his power, in consideration of a price which he demands, and which price is usually the renunciation of eternal salvation."[234]

Having studied here the operations of the devils, we can well surmise that it is they who inspire the many violent and sexually explicit movies that have prompted many of the crimes we so often hear about in the news. Likewise, we may justly consider that the devils inspire the many TV programs, soap operas and bestselling novels which depict explicit sexual encounters and the seeming "glamour" and "romance" of sexually loose living. All such immoral activity plays straight into the plan of the devil for the damnation of souls.

In addition to the productions of the movie industry, the books emerging from secular publishing companies depicting violence and explicit sexual immorality surely also have their inspiration ultimately from the devil. Many of these immoral books get onto the fiction shelves of our public and school libraries, even though they should have no place next to the classics. Such books should never be in the home of a Christian.

As we well know, Satanism is often involved in the drug trade, as indicated in a Mexican case dating from 1989, when authorities discovered gruesome evidence on a cattle ranch in the Rio Grande Valley. In addition to 75 pounds of marijuana, they discovered several makeshift graves and the remains of 13 males who had been tortured with razor blades or had their hearts removed. All had been severely mutilated: ears were cut off, genitals were removed, eyes were gouged out; and there was one body whose head was missing. Also found in a dark shed was an iron kettle that contained a charred human brain and a roasted turtle. Other vessels contained human hair, a goat's head and chicken parts.

After their arrest, the individuals confessed their belief that the satanic ceremonies they performed would draw a protective shield around their weekly 2,000 lb. marijuana distribution business. The arrestees also revealed that they tried to ingratiate themselves with the devil by boiling the brains and hearts of their victims and mixing the brew with leg and arm bones and animal heads.[235] This case shows how vile Satanism can become. There is nothing "pretty" about it.

111. Witchcraft

Witchcraft, or sorcery, is defined as a type of black magic in which evil is invoked by means of diabolical intervention. The Rev. Herbert Thurston, S.J., who has thoroughly studied the subject of witchcraft, writes:

> It is not easy to draw a clear distinction between magic and witchcraft. Both are concerned with the

> producing of effects beyond the natural powers of man by agencies other than the Divine. But in witchcraft, as commonly understood, there is involved the idea of a diabolical pact or at least an appeal to the intervention of the spirits of evil. In such cases this supernatural aid is usually invoked either to compass the death of some obnoxious person, or to awaken the passion of love in those who are the objects of desire, or to call up the dead, or to bring calamity or impotence upon enemies, rivals, and fancied oppressors.[236]

These are some of the principal purposes. The activities include fortune-telling, predicting of the future, the belief in charms and magical potions, the use of Tarot cards and speaking with the dead. These latter have surfaced throughout nearly all periods of the world's history, beginning as early as 2000 B.C., as evidenced by the Code of Hammurabi. In both ancient Egypt and in Babylonia, witchcraft played a conspicuous part, as records reveal.

In the Old Testament, witchcraft (or at least the consulting with evil spirits) is mentioned a number of times. In the book of *Deuteronomy* we find the following injunction: "Neither let there be found among you any one that shall expiate his son or daughter, making them to pass through the fire: or that consulteth soothsayers, or observeth dreams and omens, neither let there be any wizard, nor charmer, nor any one that consulteth pythonic spirits, or fortune tellers, or that seeketh the truth from the dead. For the Lord abhorreth all these things, and for these abominations he will destroy them at thy coming." (*Deut.* 18:10-12).

In the first book of *Kings* we read that Saul, on seeing the opposing forces of the Philistines, became frightened and asked God to reveal to him how to proceed in battle. When God did not answer his prayer, and when neither dreams, nor priests, nor prophets helped him, Saul said to his servants, "Seek me a woman that hath a divining spirit, and I will go to her and inquire by her. And his servants said to him: There is a woman that hath a divining spirit at Endor." (*1 Kgs.* 28:7).

Saul disguised himself with a change of clothing and, in the company of two men, visited the witch and instructed her to "divine spirits and bring me up him whom I shall tell thee." (*1 Kgs.* 28:8). Not recognizing Saul, the woman replied, "Behold thou knowest all that Saul hath done, and how he hath rooted out the magicians and soothsayers from the land. Why then dost thou lay a snare for my life to cause me to be put to death?" (*1 Kgs.* 28:9). After Saul, still in disguise, reassured her that no harm would come to her, he asked her to bring Samuel from the dead. "And when the woman saw Samuel, she cried out with a loud voice, and said to Saul: Why hast thou deceived me, for thou art Saul?" (*1 Kgs.* 28:12). It is believed that Samuel did appear, not because of the power of the witch, but by the will of God, who wanted Samuel to tell Saul of the hardships that he would endure. (*1 Kgs.* 28:18-19).

Harsh punishment is prescribed for witches in the book of *Exodus,* which states: "Wizards thou shalt not suffer to live." (*Ex.* 22:18). This is repeated in the book of *Leviticus:* "A man, or woman, in whom there is a pythonical or divining spirit, dying let them die: they shall stone them: their blood be upon them." (*Lev.* 20:27). Harsh treatment has also been meted out to witches, wizards and the like throughout history. It is noted that these people had already renounced allegiance to God and His Commandments.

In the New Testament, witchcraft is given as an evil by **St. Paul** in his letter to the *Galatians*: "Now the works of the flesh are manifest, which are fornication, uncleanness, immodesty, luxury, idolatry, witchcrafts, enmities . . ." (*Gal.* 5:19). In the *Acts of the Apostles,* mention is made of a certain man named Simon, "who before had been a magician in that city, seducing the people of Samaria, giving out that he was some great one . . . And they were attentive to him, because, for a long time, he had bewitched them with his magical practices." (*Acts* 8:9-11).

Afterwards, Simon was converted by the Apostle Philip. *The Apocalypse* also reveals that "Without are dogs, and sorcerers, and unchaste and murderers, and servers of idols, and every one that loveth and maketh a lie." (*Apoc.* 22:15).

From the earliest times, witches have been held in the lowest consideration and were at most times feared and subject to severe punishment. Both civil and ecclesiastical governments enacted laws regarding them. Among the early ecclesiastical pronouncements are those of: **The Council of Elvira** (306), which refused Holy Viaticum (Holy Communion as part of the Last Rites) to those who had killed a man by a spell, since this could not be effected "without idolatry," that is, it could not be done except by the power of the devil; **The Council of Ancyra** (314), which imposed a five-year penance upon those who consulted magicians, a practice that was regarded as paganism; and **The Eastern Council in Trullo** (692), which treated sorcery as a crime to be "visited with excommunication" until adequate penance had been performed. Later, a number of ecclesiastical bodies enacted other rules regarding the punishment of witches. They prohibited the torture and other extreme punishments that were then exercised against them.

Some of the Church officials who condemned the practice of witchcraft as evil and warned against it were: **Nicholas I** (in c. 866), the **Bishop of Worms** (in c. 1020), **Pope Gregory VIII** (in 1080), **Pope Alexander IV** (in 1258), **Pope John XXII**, **Pope Benedict XII, Pope Innocent VIII** (in c. 1484) and **Pope Gregory XV** (in 1623).

Punishments given to witches consisted variously of the ordeal of cold water, imprisonment for life or for long terms, beatings and other forms of torture, as well as hanging. The first burning of a witch seems to have taken place at Toulouse in 1275, when a woman was sentenced when she confessed "to having brought forth a monster after having relations with an evil spirit, and having nourished it with the flesh of kidnapped babies."[237] It is suggested that the woman was mentally deficient, although there have been many reports of witches and evil people, in their sleep, having relations with incubi (evil spirits in male form) and with succubi (evil spirits in female form).

Other burnings in large numbers took place throughout Europe. In Toulouse in 1335, out of the sixty-three people accused of witchcraft, 8 were burned. In Valais between 1428 and 1434, 200 alleged witches were put to death, at Briançon over 150 suffered a similar fate. In 1572 Augustus of Saxony imposed the penalty of burning for witchcraft of every kind, including simple fortune-telling. In Osnabrück in 1583, 121 people were burned during a three-month period. At Wolfenbuttel in 1593, often 10 people were burned in one day. These burnings were enacted by the secular courts, since the Church authorities in Rome always prohibited such severe punishment and often objected to the use of torture, which was often practiced against witches.

In Spain and Italy, accusations of witchcraft were handled by the Inquisition, and although torture was then a legal form of civil punishment, only a dozen persons were burned out of 5,000 put on trial. In the sixteenth century, lay tribunals condemned witches to be burned, which took place in the immediate neighborhood of Rome. In England, Stearne "the Witchfinder" boasted that he personally knew of 200 executions. Howell, writing in 1648, reports that within two years nearly 300 witches were arraigned and the majority of them executed. In Scotland during the sixteenth and seventeenth centuries, 3,400 executions are reported to have occurred. At the end of the seventeenth century, witch trials began to diminish, and in the eighteenth century they practically ceased. The last trial for witchcraft in Germany was in 1749.

After the migration of European colonists to America, the witchcraft cases in Spanish and French territories in America came under the jurisdiction of Church courts, with no one suffering death on this charge. However, in the English colonies, 19 or 20 alleged witches were burned to death as a result of the famous Salem witch trials of 1692. Another 20 people were executed between 1650 and 1710.

The existence of witchcraft, involving at times a pact with the devil and diabolical interference in human affairs, can hardly be denied. And it is somewhat surprising that many of those accused spontaneously confessed to using witchcraft and did so apparently without threat or fear of torture. But it is said that 99 out of 100 cases rested on pure delusion. We can also wonder how many people were accused of witchcraft in retaliation for simple (or even serious) personal injuries, or by neighbors after village quarrels.

Although some advocates of witchcraft profess that modern witchcraft is a form of nature religion that emphasizes the healing arts, the evil aspects of witchcraft are still notorious, and the craft is still flourishing. The number of covens is not publicly known. Witches, both male and female, are now openly professing their belief in Satan and in the virtues of witchcraft.

More recently, a witch who publicly defended Wicca (witchcraft) spirituality, declared that there is nothing evil in witchcraft. She maintains that witchcraft and wizardry are simply part of a religion that worships nature and celebrates its beliefs with rituals. But even such a supposedly "innocent" practice is idolatry, in the teaching of the Catholic Church. The *Catechism of the Catholic Church* teaches that "Idolatry consists in divinizing what is not God. Man commits idolatry whenever he honors and reveres a creature in place of God . . ." Idolatry "is therefore incompatible with communion with God." (#2113).

112. The Occult and the New Age Movement

Much has already been written in recent times about the occult and the "New Age Movement," both of which are joined hand in hand with evil and demonic influences. The word "occult" is taken from the Latin, meaning "hidden" from general view. One source defines "the occult" as "a vague term describing a wide range of activities connected with the supernatural, from seances to black magic, from reading one's horoscope in the newspaper to child abuse. The term has come to have a largely sinister connotation and association with Satanism and witchcraft. The occult sciences include the study and practice of such paranormal phenomena as telepathy and clairvoyance."[238]

As an aside, we note that in Catholic usage, "supernatural" refers strictly to those things that pertain to God, whereas "preternatural" is the word properly used to refer to those things connected with the devil or with certain powers beyond the natural scope of fallen man, including, even, those apparently latent powers within man which we can assume were lost through the Original Sin of our first parents in the Fall. These powers would include such things as great strength, unusual knowledge or talents, mental telepathy, telekenesis (moving objects by mind power through perfect concentration), astral projection (moving outside the body, while the body lies dormant), levitation, etc.

The Rev. William Kent Burtner, O. P. mentions that the New Age Movement is not easily defined. It is a "variety of non-traditional religious organizations, self-help programs, modern witches, large group awareness training and esoteric satanist groups. New Age expressions are poorly coordinated and differ widely from each other. Despite their differences, however, they share some common ideologies and behavioral manifestations that allow us to talk about them as a whole."[239] Another source defines the New Age Movement as a movement that "emphasizes the holistic view of body and mind, alternative or complementary medicines, personal growth therapies, and a loose mix of theosophy, ecology, oriental mysticism, and a belief in the dawning of an astrological age of peace and harmony . . . it includes New Age ideas such as monism and pantheism, preferring intuition and direct experience to rationality and science."[240] Given these descriptions and the activities practiced by New Agers, we can see that the New Age Movement is basically occult in nature.

New Agers do not hide the fact that they embrace the influence of Lucifer. One of the early publishers of New Age materials called itself "Lucifer Trust," but is now known as Lucis Trust or Lucis Publishing Company. (It was primarily dedicated to publishing the numerous works of the "clairvoyant" Alice Bailey.) Lucifer for New Agers is not a wicked spirit as in the

Bible, but a placid being who acts as an intermediary between man and God. In this way he replaces Jesus and is given a positive image. In the opinion of Constance Cumbey and many other writers on the subject, "the motive behind the New Age Movement is Lucifer's desire to be worshiped as God."[241]

According to Joseph Carr in his book, *The Lucifer Connection,*

> the major goal of the New Age is to force all humanity to take a 'Luciferic Initiation' in order to enter the New Age alive under the auspices of one World Religion. All people of the "old thought form" [i.e., especially Christians] who refuse the initiation will be zapped to another dimension when the New Age dawns.[242]

Any activities such as those mentioned previously, whether they be New Age or occultist, are all undeniably Luciferic.

One need only check the Internet under "Occult-Paganism" to see the large number of sites and the large numbers of people who participate in pagan on-line forums. Such websites are depressing and gloomy, and a right-living person cannot stay in them for long. One can only imagine—given the number of people who have Internet access—how many there are who do not use computers, but who know of various New Age activities and gatherings through the use of the "International Pagan Events Calendar" or who recite the prayer for the goddess, which is "a takeoff on the Christian Lord's Prayer."

One can also check the card catalog of any library system to discover the many books on occult subjects. This author discovered in one library system with 13 neighborhood libraries the following books on these occult subjects (a few of which might be duplicates because of cross-referencing): astrology, 81 books; reincarnation, 52 books; spiritualism, 48; spirit writing, 26; magic, 30, and occultism, 86. There are also books on amulets, charms, incantations, channeling, talismans, zodiacal gems, etc.

The popularity of this New Age/occult activity is demonstrated in yet another library system with 19 neighborhood branches. Distributed among these libraries are books about: astrology, 151 books; reincarnation, 100 books; spiritualism, 101 books. Some of these books have titles such as *Paranormal Borderlines of Science; Principalities and Powers; New World of the Mind; Frontiers of the Unknown; The Devil and All His Works; Forbidden Universe; Mediums, Mystics and the Occult; The New Pagan; America Bewitched; The Screaming Skull;* and *A Book of Ceremonial Magic.*

New Agers even have their own music, which consists of quiet, pleasant, relaxing sounds and melodies that can easily lull one into an altered state. In the library just mentioned there are 141 cassettes of this type of music—all with different titles, and 58 compact discs—again, all with different titles.

There can be no doubt of the devil's activity in modern times. With good reason does the Catholic Church warn the faithful of the dangers to which many are exposing themselves by indulging in satanically inspired practices as found in occultism and the New Age Movement—warnings that will be emphasized later.

Not only does the Church express concern about the occult and New Age, but many writers do so as well, with books that are readily available, such as: *Catholics and the New Age* by Rev. Mitch Pacwa, S.J.; *Cults, Sects, and the New Age* by Rev. James J. LeBar; *The New Age* by Ralph Rath; *The Hidden Dangers of the Rainbow* by Constance Cumbey; and *The Lucifer Connection* by Joseph Carr. These are but a few of the many books in print that give thorough explanations of the dangers inherent in these movements, as well as their history and other particulars.

113. Scientology and Dianetics

Dianetics: The Modern Science of Mental Health, promoted by the followers of L. Ron Hubbard, is based on the premise that we are all gods. We have only to claim our godhood. Hubbard thought to add his theories to the science of modern psychiatry, but the medical community opposed this so strongly that he developed his theories into a quasi religion, the Church of Scientology, which allowed him to seek tax-exempt status and freedom of governmental criticism and examination.

Scientology is described as "a process working through levels of self-knowledge and knowledge of past lives to awaken the primordial deity within, until a person is able to regain total godhood." Christ is a man "who achieved a state of clear, but not the higher state of operating thetan."[243] The "state of clear" mentioned in this quotation exists when one is free of "engrams." These engrams could be a criticism, words said in anger, or any situation that leaves a troubling memory in the mind. Engrams must be "erased" through dianetic therapy by an "auditor." L. Ron Hubbard states in his book, *Dianetics: The Modern Science of Mental Health,* that "there are no real demons in dianetics." The sentence is even placed in italics for emphasis.[244] A demon in this religion is "a by-pass circuit in the mind, called 'demon' because it was long so interpreted. Probably an electronic mechanism." Demons in Dianetics are "engrams" that Hubbard defines as "Any moment in greater or lesser 'unconsciousness' on the part of the analytical mind which permits the reactive mind to record the total content of that moment with all perceptics."[245]

From Dianetics, which deals with the mind and is called "a spiritual healing technology," grew Scientology, which is "an applied religious philosophy" dealing with the spirit. In other words, Dianetics and Scientology can solve all problems of both body and soul. As mentioned earlier, this religion also believes in reincarnation, a theory condemned by the Catholic Church.

114. Cults and Eastern Religions

In an on-line list called the "Cult Catalog," compiled by Computers for Christ,[246] seventy-six cults and Eastern religions are listed. Of these, thirty-three claim that Jesus was not God; many claim that *we* are gods! The Center for Spiritual Awareness teaches that "The awakening of individuals to the realization of their own Christ-nature is what will liberate man and transform society."

The Children of God believe in the occult, reincarnation and sexual permissiveness. The Church of the Living Word teaches that "What He is, we become." The Process Church of the Final Judgement believes in three gods, Jehovah, Lucifer and Satan. The Unification Church of Sun Myung Moon holds that while Jesus did redeem man spiritually, salvation can come only through a Messiah who achieves perfection by marrying and having perfect offspring. Since Christ died and resurrected before He could accomplish this, Moon is regarded as the second Messiah, who will complete what Christ supposedly failed to do—achieve a physical redemption.

The 3 HO Foundation claims that God is cosmic energy, a yin-yang. "Man has never realized he is God . . . God is a stick . . . God is a cup . . . God is a woman." Ananda Marga Yoga teaches that we must "be constantly absorbed in the thought of God, and you too will become God." Bawa Muhaiyaddeen Fellowship claims that "if man is to see God, he must become God." Eckankar "makes the biblical God into a demon who as creator is responsible for the evil in the world and defines Christ as 'god as all men are god.'" Ruhani Satsang believes that Jesus spent many of His early years in India and learned from the Yogis and Buddhist monks.

Muslims preach that Jesus was "only a prophet and not the equal of Moses and Muhammad."

As it is a despicable thing for Satanists to abuse the Holy Eucharist in their black mass, we are also confronted by another abuse practiced by many cults, that is, the use of Catholic religious objects in their ceremonies. One cult, for instance, is the Santeria religion, which has no qualms about using statues of the Blessed Mother and the Saints in their offerings to various gods. The Blessed Mother's statues, particularly the Cuban Our Lady of Charity and Our Lady of Mount Carmel, adorn ceremonial altars, as do the statues of St. Barbara, St. Francis of Assisi and

St. Lazarus. Before these holy images are placed tureens holding ceremonial rocks, nuts, shells or other articles.

Pictures in the book, *Santeria: The Religion*[247] show a statue of St. Francis of Assisi on a table "that covers Orunla's secrets." In front of the table is "a sea of coconuts, each brought to a babalawo's house by his godchildren on October 4, the saint's feastday." A chapter in the book is entitled, "Obi: The Divining Coconut."

Other pictures show a very dirty crucifix positioned behind a very dirty human skull with chains and unknown objects surrounding them. Another picture shows a doll behind a skull that has a chain dangling from its mouth and assorted dark objects clustered around—all of which is sprinkled with the blood of sacrificial animals. Lastly, there is a collection containing a statue of Our Lady of Charity, a candle with the image of Our Lady, "sacred stones," a pumpkin and money, "all of which she rules." There is also a lottery ticket tucked behind the statue of Our Lady. Other pictures show a beef tongue pierced with needles and tied with a red ribbon—an offering to another god. Other pictures show a chicken that was sacrificed, an initiate feeding on the blood of a dove while in a trance, and ceremonies being performed in which diabolical possessions are encouraged: all of this before images of Our Lady.

And this is only one "religion" mentioned here. There are many others that depend on and use Catholic pictures and objects in their rituals. We can only recall that at Fatima we were encouraged to pray in reparation for the sins committed against the Immaculate Heart of Mary. Our Lord and Our Lady are being much offended today by these false and diabolically inspired "religions." For those who would like to learn more about cults and their dangers, the book by Rev. James J. LeBar is recommended: *Cults, Sects, and the New Age.*

Needless to say, a person should be very cautious about fraternizing with members of cults, since they are very adept at gaining converts. This author knows of a devout Third Order member who made friends with a member of a cult, agreed to take only a few Bible lessons with the cult member—no doubt thinking the lessons would be taken from a Catholic Bible—and ended by leaving the Third Order *and* the Catholic Church. If this person, who was a devout Catholic, could be drawn away, then the persuasive recruiting tactics of these cult members must be very great.

115. Other Dangerous Activities

Divination is the general term used to describe types of efforts to know the future by inadequate means. "The means being inadequate, they must therefore be supplemented by some power which is represented all through history as coming from gods or evil spirits." (*Catholic Encyclopedia,* 1913). The future is known only to God, the **divine** Mind. Therefore, all efforts to know the future are called **divination**—because they are attempts to acquire a divine knowledge in this regard.

The many types of divination have been found at all times in history and among all peoples. The notable exception is where the Catholic Faith has flourished, for with the True Faith comes the realization that God holds the knowledge of the future as a divine prerogative and that He imparts only a small portion of this knowledge to man, usually through His Prophets and the Saints. Any attempt, therefore, that man makes to know the future on his own, other than what we know from Scripture and predictions of the Saints, involves *superstition* (belief in meaningless indications), *idolatry* (placing false trust in people or techniques instead of in God) and *demonology* (commerce with evil spirits). All of these are forbidden by the First Commandment of God and are therefore under the condemnation of the Catholic Church.

People who engage in divination may argue that they are employing only "natural" means, and therefore that a given practice they engage in is not sinful, as for example, consulting *psychics.* Psychics from an early age usually seem to possess an enhanced sort of preternatural sense about things which the average person does not have. Nonetheless, because the special knowledge even of psychics is extremely limited and is generally untrustworthy, they often resort to other means to enhance their "natural" (or preternatural) knowledge, and this can lead to solicitation of evil spirits. Their representations of the future are grossly inadequate and possibly positively false. In any case, it is wrong to follow their advice or to consult them.

Others engaging in various forms of divination that involve spirits may claim that they are dealing only with *good* spirits. But this is not true. The Angels normally do not communicate directly with us; such direct communication occurs *only* to relatively few people who have been privileged to see, e.g., their guardian angels or to speak with them. Because God only very rarely communicates with man by the direct influence of His angels, we have to presume that the spirits being contacted through various means of divination are in fact devils. Therefore any such solicitation of spirits is dangerous and is forbidden by the Church as sinful.

The methods of divination are many and varied. The Romans officially practiced *auspices* (analyzing the notes, flights and actions of birds) and *haruspices* (analyzing the entrails of animals) in an effort to know if it were favorable to engage in certain important actions—usually by the government—such as going to battle. *Astrology* has been universally practiced at all times, as also *chiromancy* (palmistry), throwing dice, drawing straws, cutting cards, crystal gazing and many other practices.

Psychics (soothsayers), who are so well known today with their pleasant invitations for all to "join in the fun," are those who offer "advice" and "assistance" by giving their clients tarot card or aura "readings." The aura is another term for a person's bodily halo, and various colors of the aura are taken to mean certain things about the state of the person's being. Psychics know in a mysterious way some of the events (although incomplete) in a person's past and something of their clients' present relationships, and from this vague knowledge they give advice on how to improve their clients' lives. They might also give some hints as to the person's future and a course of action they say he should take. What they practice is more or less divination: the foreseeing of future events or the discovery of hidden knowledge. This activity might also be called by the Old Testament name of soothsaying, which is strictly forbidden by Scripture: "Go not aside after wizards, neither ask anything of soothsayers, to be defiled by them: I am the Lord your God." (*Lev.* 19:31).

God alone knows what will take place in the future, and as we know, He sometimes gives the devil an insight into future happenings. Pope Benedict XIV, in writing about prophecy, explains that "the devil cannot of his own natural knowledge foretell future events which are the proper objects of prophecy, yet God may make use of him for this purpose."[248]

From whom, then, do the fortune-tellers and psychics obtain their information? As Msgr. Léon Cristiani writes, "To try to foretell the future, except in certain cases of divinely inspired prophecy, is therefore necessarily satanic, in the sense that it is an encroachment on the divine. It therefore follows that no power of prediction has been vouchsafed to the Tarot [and the like] . . . any more than in the conjunctions of stars and planets at the birth of a human being."[249]

Cristiani also notes that some neighborhood fortune-tellers, as well as others, have adopted this lucrative occupation "without the least idea that it is immoral and probably diabolic."

Since Satanists, witches, and practitioners of the occult are engaged in activities which have been inspired by Satan, it results that they are collaborators, intimates and associates of Satan, which places them and their clients in a very dangerous position indeed!

Astrology, a type of divination, is also a relative of the occult and New Age movements. It is based on the false belief that a person's character and future are influenced by the positions of the sun, moon, stars and planets at the time of birth. The horoscope which astrologers develop from their observations and plottings is a map of the heavens on which they plot the positions of the planets for a given moment. This chart bearing the 12 signs of the Zodiac is interpreted, but the "readings" vary greatly from one astrologer to another.

In 1975, according to Ralph Rath in his book *The New Age: A Christian Critique*, 192 leading scientists, including 19 Nobel Prize winners, after a thorough study, publicly disavowed astrology.

The author lists several arguments against the validity of astrology. First, astrology is based on the hypothesis that the sun circles the earth. Second, as the earth spins on its axis there is an uneven wobble, therefore a shift in the Zodiac. Horoscope readings are now inaccurate by 30 days because of changes in the celestial movements over the course of centuries. Astrologers disagree as to the number of Zodiac signs, some relying on 12, 14, or even more. Since astrology is practiced universally, even by pagan religions whose number of Zodiac signs may vary, the readings would also be different depending upon the religion of the "reader." And lastly, no planet is visible north of the Arctic Circle for several weeks of the year. Therefore, babies born in the Arctic Circle during that time would theoretically not have a horoscope.[250]

We can report that astrology, in the words of Ralph Rath, "is totally unscientific and totally illogical."

The horoscope is mentioned as far back as Old Testament times since we read in *4 Kings:* "And he destroyed the soothsayers, whom the kings of Juda had appointed to sacrifice in the high places in the cities of Juda, and round about Jerusalem: them also that burnt incense to Baal, and to the sun, and to the moon, and to the *twelve signs*, and to all the host of heaven." (*4 Kings* 23:5). (Emphasis added.)

The prophet Isaias speaks soberly of God's judgment upon Babylon: "Thou has failed in the multitude of thy counsels: let now the astrologers stand and save thee, they that gazed at the stars, and counted the months, that from them they might tell the things that shall come to thee. Behold they are as stubble, fire hath burnt them; they shall not deliver themselves from the power of the flames . . ." (*Is.* 47:13-14).

It has been noted that those who consult astrologers are usually dissatisfied and frustrated with life. They are described as being fragile and insecure and in need of a guide who will tell them what to do. Those who consult for amusement do not realize the danger in which they place themselves.

Tarot Cards are something like playing cards, each having a different design, which when dealt, are read according to their position to one another. Tarot cards date to about the first century A.D. These, too, are meant to reveal present situations and predict future events. But since the position of the cards is interpreted, would the reading be the same if the cards were re-shuffled and re-dealt, and then read by a practitioner who did not know the results of the previous reading?

Crystal Ball gazing attempts to predict the future, or to see events happening, or events that are taking place at a distance. For someone who has never gazed into a crystal ball we will tell you that all you will see is the upside-down reflection of the surrounding area. Anyone who claims to see an event taking place within the crystal ball either has a very vivid imagination or is witness to the workings of the devil.

The use or wearing of **Crystals** is said to "unlock the access-windows of awareness to horizons of light previously unimagined . . . Quartz crystals represent the sum total of material plane evolution." Ralph Rath quotes another author as recording that "Clear quartz radiates with divine white light, and by seeing, touching, wearing, using or meditating with these crystals, one can actually work with that light in a physical form."[251] The language of crystal enthusiasts and writers is so confusing that one wonders if they really understand and believe what they are saying or writing.

Some crystal enthusiasts hang crystals around their necks, suspend them from their ceilings and use them in so many varied ways that it would be tedious to list them. It is reported that a crystal enthusiast even claimed that the proper crystal could protect the wearer from contracting the AIDS virus. Needless to report, the dealers in these often very high-priced crystals are making fortunes from the foolish beliefs of their customers.

Amulets are objects worn around the neck as a charm against evil or injury and are said to be different from **Talismans**. In olden times these were either "engraved in stone or metal, or drawn upon parchment or paper, and were worn both to procure love for and to avert danger from its possessor." But now, according to *The Book of Talismans, Amulets and Zodiacal Gems,*

> with the growing knowledge of finer forces opening up new powers to mankind and to which we are slowly coming into touch, many people are prepared to admit that there may be some active power in a thought made concrete in the form of a talisman or amulet, which may be made for some specific purpose, or for particular wear, becoming to the wearer a continual reminder of its purpose and undoubtedly strengthening him in his aims and desires.[252]

These un-Christian and superstitious talismans come in various shapes like rings, brooches, or decorative pins and are either made in a specific form, such as a star, an animal or a cross, or they may be round or square, with words, letters or figures engraved on them. The purpose of wearing these objects is also varied—from warding off evil to acquiring love, producing good luck, preventing injury, or even to use as a curative device or to act as a producer of supernatural powers.

Reincarnation is the theory of the return of the soul into different bodies in subsequent lives, one after the other, in order to work off "bad karma" before being elevated to a higher plane.

Scripture plainly tells us: "It is appointed unto men once to die, and after this the judgment. So also Christ was offered once to exhaust the sins of many . . ." (*Heb.* 9:27-28). In addition, the *Catechism of the Catholic Church* clearly states: "When the single course of our earthly life is completed, we shall not return to other earthly lives . . . There is no 'reincarnation' after death." (#1013).

Also, Padre Pio has identified reincarnation as "heresy."

Transcendental Meditation, according to Ralph Rath, is a form of Hinduism in which practitioners worship Hindu gods. This worship occurs during an initiation ceremony that takes place before the "meditator" receives his personal mantra—a secret Sanskrit word he must recite over and over during his meditation. According to Ralph Rath, "Reports of demonic possession or obsession as a result of TM have surfaced."[253]

Silva Mind Control is another practice that is questionable, since it deals with altered states of consciousness. According to Ralph Rath, at the conclusion of the program of Silva Mind Control lectures, "The individual is asked to allow two demonic spirits to come into him or her and influence his or her judgments. These demonic spirits are called counselors."[254] Many authorities, however, have warned that "unwise tampering with psychic forces can lead to possession by evil spirits."

Mediums or **channelers** are those who enter into a trance state and permit a spiritual "entity" to enter their bodies. The entity, either a demon or a damned soul, speaks through the medium, usually in a different voice from his or her own. It is well known that Satan can and does counterfeit the miraculous.

Automatic writing occurs when a medium sits quietly with paper and pencil until a spirit, and certainly not a holy one, takes control of the pencil to write messages, poetry and even literary works.

Using **Ouija boards** is also a very dangerous practice. These are boards that are marked with the alphabet and various signs. A Ouija board is used with a planchette (which is, in effect, a miniature three-legged platform or table that replicates the three-legged table used in a spiritualistic seance). The planchette is gently touched by all the participants at the same time and it moves mysteriously to spell out spiritualistic and telepathic messages. It is also thought to be a connective link between the living and the dead. Presented as an innocent and harmless parlor game, the use of these boards is forbidden by the Church, since the object is to contact unseen spirits.

Heavy Metal Music is one of the most common sources of Satanic influence, and even of actual initiation into Satanic practices. The "heavy metal" or "death-metal" rock music culture—comprised mostly of young adults—is saturated with Satanism, as well as with drugs and violence. The direct influence of the devil is often the inspiration for composers of death-metal music. Their bands have names such as "Black Sabbath" and "Rotting Corpse" and their members are often avowed Satanists who intentionally use driving, angry rhythms, "demonic-sounding" voices and sick, perverted lyrics to promote blasphemy, sacrilege, lust, suicide, etc. They employ dissonant harmonies to whip their young audiences into a frenzy. Besides encouraging listeners to "mosh"—a violent dance in a "mosh pit" that involves jumping violently up and down and slamming into other "dancers," often causing serious injury—band members themselves often do things like desecrating Catholic sacramentals and engaging in acts of self-mutilation on stage.

Death-metal music is quite popular, both in the United States and abroad. The album of Marilyn Manson (a male) entitled "Antichrist Superstar" reached the #3 spot on the national *Billboard* music charts in the mid-1990's. Manson, titled "Reverend" by "Church of Satan" founder Anton Szandor LaVey, has led many young people to make a formal rejection of God and to take part in Satanic practices.

These facts show how misguided are those who dismiss the "heavy metal" culture with the comment, "It's only music."

116. Warnings

The Church has always warned against, fought against and

condemned divination, the magic arts and the like since the beginning of New Testament times and right up to the present. Also, the Bible in the Old Testament contains innumerable condemnations of these practices. In the 16th century, the **Council of Trent** (1545-1563) spelled it out for us in its document concerning prohibited books. Books that "are absolutely repudiated" are those that deal with:

Necromancy (communication with the spirits of the dead in order to tell the future or influence events, conjuration);

Sortilege (divination by means of lots, witchery, enchantment, soothsaying, the mixing of poisons, augury, auspices, sorcery, and magic arts);

Aeromancy (divination by means of air or air currents);

Chiromancy (divination by examination of the hand, palmistry);

Geomancy (divination by means of figures or lines);

Hydromancy (divination by means of water or other liquid, or the flow and ebb of tides);

Oneiromancy (the interpretation of dreams); and

Pyromancy (divination by means of fire or flames).[255]

The Church continues to repudiate these matters and states this firmly and clearly in the *Catechism of the Catholic Church:*

> All forms of divination are to be rejected: recourse to Satan or demons, conjuring up the dead, or other practices falsely supposed to "unveil" the future. Consulting horoscopes, astrology, palm reading, interpretation of omens and lots, the phenomena of clairvoyance, and recourse to mediums all conceal a desire for power over time, history and, in the last analysis, other human beings, as well as a wish to conciliate hidden powers. They contradict the honor, respect and loving fear that we owe to God alone. (#2116).

This, of course, warns against consulting psychics, a practice that is in vogue at the present time. About this, the *Catechism of the Catholic Church* states:

> God can reveal the future to his prophets or to other saints. Still, a sound Christian attitude consists in putting oneself confidently into the hands of Providence for whatever concerns the future, and giving up all unhealthy curiosity about it. (#2115).

The *Catechism of the Catholic Church* also warns:

> All practices of *magic* or *sorcery*, by which one attempts to tame occult powers, so as to place them at one's service and have a supernatural power over others . . . are gravely contrary to the virtue of religion. These practices are even more to be condemned when accompanied by the intention of harming someone, or when they have recourse to the intervention of demons. Wearing charms is also reprehensible. *Spiritism* often implies divination or magical practices; the Church for her part warns the faithful against it. (#2117).

Anyone who is attuned to world events is thereby warned about many evils that are certainly influenced and instigated by the devil, such as abortion, euthanasia and the like. Satanic worship and the horrific remains discovered after such rituals give testimony to the devil's love for blood sacrifice.

St. John of the Cross (d. 1591), a Doctor of the Church, also gives us warnings: In discerning the difference between true and false visions and locutions, he tells that it is difficult

> discerning those communications which the devil causes. For the devil's usually have resemblance to God's . . . Since the devil through conjecture makes many reasonable manifestations that turn out to be

> true, people may be easily misled, thinking that the revelations must then be from God. These people do not realize the ease with which the devil with his clear natural light knows, through their causes, many past or future events. Since his light is so vivid, he can easily deduce a particular effect from a specific cause. Yet the effect does not always materialize according to his deduction, since all causes depend upon God's will.[256]

That the devil knows many things is again stated by St. John of the Cross when he writes:

> The devil can learn and foretell that a person's life will naturally last only a certain number of years. And he can determine many other events through such various ways that we would never finish recounting them all, nor could we even begin to explain many because of their intricacy and the devil's craftiness in inserting lies. One cannot be liberated from him without fleeing from all revelations, visions, and supernatural communications.[257]

To this we might add that one must flee the revelations and communications of mediums and all those occultic activities that offer insights into the future, since these are courses of action which are harmful to souls.

St. John of the Cross concludes:

> God permits the devil to blind and delude many, who merit this by their sins and audacities. The devil is able and successful to the extent that others believe what he says and consider him a good spirit. So firm is their belief that it is impossible for anyone who tries, to persuade them of the diabolic origin.[258]

117. The Pope and the Evil Spirits

Pope Leo XIII (1878-1903), who reigned for twenty-five years and died at the age of 93 in the year 1903, had a most unusual experience with regard to the devil. During his pontificate, he became aware of the massive infiltration of atheism, occultism and all forms of evil penetrating society. He was especially troubled by the influence of the Masons, whose object is the ruination of the Catholic Church. (See #109.) The Pontiff authored the encyclical entitled *Humanum Genus* (*On Freemasonry)* which exposed the Masons, their rituals and their inclination toward materialism, occultism and humanism.

The Pope's experience involving the devil is said to have happened in the following way: While consulting with a number of Cardinals in the private Vatican chapel on October 13, 1884, he happened to pass before the altar, where he stopped suddenly and seemed to lose all awareness of his surroundings. His slender face grew pale, his eyes stared in horror, and he stood motionless for several minutes until those around him thought he was about to die. His physician rushed to his side, but in a moment or two the Pope recovered and almost painfully exclaimed, "Oh! What terrifying words I have heard." It is said that after the Pope recovered, he retired to his office, where he composed the famous prayer to the Archangel Michael:

> St. Michael the Archangel, defend us in battle, be our safeguard against the wickedness and snares of the devil. May God rebuke him, we humbly pray, and do thou, O Prince of the heavenly host, by the power of God, cast into Hell Satan and the other evil spirits who prowl about the world for the ruin of souls. Amen.

After a time, Pope Leo XIII confided what he had heard: According to the report of his vision, the devil, in a guttural voice, had boasted to God that he could destroy the Church if he were given more time and more power. He then asked God for

75 years, then 100 years. His request was granted by God, with the understanding there would be a penalty when he failed. The Pope was so worried after this experience that the prayer he composed was ordered by him to be said after all low Masses throughout the world. The prayer was recited as ordered, and was preceded by three *Hail Marys.* The recitation of these prayers after Mass was discontinued in most parishes after Vatican II when the traditional Latin Mass was replaced in 1970. However, on October 3, 1984—100 years minus 10 days after Pope Leo XIII heard the devil ask for 100 years with which to attack the Church—Pope John Paul II issued an "indult whereby priests and faithful . . . may be able to celebrate Mass by using the Roman Missal according to the 1962 edition." Thanks to this indult, the St. Michael prayer is still recited after Mass whenever the traditional Latin Mass is offered.

NOTES

— PART ONE: ANGELS —

1. St. Augustine, *The City of God* (New York: Doubleday, 1958), p. 219.
2. St. Bernard of Clairvaux, *Liber de Consideratione,* V, 4.
3. Rev. Pascal P. Parente, *The Angels: The Catholic Teaching on the Angels* (Originally published as *Beyond Space: A Book About the Angels,* New York: Society of St. Paul, 1961; Rockford, IL: TAN Books and Publishers, Inc., 1994), p. 20.
4. *Ibid.*, p. 22.
5. *Catechism of the Catholic Church* (San Francisco: Ignatius Press, 1994), #332.
6. St. Thomas Aquinas, *Summa Theologica* (Chicago: Encyclopaedia Britannica, Inc., 1952), Part I. Q. 61. Art. 2.
7. *Summa*, Part I. Q. 62. Art 8.
8. *Angela of Foligno,* Trans. Paul Lachance, (New York: Paulist Press, 1993), pp. 210-211.
9. Parente, *op. cit.,* pp. 16-17.
10. *Summa,* Part I. Q. 108. Art. 8.
11. Lady Georgiana Fullerton, *The Life of St. Frances of Rome* (New York: P. J. Kenedy and Sons), p. 60.
12. Joan Carroll Cruz, *Miraculous Images of Our Lady* (TAN, 1993), p. 426.
13. Fr. Joseph I. Dirvin, C.M., *Saint Catherine Labouré of the Miraculous Medal* (Farrar, Straus & Cudahy, Inc., 1958; TAN, 1984), pp. 86-92.
14. Fr. Juan Echevarria, *The Miracles of Saint Anthony Mary Claret, Archbishop and Founder* (Originally published as *Reminiscence of Blessed Anthony Mary Claret*) (Compton, CA: Claretian Major Seminary, 1938; TAN, 1991), pp. 69-70.
15. Fullerton, *op. cit.,* p. 60.
16. Fr. Alessio Parente, O.F.M. Cap., *Send Me Your Guardian Angel, Padre Pio* (New York: The Noteworthy Co., 1984), pp. 28-29.
17. Augusta Theodosia Drane, *The Life of St. Dominic* (London: Burns & Oates, Ltd., 1919), pp. 144-145.
18. *Ibid.*, pp. 139-140.
19. Mary Sharp, *A Guide to the Churches of Rome* (Philadelphia: Chilton Books, 1966), p. 198.
20. J. K. Huysmans, *Saint Lydwine of Schiedam,* Trans. Agnes Hastings (London: Kegan Paul, Trench, Trubner & Co., Ltd., 1923; TAN, 1979), pp. 109, 111.
21. J. C. Kearns, O.P., *The Life of Blessed Martin De Porres: Saintly American Negro and Patron of Social Justice* (New York: P. J. Kenedy & Sons, 1937), p. 80.
22. *Ibid.*, p. 100.
23. Friar Stanislaus of St. Theresa, O.C.D., *St. Theresa Margaret of the Sacred Heart of Jesus* (New York: Benziger Brothers, 1934), p. 99.
24. Echevarria, *op. cit.,* p. 70.
25. Ven. Mary of Agreda, *The Mystical City of God,* Abridged. Trans. Fiscar Marison (So. Chicago: The Theopolitan, 1913), Book One, Chapter XXIII, # 362.
26. Lucia of Fatima, *Fatima in Lucia's Own Words: Sister*

Lucia's Memoirs, Ed. Louis Kondor, S.V.D. (Fatima, Portugal: Postulation Centre, 1976), p. 62.
27. *Ibid.*, pp. 62-64.
28. Rev. Alban Butler, *The Lives of the Saints* (New York: P. J. Kenedy & Sons, 1933), Vol. IV, pp. 304-305.
29. Omer Englebert, *The Lives of the Saints,* Trans. Christopher and Anne Fremantle (New York: Collier Books, 1964), pp. 488-489.
30. Drane, *op. cit.*, pp. 99-100.
31. *Ibid.*, pp. 100-101.
32. *Ibid.*, p. 143.
33. Ven. Mary of Agreda, *The Mystical City of God* (Abridged) (TAN, 1978), p. 225-226.
34. Agreda, The Theopolitan, 1913, p. 36.
35. Fullerton, *op. cit.*, pp. 59-63.
36. Frances Parkinson Keyes, *Three Ways of Love* (New York: Hawthorn Books, 1963), p. 87.
37. *Ibid.*, pp. 120-121.
38. Comte Paul Biver, *Père Lamy* (Dublin: Clonmore & Reynolds Ltd., 1951; TAN, 1973), p. 183.
39. *Ibid.*, pp. 100-101.
40. St. Teresa of Avila, *The Autobiography of St. Teresa of Avila*, Trans. David Lewis, Re-edited by Very Rev. Benedict Zimmerman, O.C.D. (London: Thomas Baker, 1921; TAN, 1997), Chapter XXIX, # 16-17.
41. Rev. Prosper Gueranger, *Life of Saint Cecilia, Virgin and Martyr* (Philadelphia: Peter F. Cunningham, Catholic Bookseller, 1879), p. 71.
42. Lucia of Fatima, *op. cit.*, p. 62.
43. Fr. Paul O'Sullivan, *All About the Angels* (Lisbon: Edições do Corpo Santo, 1945; TAN, 1990), p. 29.
44. William D. Coyne, *Our Lady of Knock* (New York: Catholic Book Publishing Company, 1948), pp. 28-29.
45. Gueranger, *op. cit.*, p. 71.
46. St. Gertrude the Great, *The Life and Revelations of Saint Gertrude* (Westminster, Maryland: The Newman Press, 1949), p. 476.
47. Passionist Nuns, *A Lover of the Cross: St. Gemma Galgani* (Lucca, Italy: Monastero-Santuario di S. Gemma Galgani, 1940), p. 127.
48. Very Rev. K. E. Schmoeger, C.SS.R., *Life of Anne Catherine Emmerich* (Los Angeles: Maria Regina Guild, 1968; TAN, 1976), Vol. II, p. 214.
49. C. Bernard Ruffin, *Padre Pio: The True Story* (Huntington, Indiana: Our Sunday Visitor, Inc., 1982), p. 105.
50. Schmoeger, *op. cit.,* Volume 2, p. 207.
51. *Ibid.*, p. 213.
52. Thomas of Celano, *St. Francis of Assisi* (Chicago: Franciscan Herald Press, 1988), Part I, Chap. III, # 94, p. 84-85.
53. Parente, *op. cit.,* pp. 96-97.
54. Coyne, *op. cit.*, p. 29.
55. Agreda, The Theopolitan, 1913, p. 36.
56. St. Teresa of Avila, *The Relations.* Included in *The Autobiography of St. Teresa of Avila,* Trans. David Lewis (TAN, 1997), Rel. III, #16, p. 449-450.
57. Dirvin, *op. cit.,* pp. 84-86.
58. *Summa*, Part I, Q. 113, Art. 2.
59. Edward Van Speybrouck, *Father Paul of Moll* (Clyde, MO: Benedictine Sisters of Perpetual Adoration, 1910; TAN, 1979), p. 256.
60. St. Teresa of Avila, *Autobiography, op. cit.*, Chapter XXIX, #16.
61. Biver, *op. cit.*, p. 93.
62. *Ibid.*, p. 100.

63. *Summa,* Part I. Q. 57. Art. 3.
64. *Ibid.*
65. St. Augustine, *op. cit.*, p. 182.
66. *Summa,* Part I. Q. 57. Art. 4.
67. Fullerton, *op. cit.,* p. 63.
68. *Summa,* Part I. Q. 107. Art. 1.
69. St. John Damascene, *De Fide Orth.,* II, 3.
70. Parente, *op. cit.,* p. 33.
71. Joan Carroll Cruz, *The Incorruptibles* (TAN, 1977), p. 74.
72. Keyes, *op. cit.*, p. 121.
73. Fullerton, *op. cit.*, p. 117, 129.
74. Emily Mary Shapcote, *Legends of the Blessed Sacrament* (London: Burns & Oates, Ltd., 1877), pp. 143-145.
75. Fr. Pius of the Name of Mary, *The Life of Saint Paul of the Cross* (New York: P. O'Shea, 1924), pp. 189-190.
76. Rev. Angelo Pastrovicchi, O.M.C., *St. Joseph of Copertino* (St. Louis: B. Herder Book Co., 1918; TAN, 1980), p. 13.
77. Butler, *op. cit.,* Vol. II, p. 350.
78. *Ibid.*, p. 200.
79. *Ibid.*, Vol. III, p. 103.
80. *Ibid.*, Vol. V, p. 261.
81. Passionist Nuns, *op. cit.*, pp. 130-132.
82. The Companions of Jesus and Mary, *Sister Mary Martha Chambon: Religious at the Monastery of the Visitation, Chambery* (Montreal: The Companions of Jesus and Mary, 1924), p. 12.
83. Alessio, *op. cit.*, p. 105.
84. Biver, *op. cit.*, p. 101.
85. Pastrovicchi, *op. cit.*, p. 106.
86. Fr. Joseph Sicardo, O.S.A., *St. Rita of Cascia, Saint of the Impossible* (Originally published as *Life of Sister St. Rita of Cascia*) (Chicago: D. B. Hansen & Sons, 1916; TAN, 1990), p. 76.
87. Cruz, *The Incorruptibles,* p. 164.
88. Drane, *op. cit.*, pp. 212-213.
89. Parente, *op. cit.,* p. 38.
90. O'Sullivan, *op. cit.*, p. 39.
91. *Summa,* Part I. Q. 53. art. 3.
92. Biver, *op. cit.*, p. 100.
93. Lucia of Fatima, *op. cit.*, p. 64.
94. *Ibid.*, p. 64.
95. Schmoeger, *op. cit.*, pp. 205-206.
96. Cruz, *The Incorruptibles,* p. 74.
97. Huysmans, *op. cit.,* p. 111.
98. *Ibid.*, p. 93.
99. *Ibid.*, p. 93.
100. *Ibid.,* pp. 182-183.
101. St. Teresa of Avila, *The Life of Teresa of Jesus,* Trans. E. Allison Peers (Garden City, New York: Image Books, 1944), pp. 273-274.
102. *Ibid.*, p. 384.
103. Rev. J. Spencer Northcote, D.D., *Celebrated Sanctuaries of the Madonna* (Philadelphia: Peter F. Cunningham & Son, 1868), pp. 163-176.
104. Joan Carroll Cruz, *Miraculous Images of Our Lady* (TAN, 1993), p. 413.
105. *Ibid.*, p. 179.
106. William J. Walsh, *The Apparitions and Shrines of Heaven's Bright Queen* (New York: Carey-Stafford Company, 1904), Volume II, pp. 50-51.
107. Francis Johnston, *The Wonder of Guadalupe* (Published by TAN in conjunction with Augustine Publishing Co., Chulmleigh, Devon: England, 1981), p. 26.
108. Butler, *op. cit.,* Volume III, pp. 18, 40.
109. Huysmans, *op. cit.,* pp. 182-183.
110. St. Margaret Mary Alacoque, *The Autobiography of St. Margaret Mary Alacoque* (England: Sisters of the Visitation, 1930;

TAN, 1986), p. 113.
111. Drane, *op. cit.*, pp. 158-159.
112. Echevarria, *op. cit.,* pp. 260-261.
113. Schmoeger, *op. cit.,* p. 214.
114. Sr. Mary Jean Dorcy, O.P., *Saint Dominic's Family* (Dubuque: The Priory Press, 1964; TAN, 1983), p. 130.
115. Biver, *op. cit.,* p. 101.
116. Parente, *op. cit.,* p. 129.
117. *Ibid.*, pp. 130-131.
118. Huysmans, *op. cit.,* p. 182.
119. Thomas of Celano, *op. cit.,* pp. 241-242.
120. Fr. Michael Muller, C.SS.R., *The Blessed Eucharist: Our Greatest Treasure* (Baltimore: Kelly and Piet, 1868; TAN, 1994), p. 32-33.
121. Henri-Marie Boudon, *Devotion to the Nine Choirs of Holy Angels, Especially to Angel-Guardians* (London: Burns and Oates, 1911), p. 41.
122. St. Ignatius Martyr, *Epistle to the Trallians,* 5.
123. St. Gregory the Great, *Hom. 34 in Evang.*
124. Dionysius the Areopagite, *On the Celestial Hierarchies,* Trans. J. Parker (London, 1897). As found in Migne's *Patrologia Graeca.*
125. St. Teresa of Avila, *Autobiography*, Chapter XXIX, #16.
126. Fullerton, *op. cit.*, p. 60.
127. *Ibid.*, p. 60.
128. Boudon, *op. cit.,* pp. 147-148.
129. St. Teresa of Avila, *Autobiography,* Chapter XXIX, # 216-217.
130. Boudon, *op. cit*., pp. 148-149.
131. St. Dionysius the Areopagite, *op. cit.*
132. Boudon, *op. cit*., p. 144.
133. *Ibid.*, p. 16.
134. St. Dionysius the Areopagite, *op. cit.*
135. *Ibid.*
136. Boudon, *op. cit.,* pp. 127-129.
137. *Ibid.*, p. 127.
138. *Summa,* Part I, Q. 108. Art. 6.
139. St. Dionysius the Areopagite, *op. cit.*
140. *Epistle to Diognetus,* from *The Didache* (Ancient Christian Writers), Trans. James A. Kleist, S.J. (New York: Paulist Press, 1948), pp. 140-141.
141. Boudon, *op. cit.*, p. 127.
142. Fullerton, *op. cit.,* p. 60.
143. Boudon, *op. cit.,* p. 127-129.
144. *Ibid.,* p. 127.
145. *Saint Michael and the Angels* (South Bend: Marian Publications, 1977, under the title *The Precious Blood and the Angels;* TAN, 1983), p. 24.
146. *The Catholic Encyclopedia* (New York: The Encyclopedia Press, Inc., 1913), Vol. I, p. 478.
147. Thomas of Celano, *op. cit.,* Part II, Chapter CXLIX, #197, pp. 295-6.
148. Fr. Pius of the Name of Mary, *The Life of Saint Paul of the Cross* (New York: P. O'Shea, 1924), p. 78.
149. Agreda, TAN, 1978, p. 225-226.
150. Biver, *op. cit.,* p. 101.
151. *Ibid.*, pp. 102-103.
152. Echevarria, *op. cit.,* p. 43.
153. Schmoeger, *op. cit.,* Book II, p. 213.
154. Biver, *op. cit.,* p. 101.
155. *Ibid.*, p. 103.
156. St. Basil the Great, *Contra Eunomium,* III, 1.
157. *The Guardian Angels, Our Heavenly Companions* (Originally published under the title, *Our Heavenly Companions)* (Clyde, Missouri: Benedictine Sisters of Perpetual Adoration, 1956; TAN, 1996), p. vi.

158. Fr. Franciscus Suarez, S.J., *Opera Omnia,* Vol. II: *De Angelis* (Paris: Edition Vives, 1856), VI, 17.
159. *The Guardian Angels, Our Heavenly Companions,* p. 16.
160. St. Margaret Mary Alacoque, *The Letters of St. Margaret Mary Alacoque*, Trans. Fr. Clarence A. Herbst, S.J. (Chicago: Henry Regnery Co., 1954; TAN, 1997), p. 127.
161. Passionist Nuns, *op. cit.,* p. 127.
162. *Ibid.*, p. 128.
163. C. Bernard Ruffin, *Padre Pio: The True Story* (Huntington, IN: Our Sunday Visitor Publishing Division, 1991), p. 315.
164. *Ibid.*, p. 315.
165. Agreda, *op. cit.,* p. 37.
166. *Summa,* The Theopolitan, 1913, Ia IIae. Q. 113. Art. 5.
167. St. Jerome, *In. Matt.,* 18, 10.
168. St. Anselm, *Elucid.,* II, 31.
169. *Summa,* First Part. Q. 113. Art 7.
170. *The Guardian Angels, Our Heavenly Companions,* p. 44.
171. Passionist Nuns, *op. cit.*, p. 128.
172. *Summa,* First Part. Q. 113. Art 3.
173. St. Dionysius the Areopagite, *op. cit.*
174. *Summa,* Part I. Q. 113. Art. 3.
175. Pastrovicchi, *op. cit.,* p. 80.
176. Schmoeger, *op. cit.,* Vol. II, p. 205.
177. Butler, *op. cit.,* Vol. V, p. 191.
178. *The Guardian Angels, Our Heavenly Companions*, p. 26.
179. Thomas of Celano, *op. cit.,* Part II, Chap. CXLIX, #197, p. 295.
180. Sr. Mary Minima, *Seraph Among Angels: The Life of St. Mary Magdalene de'Pazzi* (Chicago: The Carmelite Press, 1958), pp. 47-48.
181. Butler, *op. cit.,* Vol. VI, p. 192.
182. Cruz, *The Incorruptibles,* p. 31-32.
183. Biver, *op. cit.,* p. 183.
184. Sr. M. Faustina Kowalska, *Divine Mercy in My Soul: The Diary of the Servant of God Sister M. Faustina Kowalska* (Stockbridge, Massachusetts: Marian Press, 1987), p. 212.
185. Rev. Gabriel Locher, O.S.B., *A Brief Biography of Sister Mary Fortunata Viti* (Clyde, Missouri: Benedictine Convent of Perpetual Adoration, 1940), p. 111.
186. *Summa,* Part I. Q. 108. Art. 7.
187. Nilles, *Kalendarium Manuale utriusque Ecclesiae Orientalis et Occidentalis,* Innsbruck, 1896.
188. Agreda, The Theopolitan, 1913, *Our Heavenly Companions*, pp. 36-37.
189. Biver, *op. cit.,* p. 100.
190. *The Guardian Angels, Our Heavenly Companions*, p. 31-32.

— PART TWO: DEVILS —

1. *Genesis* 3:1-5 and 3:13-15.
2. *Leviticus* 17:7.
3. *Deuteronomy* 32:17.
4. *Judges* 9:23.
5. *1 Kings* [*1 Sam.*] 16:14-16, 23. *2 Kings* [*2 Sam.*] 19:22. *3 Kings* [*1 Kgs.*] 21:13. *4 Kings* [*2 Kgs.*] 1:2,3,6,16.
6. *Paralipomenon* 11:15; 21:1.
7. *Tobias* 3:8; 6:8,14,16,17,19; 8:3; 12:3,14.
8. *Job* 1:6,9,12; 2:1-4, 6,7.
9. *Psalms* 90:6; 95:5; 105:37; 108:6.
10. *Ecclesiasticus* 21:30.
11. *Wisdom* 2:24.
12. *Isaias* 14:12-14.
13. *Baruch* 4:7, 36.
14. *Habacuc* 3:5.
15. *Zacharias* 3:1-2.
16. *1 Machabees* 1:38.
17. *Matthew* 4:1-11, 24 (5 refer-

ences); 8:16,28,31,33 (4 refs.); 9:32-34 (4 refs.); 10:25 (1 ref.); 12:24,27 (6 refs.); 15:22 (1 ref.); 17:17 (1 ref.).
18. *Mark* 1:13,32,34,39 (4 refs.); 3:15,22 (4 refs.); 5:15-18 (3 refs.); 6:13 (1 ref.); 7:26-30 (3 refs.); 9:37 (1 ref.); 16:9 (1 ref.).
19. *Luke* 4:2-5,13,33,35 (6 refs.); 7:33 (1 ref.); 8:2 (1 ref.); 9:1, 42, 49 (3 refs.); 10:17 (1 ref.); 11:14 (2 refs.); 22:3 (1 ref.).
20. *John* 6:71 (1 ref.); 7:20 (1 ref.); 8:44,48-52 (4 refs.); 10:20-21 (3 refs.); 13:2,27 (2 refs.).
21. *Acts of the Apostles* 5:3; 10:38; 13:10; 19:13; 26:18.
22. *Romans* 16:20.
23. *1 Corinthians* 5:5; 7:5; 10:20-21.
24. *2 Corinthians* 2:11; 11:14; 12:7.
25. *Ephesians* 4:27; 6:11.
26. *1 Thessalonians* 2:18.
27. *2 Thessalonians* 2:9.
28. *1 Timothy* 1:20; 3:6-7; 4:1; 5:15; 6:9.
29. 2 *Timothy* 2:26.
30. *Hebrews* 2:14.
31. *James* 2:19; 4:7.
32. *1 Peter* 5:8.
33. *1 John* 3:8,10.
34. *Jude* 1:9.
35. *Apocalypse* 2:9, 10, 13,24; 3:9; 9:20; 12:9,12; 16:14; 18:2; 20:2,7,9.
36. *Matt*. 4:10; 7:22; 10:8; 11:18; 13:39; 16:23; 25:41. *Mark* 16:17. *Luke* 8:12; 10:18; 11:15-19; 13:32. *John* 6:71; 8:44, 49.
37. St. Thomas Aquinas, *Summa Theologica* (Chicago: Encyclopaedia Britannica, 1955). Part I. Q. 109. Art 2.
38. *Catechism of the Catholic Church* (San Francisco: Ignatius Press, 1994), #390.
39. *Apocalypse* 12:10.
40. *John* 8:44.
41. *John* 8:44.
42. *John* 13:2.
43. *1 Peter* 5:8.
44. *Apocalypse* 2:9.
45. *Apocalypse* 20:7.
46. *Gen*. 3:13.
47. *John* 10:10.
48. *1 Timothy* 4:2.
49. *Numbers* 5:14,30.
50. *Matt*. 8:28.
51. *1 Kgs*. [*3 Kgs*.] 16:15.
52. *Ezech*. 28:17.
53. *Matt*. 17:15; *Mark* 1:26.
54. *Matt*. 12:45; *Luke* 11:26.
55. *Canons and Decrees of the Council of Trent,* Trans. Rev. H. J. Schroeder, O. P. (St. Louis, Missouri: B. Herder Book Co., 1941; TAN, 1978), p. 21. (From the Fifth Session of June 17, 1546.)
56. *The Documents of Vatican II,* Ed. Rev. Walter M. Abbott, S.J. (New York: Guild Press, 1966), p. 596.
57. Very Reverend Adolphe Tanquerey, S.S., D.D., *The Spiritual Life: A Treatise on Ascetical and Mystical Theology* (Westminster, Maryland: The Newman Press, 1930), pp. 115-116.
58. *Ibid.*, p. 119.
59. *Ibid.*, p. 116.
60. Ralph Rath, *The New Age: A Christian Critique* (South Bend, Indiana: Greenlawn Press, 1990), p. 154.
61. Fr. Delaporte, *The Devil: Does He Exist? And What Does He Do?* (Originally published in 1871; TAN, 1982), p. 126.
62. *The Documents of Vatican II, op. cit.*, p. 235.
63. *Catechism of the Council of Trent,* Trans. John McHugh, O.P. and Charles Callan, O.P. (New York, 1923; TAN, 1982), pp. 568-569.
64. *Ibid.*, p. 569.
65. *Summa, op. cit.,* Part I. Q. 64. Art. 1.

66. St. John of the Cross, *The Collected Works of St. John of the Cross,* Trans. Kieran Kavanaugh and Otilio Rodriguez (Washington, D.C.: I.C.S. Publications, 1973), *Ascent of Mount Carmel,* Bk. II, Ch. 21, #7.
67. *Summa, op. cit.,* Part I. Q. 64. Art. 9.
68. C. Bernard Ruffin, *Padre Pio: The True Story* (Huntington, Indiana: Our Sunday Visitor, Inc., 1991), p. 141.
69. *Ibid.*, p. 367.
70. Very Rev. K. E. Schmoeger, C.SS.R., *Life of Anne Catherine Emmerich* (TAN, 1976), Vol. II, p. 206.
71. St. Athanasius, *St. Antony of the Desert* (Titled *St. Antony the Hermit* by Benziger) (New York: Benziger Bros., 1924; TAN, 1995) pp. 13-15.
72. *The Catholic Encyclopedia* (New York: The Encyclopedia Press, Inc., 1913), Vol. XV, p. 478.
73. St. Gregory the Great, *Life of St. Benedict,* as found in the book, (*The Very Rev.*) *Father Paul of Moll* by Edward van Speybrouck (Clyde, MO: Benedictine Convent, 1910; TAN, 1979), p. 305.
74. Augusta Theodosia Drane, *The Life of St. Dominic* (London, England: Burns & Oates, Ltd., 1919), pp. 134-135.
75. *Ibid.*, p. 196.
76. Mother Mary Francis, *Walled in Light: Saint Colette* (Chicago: Franciscan Herald Press, 1985), p. 223.
77. Albert Paul Schimberg, *Tall in Paradise: The Story of Saint Coletta of Corbie* (Francestown, New Hampshire: Marshall Jones Company, 1947), pp. 50-51.
78. *Ibid.*, p. 159.
79. St. Teresa of Avila, *The Life of Teresa of Jesus* (Garden City, New York: Image Books, 1944), p. 287.
80. *Ibid.*, p. 290.
81. *Ibid.*, p. 370.
82. Rev. Angelo Pastrovicchi, O.M.C., *St. Joseph of Copertino* (St. Louis, Missouri: B. Herder Book Co., 1918; TAN, 1980), pp. 81-82.
83. Thomas of Celano, *St. Francis of Assisi* (Chicago: Franciscan Herald Press, 1988), pp. 166-167.
84. St. Margaret Mary Alacoque, *The Autobiography of St. Margaret Mary Alacoque* (Roselands, Walmer, Kent, England: Sisters of the Visitation, 1930; TAN, 1986), p. 80.
85. Lay Brother of the Congregation of the Most Holy Redeemer, *Life, Virtues and Miracles of St. Gerard Majella* (Boston: Mission Church, 1907), p. 189.
86. Fr. Pius of the Name of Mary, *The Life of Saint Paul of the Cross* (New York: P. O'Shea, 1924), pp. 222-223.
87. Rev. Father F. X. Schouppe, S.J. (and Thomas A. Nelson), *Hell* (plus *How to Avoid Hell*) (New York: Hickey & Co., 1883; TAN, 1989), p. 72.
88. Edward Van Speybrouck, *The Very Rev. Father Paul of Moll* (Clyde, Missouri: Benedictine Convent, 1910; TAN, 1979), p. 230.
89. Sr. Mary Jean Dorcy, O.P., *Saint Dominic's Family* (Dubuque, Iowa: The Priory Press, 1964; TAN, 1983), p. 46.
90. Sr. Mary Minima, *Seraph Among Angels: The Life of St. Mary Magdalene De'Pazzi* (Chicago: Carmelite Missions, 1958), pp. 82-83.
91. Fr. Genelli, *The Life of St.*

Ignatius of Loyola (New York: Benziger Brothers, 1917; TAN, 1988), pp. 60-61.
92. Cecil Kerr, *Teresa Helena Higginson* (Academy of California Church History, 1926), p. 155.
93. *Ibid.*, p. 156.
94. *Ibid.*, p. 65.
95. Fr. Juan Echevarria, *The Miracles of St. Anthony Mary Claret* (Originally published as *Reminiscences of Blessed Anthony Mary Claret,* Compton, California: Claretian Major Seminary, 1938; TAN, 1992), p. 29.
96. Rev. Alban Butler, *The Lives of the Saints* (New York: P.J. Kenedy & Sons, 1937), Vol. VI, pp. 233-235.
97. Alden Hatch, *The Miracle of the Mountain* (New York: Hawthorn Books, Inc., 1959), p. 70.
98. Comte Paul Biver, *Père Lamy* (Dublin: Clonmore & Reynolds, Ltd., 1951; TAN, 1973), p. 104.
99. Sr. Josefa Menendez, *The Way of Divine Love* (Westminster, Maryland: The Newman Press, 1950), p. xxvii.
100. Ruffin, *op. cit.*, p. 85.
101. *Ibid.*, p. 413.
102. Lucia of Fatima, *Fatima in Lucia's Own Words* (Fatima, Portugal: Postulation Centre, Fatima, 1976), p. 108.
103. *Ibid.*, p. 143.
104. *Ibid.*, pp. 143-144.
105. E. Cobham Brewer, *A Dictionary of Miracles* (New York: Cassell and Company, Ltd., 1884), p. 12.
106. *Ibid.*, p. 96.
107. *Ibid.*, p. 97.
108. Schimberg, *op. cit.*, p. 159.
109. St. Teresa of Avila, *op. cit.*, p. 291.
110. *Ibid.*, pp. 370-371.
111. *Ibid.*, p. 287.
112. Lady Georgiana Fullerton, *The Life of St. Frances of Rome* (New York: P. J. Kenedy and Sons), p. 42.
113. Zsolt Aradi, *The Book of Miracles* (New York: Farrar, Straus & Cudahy, 1956), pp. 179-180.
114. Charles Warren Stoddard, *Saint Anthony, The Wonder Worker of Padua* (Notre Dame, Indiana: The Ave Maria, 1896; TAN, 1971), p. 58.
115. Fr. Pius of the Name of Mary, *op. cit.*, p. 120.
116. *Ibid.*, p. 79.
117. Hatch, *op. cit.,* p. 129.
118. Rev. Gabriel Locher, O.S.B., *A Brief Biography of Sister Mary Fortunata Viti* (Clyde, Mo: Benedictine Convent of Perpetual Adoration, 1940), pp. 128-129.
119. *Ibid.*, p. 131.
120. *Ibid.*, p. 130.
121. Ruffin, *op. cit.*, p. 101.
122. A School Sister of Notre Dame, *Mother Caroline and the School Sisters of Notre Dame in North America* (Saint Louis, Missouri: Woodward and Tiernan Company, 1928), Vol. I, p. 95.
123. *Ibid.*, p. 95.
124. *Ibid.*, pp. 96-97.
125. *Ibid.*, p. 97.
126. St. Athanasius, *op. cit.,* p. x.
127. *Ibid.*, pp. 13-14.
128. Drane, *op. cit.*, p. 160.
129. *The Little Flowers of St. Francis,* Trans. Raphael Brown (Garden City, New York: Image Books,1958), p. 175.
130. Thomas of Celano, *op. cit.,* p. 236.
131. Bl. Raymond of Capua, *The Life of St. Catherine of Siena* (New York: P. J. Kenedy & Sons, 1960), pp. 373-374.

132. Butler, *op. cit.*, Volume XI, pp. 75-77.
133. Schimberg, *op. cit.*, p. 159.
134. James A. Carrico, *Life of Venerable Mary of Agreda, Author of the Mystical City of God, the Autobiography of the Virgin Mary* (San Bernardino, California: Crestline Book Company, 1959), pp. 19-20.
135. Minima, *op. cit.*, p. 74.
136. Paul Van Dyke, *Ignatius Loyola: The Founder of the Jesuits* (New York: Charles Scribner's Sons, 1926), p. 289.
137. *Ibid.*, p. 290.
138. John of St. Samson, O.Carm., *Prayer, Aspiration and Contemplation* (New York: Alba House, 1975), pp. 8-9.
139. Alacoque, *op. cit.*, pp. 80-81.
140. Fr. Pius of the Name of Mary, *op. cit.*, p. 223.
141. Albert Bessieres, S.J., *Wife, Mother and Mystic: Bl. Anna Maria Taigi* (London: Sands & Co., Ltd., 1952; TAN, 1970), pp. 104-106.
142. *Ibid.*, pp. 150-151.
143. *Ibid.*, p. 153.
144. Abbe Francis Trochu, *The Cure d'Ars, St. Jean-Marie-Baptiste Vianney* (London: Burns, Oates and Washbourne, 1927; TAN, 1977), p. 239.
145. *Ibid.*, p. 243.
146. Echevarria, *op. cit.*, pp. 78-79.
147. Kerr, *op. cit.*, pp. 62-63.
148. *Ibid.*, p. 67.
149. Menendez, *op. cit.*, p. xxvii.
150. Ruffin, *op. cit.*, p. 102.
151. *Ibid.*, p. 366.
152. *Ibid.*, p. 367.
153. A. Poulain, S.J., *The Graces of Interior Prayer* (St. Louis: B. Herder Book Company, 1907), p. 441.
154. Fr. Joseph Sicardo, O.S.A., *St. Rita of Cascia, Saint of the Impossible* (Chicago: D. B. Hansen & Sons, 1916; TAN, 1990), p. 106.
155. Minima, *op. cit.*, p. 216.
156. Fr. Pius of the Name of Mary, *op. cit.*, p. 222.
157. Echevarria, *op. cit.*, p. 107.
158. Hatch, *op. cit.*, p. 158.
159. André Legault, C.S.C., *Brother André of the Congregation of Holy Cross* (Montreal, Canada: Saint Joseph's Oratory), p. 22.
160. *Ibid.*, pp. 129-130.
161. Kerr, *op. cit.*, p. 157-158.
162. St. Teresa of Avila, *op. cit.*, p. 289.
163. Schouppe, *op. cit.*, p. 70.
164. Van Dyke, *op. cit.*, p. 289-290.
165. Locher, *op. cit.*, p. 131.
166. St. Gregory the Great, *op.cit.*, p. 311.
167. Bede the Venerable, *The Ecclesiastical History of the English Nation* (London: J. M. Dent & Sons, 1958), pp. 304-305.
168. Trochu, *op. cit.*, p. 246.
169. Kearns, *op. cit.*, p. 99.
170. Kerr, *op. cit.*, p. 61.
171. St. Teresa of Avila, *op. cit.*, Chapter XXXI, p. 287.
172. Msgr. Léon Cristiani, *Evidence of Satan in the Modern World* (England: Barrie & Rockliff, 1961; TAN, 1974) p. 42.
173. *Ibid.*, p. 43.
174. *Ibid.*, p. 49.
175. *Ibid.*, p. 48.
176. *Ibid.*, p. 50.
177. *Ibid.*, p. 52.
178. *Ibid.*, p. 55.
179. *Ibid.*, p. 56.
180. Kearns, *op. cit.*, p. 98.
181. Sicardo, *op. cit.*, p. 106.
182. Poulain, *op. cit.*, p. 443.
183. Fr. Pius of the Name of Mary, *op. cit.*, pp. 115-116.
184. *Ibid.*, p. 116.

185. Biver, *op. cit.,* p. 105.
186. St. Teresa of Avila, *op. cit.*, pp. 370-371.
187. *The Autobiography of St. Teresa of Avila,* Trans. David Lewis (New York: Benziger Bros., 1916; TAN, 1997), p. 287.
188. Bessieres, *op. cit.*, p. 151.
189. Tanquerey, *op. cit.,* p. 117.
190. J. K. Huysmans, *Saint Lydwine of Schiedam* (London: Kegan Paul, Trench, Trubner & Co., Ltd., 1923; TAN, 1979), pp. 198-199.
191. Trochu, *op. cit.*, p. 249.
192. Paul Van Dyke, *op. cit.,* p. 295.
193. *The Mystical City of God,* Trans. Fiscar Marison (So. Chicago, Illinois: The Theopolitan, 1913), Vol. I, pp. 192-193.
194. St. Teresa of Avila, *Interior Castle,* Trans. and Ed. E. Allison Peers (Garden City, New York: Image Books, 1961), Fifth Mansion, pp. 121-122.
195. St. Teresa of Avila, *The Autobiography of St. Teresa of Avila,* Trans. and Ed. E. Allison Peers (Garden City, New York: Image Books, 1944), pp. 290-291.
196. Louis Moden, S.J., *Signs and Wonders* (New York: Desclee Company, 1966), pp. 163-164.
197. *Ibid.*, p. 165.
198. Tanquerey, *op. cit.*, pp. 720-721.
199. Cristiani, *op. cit.*, p. 123.
200. *Ibid.,* p. 77.
201. Tanquerey, *op. cit.*, p. 721.
202. *Ibid.,* p. 722.
203. Cf. Poulain, *op. cit.*, p. 429.
204. *Matt.* 8:16; 9:32-33; 12:22; 15:22-28; 17:14-17. *Mark* 1:23-27, 32-34, 39. *Luke* 4:33-35, 41; 9:42-43, 11:14.
205. *Matt.* 8:28-33; *Mark* 5:2-17; *Luke* 8:27-38.
206. Tanquerey, *op. cit.*, pp. 725-726.
207. John Patrick Gillese, *Begone, Satan!* (Huntington, Indiana: Our Sunday Visitor, 1974), pp. 17 to 64.
208. Butler, *op. cit.,* Vol. VI, p. 112.
209. Cristiani, *op. cit.,* p. 65-68.
210. St. Gregory the Great, *op. cit.,* pp. 310-311.
211. Thomas of Celano, *op. cit.,* p. 226.
212. Drane, *op. cit.*, p. 35.
213. *Ibid.*, p. 133.
214. Pastrovicchi, *op. cit.,* pp. 65-66.
215. Minima, *op. cit.*, pp. 216-217.
216. Trochu, *op. cit.,* p. 249.
217. *Ibid.*, p. 250.
218. *Ibid.*, pp. 250-251.
219. Richard N. Ostling, TIME Magazine, March 19, 1990, Vol. 135, #12, p. 55.
220. *Code of Canon Law* (Washington, D.C.: Canon Law Society of America, 1983), #1172.
221. *The Current Norms Governing Exorcisms,* The Congregation for the Doctrine of the Faith, September 29, 1984.
222. St. Louis-Marie Grignion de Montfort, *True Devotion to Mary* (Fathers of the Company of Mary, 1941; TAN, 1985), #52, p. 31.
223. St. Alphonsus de Liguori, *The Glories of Mary* (St. Louis: Redemptorist Fathers, 1931), p. 223.
224. *Ibid.*, p. 225.
225. *Ibid.*, p. 149.
226. *Ibid.*, p. 149.
227. *Ibid.*, pp. 149-150.
228. Cristiani, *op. cit.*, p. 145.
229. *Ibid.*, p. 204.
230. *Catholic Almanac,* 1999 Ed. (Huntington, IN: Our Sunday Visitor, Inc.), p. 281.
231. Taken from the article, "An Anthropological View of Satanism" that appeared in the

Vatican newspaper *L'Osservatore Romano*, March 12, 1997.
232. Article by Giuseppe Ferrari, *L'Osservatore Romano,* Vatican City, January 29, 1997.
233. *Ibid.*
234. Delaporte, *op. cit.*, p. 61.
235. TIME Magazine, April 24, 1989, Vol. 133, #17, p. 30.
236. Herbert Thurston, S.J., article in *The Catholic Encyclopedia (*New York: The Encyclopedia Press, Inc., 1912), Vol. XV, p. 674.
237. *The Catholic Encyclopedia*, *op. cit.*, p. 675.
238. Hutchinson Online Encyclopedia, Helicon Publishing Co., Ltd., 1996.
239. Rev. James J. LeBar, *Cults, Sects, and the New Age* (Huntington, Indiana: Our Sunday Visitor, Inc., 1989), p. 152.
240. *Ibid.*, p. 152.
241. Constance D. Cumbey, *The Hidden Dangers of the Rainbow* (Shreveport, Louisiana: Huntington House, Inc., 1983), p. 25.
242. Joseph Carr, *The Lucifer Connection* (Lafayette, LA: Huntington House, Inc., 1987), p. 79.
243. *Certainty* magazine, Vol. 5, No. 10.
244. L. Ron Hubbard, *Dianetics, the Modern Science of Mental Health: A Handbook of Dianetic Procedure* (United States: Publications Org., 1976), p. 86.
245. *Ibid.*, p. 422.
246. A comprehensive "Index of Cults and Religions" can be found through the Watchman Fellowship's home page, at www.watchman.org.
247. Migene Gonzalez-Wippler, *Santeria: The Religion—Faith, Rites, Magic* (St. Paul, Minnesota: Llewellyn Publications, 1996).
248. *The Catholic Encyclopedia*, *op. cit.*, Vol. XII, p. 474.
249. Cristiani, *op. cit.*, p. 184.
250. Rath, *op. cit.*, pp. 74-75.
251. *Ibid.,* p. 77.
252. William Thomas and Kate Pavitt, *The Book of Talismans, Amulets and Zodiacal Gems* (London: Bracken Books, 1993), p. 11.
253. Rath, *op. cit.*, pp. 131-133.
254. *Ibid.*, p. 135.
255. Schroeder, *op. cit.*, p. 276.
256. St. John of the Cross, *op. cit., The Ascent of Mount Carmel*, Book II, #7, p. 175-176.
257. *Ibid.*, Book II, #11, p. 177.
258. *Ibid.*, Book II, #12, p. 177.

One of the most amazing subjects of any book . . .

MYSTERIES MARVELS MIRACLES

by Joan Carroll Cruz

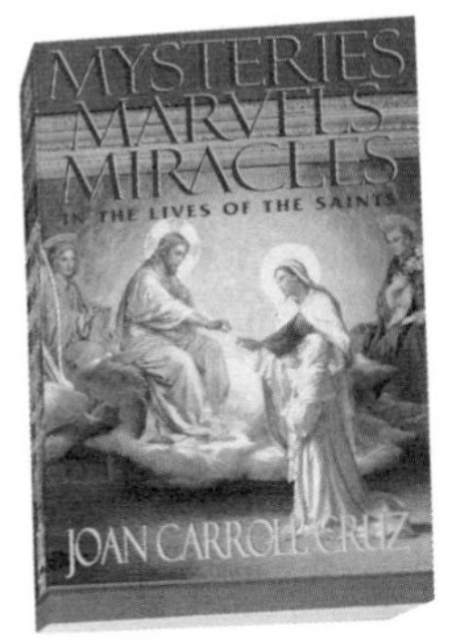

No. 1383. 581 Pages. 77 Illus. PB. Impr. ISBN-5417.

24.00

Mysteries, Marvels, Miracles is one of the most amazing Catholic books of the century, for here in one volume are hundreds of true stories of miraculous phenomena in the lives of the Saints. Although easy to read, the book is referenced and indexed, making it a real treasury of miracles.

Mrs. Cruz—a now-famous writer—scoured through libraries and wrote to shrines all over the world for the material for this remarkable book.

The wonders described here include bilocation, levitation, odor of sanctity, odor of sin, transverberation and other miracles of the heart, miraculous transport, money mysteriously provided, multiplication of food, mystical marriage and heavenly jewelry, miraculous protection, lights and rays of love, fire and heat of love, prophecy, invisibility, Saints who knew the date of their death, the stigmata (wounds of Christ), gift of tongues, mystical fasts, mystical knowledge, incorruption of bodies after death, bodies transformed after death, blood miracles, voices of the dead, death warnings and other signals from the dead, "manna" and perfume from the bodies of the Saints after death, and miracles of the Saints involving earth, sea, sky, rain, snow, ice, plants, fruits and flowers, birds, bees, bugs, animals, reptiles, springs, wells, Holy Water and fire.

Mysteries, Marvels, Miracles is a tremendous contribution to Catholic literature and a wonderful asset to the Catholic world. Miracles are one of the marks of Christ's true Church, and here the reader sees a vast panorama of Catholic miracles reaching back for centuries.

No one can read *Mysteries, Marvels, Miracles* without seeing that God has indeed favored the Saints with amazing gifts and marvelous powers over nature—testifying to His own almighty power and to the truth of the Catholic Church.

Joan Carroll Cruz is a native of New Orleans and was educated by the School Sisters of Notre Dame. She attended grade school, high school and college under their tutelage. About her teachers Mrs. Cruz says, "I am especially indebted to the sisters who taught me for five years at the boarding school at St. Mary of the Pines in Chatawa, Mississippi. I cannot thank them enough for their dedication, their fine example and their religious fervor, which made such an impression on me." Mrs. Cruz has been a tertiary in the Discalced Carmelite Secular Order (Third Order) for the past 30 years. She is married to Louis Cruz, who owns a swimming pool repair and maintenance business. They are the parents of five children.

Other books by Mrs. Cruz include *Mysteries, Marvels, Miracles, Miraculous Images of Our Lord, Miraculous Images of Our Lady, Prayers and Heavenly Promises, Secular Saints, The Incorruptibles* and *Eucharistic Miracles,* all published by TAN Books and Publishers, Inc.; *The Desires of Thy Heart,* a novel with a strong Catholic theme published in hardcover by Tandem Press in 1977 and in paperback by Signet with an initial printing of 600,000 copies; and *Relics,* published by Our Sunday Visitor, Inc. For her non-fiction books Mrs. Cruz depends heavily on information received from foreign shrines, churches, convents and monasteries. The material she receives requires the services of several translators. Mrs. Cruz is currently working on another book which also involves a great deal of research.